The
Insider's
Guide to
Franchising

The Insider's Guide to Franchising

Bryce Webster

amacom

American Management Association

This book is available at a special
discount when ordered in bulk quantities.
For information, contact Special Sales Department,
AMACOM, a division of American Management Association,
135 West 50th Street, New York, NY 10020.

Library of Congress Cataloging-in-Publication Data

Webster, Bryce.
    The insider's guide to franchising.

    Bibliography: p.
    Includes index.
    1. Franchises (Retail trade)—United States.
2. Franchises (Retail trade) I. Title.
HF5429.235.U5W43   1986   658.8'708   85-48212
ISBN 0-8144-5660-X

Printing number

10 9 8 7 6 5 4 3 2 1

To
George Ballas,
Houston entrepreneur and an inspiration to me early on.

Acknowledgments and Author's Note

I wish to thank Stephen Wagner, Editor, *Income Opportunities* magazine. The franchise columns I write for him form the foundation of this book. His presence in the publishing world is a delight to his authors and his readers alike. I would also like to acknowledge Publisher Rob Kaplan, Acquisitions Editor Karl Weber, and Associate Editor Barbara Horowitz of AMACOM. I thank them for being the most pleasant, competent, and professional group I have encountered in 15 years as an author. For their vast help with the content of this book, often responding to requests on a moment's notice, I extend my gratitude to Benjamin Thayer, Executive Director, National Alliance of Franchisees and to Meg Whittemore, Director of Communications of the International Franchise Association and numerous members of her staff.

I would like to point out to readers that I have used the pronoun *he* to connote both genders. It should be emphasized, however, that this has been done solely in the interests of avoiding awkwardness and that such passages are of course intended to apply equally to both genders.

Contents

Part I
Secrets of Buying a Franchise

1

Franchising: Debunking the Myths

McDonald's. Midas Muffler. Servicemaster. Doktor Pet Care Centers. Lawn Doctor. General Business Services. Holiday Inn. Postal Instant Press. To many people, these are common household words, words they may use every day—words as much a part of their lives as color television, convenience foods, and jogging. Indeed, these companies—despite their high "national brand recognition," as those in advertising might say—are part of our daily lives, integral parts of our communities. For the most part, they are locally owned and run by neighbors and friends, not by moguls from Manhattan, Hollywood, or even Las Cruces.

All of these and almost 2,000 more companies, both the very visible and the hardly noticed, do business through *franchises*. The term itself conjures up many things to many people. Some regard franchising as a license to print money; others view franchises as slightly shady operations to beware of, either when running one or even when buying goods from one.

The truth is, naturally, not so clear-cut. Certainly there have been franchises that did not operate on strictly ethical lines; there probably still are. These gave rise to legislation, however, that limits how shoddy such operations can be.

But there have been and still are dozens of well-run franchises that arrived in the marketplace at precisely the right time, in precisely the right place, with precisely the right product, and offered people a chance to fly to the financial moon with them. Stories from this group have caused many people—maybe you—to dream of owning a franchise someday. Realistically, though, you'll have to understand just what a franchise is (no, it does not offer a printing press and green ink) and what it is not (no, you won't automatically become an "unprincipled, back-stabbing sleazeball" by buying a franchise). A few definitions, therefore, are in order.

3

What Is a Franchise?

First, a *franchise* is nothing more than a method of distributing products and services to the buying public. For example, buying a McDonald's franchise gives buyers the right to sell the hamburgers the way McDonald's makes them and to use the McDonald's trademark, logo, and business system. That's all. Technically, because every company owns its name, its own way of doing business, and possibly patents or trademarks on its products, any company could sell the right to use its methods through a franchise. Imagine that your Aunt Patty has been baking birthday cakes, free-lance, for years. Not liking to beat the bushes herself for customers—she's over 80—she sells her cakes to local caterers who would rather not handle the baking in house. If she wanted to expand without enlarging her own little bakery, your aunt could sell the right to use the name Aunt Patty Cakes, her secret recipes, and her business methods to others who wanted to operate a wholesale bakery. Presto! Top caterers all over the country can be supplied with the always delicious Aunt Patty Cakes for weddings, society parties, and Irish wakes. Your Aunt Patty would be a *franchisor*.

In other words, a *franchisor* is the person or company that grants the buyer of the franchise the right and license to operate the business along the lines and with the products the franchisor has developed. Indeed, in other contexts, the word *franchise* itself means *right*. Example: When women gained voting rights, they became *enfranchised*.

Suppose you think Aunt Patty has a good deal going, and you decide to buy in. You are the *franchisee*. Easy as pie (or cake). Well, almost.

It's important to keep these terms straight, as they are frequently used in franchise contracts. Understanding this distinction is crucial to understanding your responsibilities and rights as the buyer of a franchise. Again, a *franchisor* is the company that owns the franchise and grants the rights and licenses—the one that controls the franchise. (In other words, Aunt Patty.) The *franchisee* is the person or company that pays the owner, or franchisor, for the franchise and the right to use it. (You.)

The *franchise* is the right to use that collection of products, trademarks, and business systems the franchisor has created. And, *franchise* sometimes refers, in the vernacular, to the physical plant. "Hey, Mary! Wanna go to that new ice cream shop downtown? It's a franchise. It's real nice, just like the one in Seattle."

What Is a Franchise Not?

Franchising is not a distributorship or dealership, and it differs from them in several important ways. In a *distributorship*, the manufacturer sells its products to you, the *distributor,* at a wholesale price. You simply resell them to dealers at a higher price, or you might sell them directly to the public at retail prices. In a legal sense, your relationship with the manufacturer probably begins and ends there. (The manufacturer may provide a certain amount of support such as training or advertising allowances in the interest of getting you to sell a lot of its goods; it does not, however, force you to follow a preset business method, nor does it require you to pay it a royalty or percentage of your gross profits.)

A *dealership* is similar to a distributorship, but is usually the business that sells to the general public at retail prices. A dealer may buy from either a manufacturer or a distributor. In most cases, dealers and distributors have the power to change the kinds of products and services they sell, and each may even sell a range of competing similar products, unless they have agreed not to do so with one or more manufacturers. These agreements are often of short duration—a year or less—and must be renewed by mutal consent. Without such an agreement, you could, for instance, offer your clients both Fred's Furnance Fittings and Herman's Heating Helpers.

The same is not true with franchises. Although you may be able financially and physically to own and operate two different franchises, you most certainly could not mix and match their products—selling Whoppers at your McDonald's, for instance. In other words, with a franchise, you are restricted by the franchise agreement to the types of products and services you may offer, how you may offer them, and sometimes even when.

And franchisors tend to require contracts with 5-, 10-, or even 15-year terms, often with options to extend the agreement beyond that. While it is no longer legal for a franchisor to require that the franchisee purchase only from the franchisor, it can require the franchisee to create and offer for sale products exactly similar to those of all the other franchisees—the product created by the franchisor. For example, if a franchisee does elect to buy beef from his own supplier, it had better match precisely the franchisor's grade. Or if the franchisee has his own logo napkins printed, the colors and type will have to match *exactly* to pass quality-control muster.

In 1970, a federal court ruling stated that franchisors could no longer force a franchisee to make purchases of supplies, equipment, real estate, and so on, from the franchisor; this arrangement had been common before that. In the late 1970s, in an even more important decision, another federal court ruled that it was illegal for Dunkin' Donuts to *influence or persuade* franchisees to buy supplies, equipment, real estate, and so on, from the parent company. The federal court reasoned that a large company like Dunkin' Donuts could, through legal muscle and economic pressure, force a one-shop operator to buy from it although the operator could probably buy supplies at a lower price from another vendor. The franchisee would lack the resources to wage an effective fight.

As a result, some franchisors no longer even sell raw materials to franchisees, preferring to operate quality-control checks more stringently instead. Some franchisors offer a choice, which can be to the franchisee's advantage when the quality is high and price competitive with independent vendors' prices.

There may, of course, be other sorts of restrictions on what a franchisee can do. And there are also the obligations of the franchisor to the franchisee to be spelled out. All this is found in the fine print in the franchise contract. A later chapter in this book is devoted to dissecting it and determining what each type of clause means to you, the franchisee.

Types of Franchises

Because of the highly visible boom in fast-food outlets and running-shoe stores, especially in the last ten years, most people have come to believe franchises are concerned only with retail operations. This is not the case. In fact, franchising has been used in two additional areas—and possibly a third—since the concept was first developed. Today these are governed by the Federal Franchise Disclosure Rule adopted as Rule 436 in 1979 by the Federal Trade Commission (FTC). The three kinds of franchising are:

• *Product Franchising.* Franchising first became popular in this country during the early 1900s as a way to sell automobiles and gasoline. At that time, franchises were created at the distributor level. This assured the manufacturers that their products would reach the public in exactly the way they desired, creating the widespread brand recognition and loyalty they desired. Since then, automobile and gasoline companies have changed their way of doing business, so that today they are not considered franchisors, nor do they have to meet the federal franchise disclosure laws. There are, however, other companies using franchising as a method of distributing their wares.

Under the federal disclosure law, this means of doing business is called a *product franchise*. Such a franchise distributes goods produced by the franchisor, or under its authority, and that carry the franchise trademark. The franchisee pays the company for the right to sell trademarked goods either by buying certain amounts of products or by paying a fee for the right to sell them. Today this type of franchising is still represented in the automotive industry by several tire dealerships; many swimming pool distributors are also this type of franchise. The federal rule does not cover any products or services not protected by a trademark.

• *Manufacturing Franchises.* The industry most often associated with franchising as a method of manufacturing is the soft drink industry. Each local or regional bottling plant is a franchisee licensed by the parent company. Coca-Cola, Pepsi, et al. sell the concentrates and associated products and supplies to their local bottlers, who then mix the concentrates with other ingredients, largely soda water, and bottle or "can" the beverage for distribution to retail dealers. Needless to say, it is necessary that these products be exactly similar from region to region. In these franchises, where a secret ingredient is the basis for the franchisor's product, it is possible that an ingredient may be "single-sourced" without being illegal.

• *Business Format Franchising.* This, of course, is the most popular method today for most franchisors. A franchisor licenses an individual (or, increasingly, another corporation) to open a retail shop, store, or chain to sell to the public various products and services under the franchisor's name.

Business format franchises are the highly visible retail operations most of us think of when we hear the word *franchise*. The franchisor licenses the business methods it has established and that are identified by its trademark. The franchisee's methods of operation are significantly controlled by the franchisor. The franchisor most often provides significant assistance to the franchisee in the operation of the business, under the guidelines of the federal disclosure rule. The franchisee is required to pay ongoing fees or royalites to the franchise company.

A fourth category of business, *business opportunity ventures,* is covered by the FTC rule under certain circumstances. These businesses are often vending-machine routes, rack-jobber opportunities, and distributorships. To be governed by the FTC rule, these ventures must meet all three of these criteria set by the government: (1) the franchisee must be required to sell goods or services provided by a franchisor, its affiliates, or a supplier required by the franchisor; (2) the franchisor is engaged in providing retail outlets or accounts for the franchisee; and (3) the franchisee must pay the franchisor a fee or other consideration for the right to obtain the franchised business.

Continuing Boom in Franchising

The modern franchising era can be said to have begun during the late 1940s and early 1950s. Most of today's major popular retail franchises were founded during that period. Here's a star-studded partial list:

McDonald's (1955), Burger King (1955), Carvel Ice Cream (1945), Putt-Putt Golf (1954), Midas Muffler (1956), Hanna Car Wash (1955), Great Bear Auto Centers (1947), Manpower Temporary Services (1955), John Robert Powers (1955), Kentucky Fried Chicken (1952), Pizza Hut (1959), Pepperidge Farm (1941), Dunkin' Donuts (1955), Mister Donut (1956), Dairy Queen (1941), Tastee-Freez (1950), Holiday Inn (1954),

Best Western (1946), Quality Inn (1950), H&R Block (1958), Duraclean (1947), Servicemaster (1948), and One Hour Martinizing (1949). Roto-Rooter and Arthur Murray Dance Studios were real pioneers, beginning in 1935 and 1938 respectively.

The boom in franchising has continued unabated through the 1960s, 1970s, and into the 1980s, resulting in remarkable growth, according to U.S. Department of Commerce statistics. In early 1985, there were almost 2,000 companies using franchising as all or part of their sales efforts. Almost one-third of *all* retail sales in this country—nearly $500 billion—were made in franchise operations during 1983 and 1984. And franchising's share of retail sales continues to rise each year. Further, almost 5 million people were employed, either full- or part-time, by more than 489,000 franchised outlets in 1984. Franchising's growth rate, however, has slowed somewhat during the 1980s from the "go-go" days of the 1960s and 1970s. And the emphasis has shifted from the small mom-and-pop storefront to the large regional or territorial franchises bought by investors and syndicates.

The U.S. Department of Commerce puts a bit of chilly icing on the franchise cake, as far as individuals are concerned. "Continuing economic improvement, stable prices, slower growing population, and increased competition for market share," it states, "will turn many large corporations and manufacturers to franchising, influenced by changing tastes of consumers and demographic shifts." Sounds good at first; more companies offering franchises, more opportunity for you. Right? A cautious *maybe* is the answer. This new-wave boom could drive some of the less expensive, hospitable-to-individuals companies out of the business, and it could draw business from already established franchisees.

In fact, only 55 companies, or slightly more than 4 percent of all franchisors, already account for almost half (49 percent) of all sales and for more than half (51 percent) of all franchise establishments. This is a very heavy concentration for such a rapidly growing method of doing business, and it makes the top 50 franchisors (in terms of size) very lucrative to own, but very expensive to buy.

When still more large companies looking for new outlets enter the fray, there could be more bad news on this front. For the major franchise companies, the trend is already away from individual ownership and toward what is called "multiunit ownership" by franchisees and the sale of regional territories to franchise distributors. The regional distributors, in turn, sell local franchises and receive a share of the income from these local operations. Significant too is the government's expectation that larger franchisors will buy up existing chains rather than open new stores.

This increasingly corporate-style ownership is on the rise for the same reasons you would cite in choosing a franchise to build your personal fortunes. They also believe a franchise offers very good prospects for success, good cash flow, tax advantages, potential for long-term capital appreciation (that is, the business becomes worth more as the years go by), and relatively little risk of complete failure. Even if failure happens, the franchisor will often buy out the franchisee and keep the outlet operating to prevent damage to the company's reputation. (Although government statistics show company ownership is usually temporary, no figures exist to determine whether the outlets are resold to individuals or corporate owners.)

If the major franchises do go on an acquisition binge during the next decade, it could mean several things for the individual franchisee, most of them bad. First, it could reduce competition in local markets and raise prices for the public. Second, it could prevent many prospective franchisees from buying one of the better-quality franchises because the price would be so high. Third, it could increase the number of company-owned and operated franchises, again limiting the chances for "new blood" to get in on the action. Fourth, it could become much more expensive to buy a high-quality franchise, since the franchise company would have less incentive to sell franchises than it had in the past. Fifth, it could force the average franchise buyer to seek out poor-quality or even exploitative franchise companies, and thus face a much greater risk of failure and of losing his investment.

In sum, you should understand that franchisors have found there are many ways to sell franchises—which is, after all, their business. Some of these are more profitable than others. Because of the large sums they receive immediately, franchisors often prefer to deal with companies or limited partnerships formed for the purpose of buying regional franchises and selling local franchises. They may prefer to work with wealthy investors or investor syndicates, which will hire professional management to operate the franchise while the investor/partner is not directly involved. They often prefer to help existing and successful franchisees to expand by opening new franchises, instead of welcoming new franchisees into the fold. With new franchisees, there are additional training costs and downside risk (risk of failure of an outlet) that they are assuming along with the franchisee. As an individual, you may well be at the bottom of the ladder of people who want to climb the mountain of potential profits by franchising.

But this does not mean the would-be small businessman or woman is going to be left out. Think of Aunt Patty and her dough! The Commerce Department also predicts that "with long-term prospects for franchising extremely bright, *growing numbers of smaller companies, operating in local or regional markets, will turn to franchising for new ways to distribute their goods and services.* [Emphasis added.] These small new franchising companies will quickly react to changing market conditions and seek out new services and merchandising alternatives in order to broaden their appeal and attract greater patronage."

Does this, then, offer a bonanza for the individual owner? Again, a cautious *yes*. There will be more opportunities and they are likely to require less investment than the big nationals. But remember, these will be untested franchises. You might still end up as a grim statistic, a victim of a franchisor who founders.

The Advantages of Owning a Franchise

Still want to own a franchise? Good. Because there are lots of bright sides to look at. Here are a dozen reasons, definite business advantages franchising offers you over starting your own enterprise:

- You receive the advantages of a well-known trademark, either regionally or nationally, and its cumulative goodwill.
- You receive the standard quality and uniformity of the franchisor's product or service and, in a successful outfit, its desirability.
- You receive all the details of a proven, existing, and successful system of marketing and bookkeeping.
- You receive proven advice on site location, outlet design, operation, marketing, and capitalization.
- You receive a business framework that minimizes the startup problems and guesswork, saving time and trouble in finding suppliers of needed products and equipment.
- You obtain proven operating methods and procedures for creating and selling the product.
- You get customers familiar with your wares, avoiding the hard sell you might otherwise have to engage in; usually, customers are already buying exactly the same products at similar locations in different areas.
- You receive, in exchange for your fee, vital information about competition, product demand, seasonal variations, community attitudes, and much more.
- You receive well-tested sources of supply and service.
- You can call on the services of well-trained and professional support people.
- You may receive significant cost savings, in some franchises, by taking advantage of franchisor discounts and a centralized purchasing system.
- And from some franchises, you can receive direct financial assistance or help in finding adequate sources of financial assistance.

Franchising has been and will remain—for the right type of person—a lucrative way to start and succeed in your own business. Nor are you limited to flipping pancakes, stacking hamburgers, or dipping ice cream cones to do it. Contrary to popular belief, not all—not even most—franchises deal with food. In fact, franchising has spread so widely, both through retail and wholesale industries, that there are almost bound to be a few franchises to fit your business and professional background, even if you've never handled food a day in your life (except to eat it). In fact, the International Franchise Association (IFA) identifies 49 types of franchised businesses. And there are several others not included in the IFA list. All of these are listed and briefly described at the end of this chapter.

A Jungle Book

It is obvious to you by now that while franchising often provides excellent opportunities, it also has some drawbacks. Franchises can fail, at either the franchisee's or franchisor's end, and there is a crunch coming in some areas of franchising. There are, in short, pitfalls here and there. Franchising is, like any business, a financial jungle.

But there are paths through the tangle of vines; if you take them, and arm yourself with knowledge, the lion won't snag you blundering through.

Following are a number of franchising fables. Take them to heart, and learn from the morals at the end.

Fable Number One: *You get filthy rich owning a franchise.* This myth is believed by most of the tens of thousands of people who want to own a franchise. They dream of owning their own McDonald's or Burger King or any one of hundreds more fast-food emporiums and of living the rest of their days in wealth and leisure.

Hold on. First, consider this: Although it is true that some franchisees become millionaires, most do not. Many make more money than was possible in their former careers or jobs. Some make less. Some fail.

Franchisors, however, have a very good chance of becoming very rich. The late Ray A. Kroc, who led McDonald's to become the best-known franchise in the country, became one of the country's 400 wealthiest men, according to *Forbes* magazine. The chairman and founder of ComputerLand has also become one of the nation's wealthiest men. The franchisor and its principal stockholders are the people who make the most money from franchising. Why?

Because they've gotten a good deal of your money up front, any royalties you owe them, and someone to perform the labor of getting them another outlet in the marketplace. If you fail, despite their help, they will take over the operation at a fraction of the cost of beginning one new.

Moral Number One: While you may make a good deal of money in franchising, you may not. But whether you succeed or fail, it's likely the franchisor will make more money than you do. This doesn't mean you should begrudge it that fact; just be sure you stand to reach your own goals with it through reasonable effort. If you want to become a multimillionaire, think about becoming a franchisor rather than a franchisee, developing your own business from the ground up and selling rights to it to others. Or have as your goal becoming at least a multiple franchisee. Or invest in a franchisor.

Fable Number Two: *Franchises are failure-proof.* Dozens of franchisors and thousands of franchisees fail each year. The Department of Commerce reports that during 1984 alone, 56 franchisors, with 2,165 outlets, failed, *and* an additional 63 franchisors decided to stop franchising. These 63 operated 1,168 outlets. The franchisees are often left high and dry after these failures or discontinuations.

Furthermore, the government reports that during 1983, more than 6,900 franchise agreements were terminated. Of these, about 2,600 were terminated by the franchisor for various reasons, almost 3,900 were terminated by franchisees, and 462 were ended by mutual consent. And more than 3,500 franchisees asked for permission to sell their franchise licenses. The last of the grim statistics is that almost 1,150 agreements that came up for renewal during 1983 were not renewed. The total failures equal almost 10,000 franchised outlets during 1983.

Franchisors are very fond of quoting Small Business Administration statistics that show that as many as 65 percent of all new businesses fail within the first five years of operation. And they compare that to the less than 5 percent per year of new franchises that fail. But there are also hidden facts behind the alarmingly high failure rate for nonfranchised businesses, the sort of statistic-skewing factors that make so many numbers meaningless. For instance, the "failure" statistics include businesses whose *modus operandi* is now and ever has been filing for bankruptcy one day, opening doors as a new entity the next. For many of these, the failure is for accounting purposes only—and those purposes may not be ethical. The figures also include as "failures" businesses that, perfectly ethically, simply want to change their name, kill off the old business entity for any of a number of reasons, and begin under a name they like better. While a business has ceased to exist under that name, it has not failed; it has merely chosen a successor in interest.

But even taking into account the pseudo-failures, franchising can still be reasonably considered a safer form of getting into business than going out on a limb on your own. And well it should, for several reasons.

First, although anyone can open his own business, franchisors only allow the pick of the litter, so to speak, to become a franchisee. Just as you will, after reading this book, thoroughly examine the franchisor, so will you be thoroughly vetted by the franchisor.

Second, the franchisor will put you through in-depth training and give you follow-up support. This is far more assistance and encouragement than the average new business owner has or dreams of receiving.

Third, few independent small-business owners have enough capital to overcome their lack of management experience. Not only will the franchisor refuse to take you on if you lack the needed capital, it will provide management experience for you, in many cases, if you have problems in that area.

In my opinion, a small-business person who starts his own business with enough capital, a good background in his chosen line of business, good common sense, and a willingness to work has a chance to succeed equal to that of a franchisee.

So don't sell yourself short, and do *not* look at a franchise as a way to save you from yourself. Before you start looking for a franchise, consider whether you have what it takes to go it alone. And if you do, consider then whether owning a franchise—and using the franchisor's experience and support to your advantage—will put you that much more ahead of the competition. Or you may decide to go ahead and open your own business without a franchisor's backing.

If you look for a franchise as a crutch, you are unlikely to succeed for two reasons: First, it is unlikely the franchisor will let you buy in; and second, a franchisor cannot prevent incompetence from causing failure. A franchisor may bail you out to preserve its reputation and keep a store open, but you still carry the burden of success or failure. In the end, your store may live on without you.

Moral Number Two: Franchisees can and do fail; their eventual demise may be lengthened, however, as the franchisor tries to protect its reputation and profits. A franchisor cannot and will not make up for incompetence; expect to prove your competence if you want to be a successful franchisee.

Fable Number Three: *Franchises are recession-proof.* Nothing is recession-proof, with the possible exception of government employment. During the 1982–83 recession, dozens of franchisors, especially those in the service industries, showed sharp reductions in the number of franchises in operation. Some, of course, did extremely well during that recession, especially fast-food restaurants.

Nor are franchises "failure-proof" in nonrecession years; each industry may have its own recession. During 1985, computer-store franchises suffered enormous losses and setbacks.

There are no guarantees that during the next recession (and another is inevitable at some point in the future) or when the latest fad dies out, the franchises will not suffer reduced sales or go out of business. In late 1985, as this was being written, there was a glut of video rental stores, and it appeared a video shakeout could happen during 1986. So give serious study to your chosen marketplace and its long-term direction *before* you buy a franchise.

Moral Number Three: There are no guarantees; you'll have to choose a franchise as wisely as you would choose a direction for an independent business—and that's very carefully indeed.

Fable Number Four: *As a franchisee, you can leave the management to others.* Unless you are just one partner in a syndicate or partnership that can afford to hire professional managers for your industry, you will need to exercise day-to-day management authority over your franchise. Most franchises, being retail outlets, are cash businesses; unless you or someone you trust with your life is in the store, cash tends to disappear from cash registers. You would need a sophisticated electronic cash register like the kind they use in the major fast-food franchises to overcome the increasingly widespread employee theft problem. Such a unit keeps electronic track of every item sold and gives exact counts of how much of each item is sold, when, and for how much. With a standard manual or even electric or electronic cash register, you get less data. What of employee theft? In a word, cash is simply too tempting.

Franchisors do provide elegant bookkeeping systems designed to help you—and them—keep track of how much you make. After all, the franchisors want to make sure they get the exact amount of royalties you owe them. But even this cannot prevent employee theft.

Equally important, you must manage your operation to make sure it runs the way you want it to run. If you doubt this truism, visit your favorite restaurant on different days of the week. On those days you receive poor service or merchandise not quite up to the usual standard, find out whether the owner is in. With only one exception, my own experience has taught that when the owner is not around, the service and even the product itself will suffer. And so will I. As a consumer, I avoid going to stores and restaurants where no one is in charge. I'm not alone. And this can cost you money beyond what disappears from the till.

Moral Number Four: To achieve the best results, you must manage your franchise operation on a day-to-day basis.

Fable Number Five: *The franchisor takes care of the messy details of running a franchise—the bookkeeping, payroll and sales taxes, unemployment compensation, and so forth.* This is not so. The franchisor only provides you with a bookkeeping system you are required or expected to follow. You, or your bookkeeper or accountant, must do the actual work and pay the bills, balance the books, and pay the taxes as they come due.

Moral Number Five: Want to make Aunt Patty Cakes? Fine. But when you've made and sold them, you still must take care of the boring details of bookkeeping and accounting, not to mention shipping part of your gross to your Uncle Sam. Many people consider him to be in business with them, more so than Aunt Patty.

Fable Number Six: *Franchises are easy to own and operate.* Yes, the franchisor helps you get started. However, once you've opened your doors, you'll be faced with the same juggling act anyone in the small-business arena must cope with. Although you may have gotten a set of hiring guidelines from the franchisor, you'll have to interview, hire, and train your help. You'll have to nurse them through their break-in period, accept their personality quirks. You'll have to deal with the local business groups, disgruntled customers (even with franchises, there are some), and salesmen from Gew-Gaw and Gimcrack, Inc., purveyors of clutter for your walls. You'll have to turn down the eighteenth Robin Cadet who asks you for a donation so the group can go to wilderness camp via the Space Shuttle. You'll have to put up with the loudmouth who almost frightens your other customers away. Your number will be the one that's called when a drunk smashes your plate glass one night; you'll have to call the insurance company and tell them. And you'll have a certain number of responsibilities to the franchisor as well. If you don't fulfill these in a timely and appropriate manner, the franchisor can rescind the agreement and take your license away. It may throw you out of the store and take control of its contents and inventory; this too varies from agreement to agreement, and must be carefully negotiated.

Moral Number Six: Franchises may be easier to get started than independent businesses, but they bear all the usual "costs" of doing business, both personal and financial, and they bring the additional responsibilities to the franchisor that independent businesses lack. Be certain that you're truly ready to accept the drawbacks of franchising as well as its potentially great rewards.

Fable Number Seven: *The rights of franchisees are protected by law.* Yes and no. The federal disclosure rule, which will be discussed in great detail in Chapter 3, explains exactly what a franchisor must tell a prospective franchisee. And 15 states have their own somewhat tougher franchise disclosure rules. But once you sign the franchise agreement and money changes hands, you must abide by that agreement unless the franchisor breaks the terms and conditions of that agreement or you are able to negotiate a mutually satisfactory alternate arrangement if you want to get out. Your legal remedies in most states are really no different than those available to any distributor or company with a contractual dispute with another company. Frankly, most state laws and courts tend to favor the franchisor. This is why many franchisees have banded together in associations to put pressure on franchisors. The National Franchisee Association (NFA) represents the rights of individual franchisees and these associations on a national level.

Moral Number Seven: In many disputes about day-to-day operations and how a contract is interpreted, a franchisee must do battle with the franchisor alone or together with other franchisees. The law, either federal or state, often does not cover the important details.

Fable Number Eight: *Franchisors have the best interests of their franchisees at heart.* Again, yes and no. As long as your interests do not conflict with their best interests, franchisors will indeed help you. At least, reputable franchisors will. Should your interests fail to converge with theirs, however, any franchisor will look out for itself first—anyone would.

And there are many ways franchisors may try to take advantage of a franchisee, prospective, new, or established. (Only a few do, naturally.) Here are several examples:

• Franchise companies may divert royalties and fees for advertising into their own general operating funds, rather than providing the local or national media coverage you were led to expect. You're paying for advertising you have not received.

• Franchisors may take "rebates" or kickbacks from approved suppliers, and sell the supplies to you at inflated prices. (This was prevalent for a while, and led to stringent laws in some states prohibiting it. It is very difficult to get away with now.)

• Franchisors may sell used or refurbished equipment to franchisees at new-equipment prices.

• Franchisors may force you to accept large numbers of discount coupons. The discounts may reduce or eliminate your profit margin, but you will still have to pay royalties to the franchisor based on the increased gross sales figures that included the value of the coupons.

For instance, suppose you were selling an average of 100 hamburgers at $1 each. You made a $20 gross profit and paid the franchise company a 7 percent royalty, or $7 out of the $100. You maximum net profit would be $13. Now, suppose the franchisor flooded your market with half-price coupons. This week, you sold 200 burgers at 50 cents each. Your sales still amounted to $100. You still have to pay the franchisor $7, the royalty on the value of the burgers at sale price. But your cost to produce twice as many burgers was probably higher—more staff time, more fuel, and so on. Worse, you might have to pay the franchisor $14, or the royalty based on the value of the goods without coupons. These and many similar unscrupulous tactics will be explored in Chapters 3, 5, 6, and 10.

Moral Number Eight: Franchisors have their own best interests at heart. They have franchisees' best interests at heart when the latter coincide with their own.

Fable Number Nine: *Owning a franchise is great for a true entrepreneur, a "free spirit" type of person.* Wrong. A certain amount of tension exists between the franchisor and franchisee, although not quite as much as between employer and employee. The franchisor seeks to exert control to protect its reputation, its market share, its profits. The franchisee, on the other hand, wants to run his own show. As a franchisee, you will be subjected to time-consuming, often annoying, reporting and supervisory requirements. Frankly, if you chafe under authority, or are the type of person who must do things your own way, a franchise may not be best for you. It is likely you will be very dissatisfied and feel as if you have traded one boss—the one in your old job or career—for another, the franchisor.

Remember, too, that franchise companies often *do not want* true entrepreneurs in their organizations. The only true entrepreneur they needed *founded* the franchise. And franchisors' professional managers—the bean-counters—may not want the trouble of dealing with independent, argumentative, if not ornery, entrepreneurs "improving" their system.

Moral Number Nine: Franchising is usually not the best business method for a true entrepreneur to follow. Look into it if you classify yourself a "modified" free spirit.

Now that you're seeing the realities of franchising, rather than the myths, whet your appetite with a smorgasbord of franchising possibilities. There's something for every palate.

55-Plus Franchise "Flavors"

Advertising. Not a big category but available all the same, advertising franchises usually involve selling direct-mail, direct-response, or mail-order advertising services to small businesses and professional offices. The only IFA member listed under advertising was American Advertising Distributors, but others include Badgeman International, Money Mailer, Rent-A-Robot, Metro Lists, and Trimark Direct Mail Advertising.

Auto and Truck Rentals. One of the largest, best known, and most prosperous categories, automobile and truck rental franchises involve the lease and rental of autos, trucks, vans, and related products and services to the general and business public. Hertz, Avis, National, and Budget Rent-A-Car are the major national franchises for new cars, but less expensive franchises in used-car rentals, such as Rent-A-Wreck, Ugly Duckling, Rent-a-Heap Cheap, and Rent-A-Dent, are also popular.

Automotive Parts and Services. This too is among the most popular, best established, and oldest types of franchises. It includes a wide range of businesses. The examples in the following list have been divided into several major categories:

- *Auto Parts Stores.* Western Auto, Parts Plus, Champion Auto Stores.
- *Automobile/Truck Sales.* National AutoFinders operates a used-car finders' service, and is typical of the few franchises remaining in automobile sales today. AIN Leasing Corp. offers long-term auto leasing franchises.
- *Brake and Muffler Services.* Midas Mufflers, Meineke Discount Mufflers, and Speedy Muffler King.
- *Body Work, Painting, and Rustproofing.* Maaco Auto Painting, Ziebart, Tuff-Kote Dinol, and Tidy Car.
- *Car Washes.* Hanna Car Wash, Robo Car Wash, Classic Car Wash, and Sparky Coin-Op Wasmobile.
- *Lubrication and Oil Changes.* Jiffy Lube, Grease Monkey, Minit-Lube, and Precision Lubrication.
- *Repair Services.* Great Bear Automotive Center, Drive Line Service, Der Wagen Haus (foreign car repair), Mastercare by Firestone, and King Bear.
- *Tires and Tire Retreading.* B. F. Goodrich, Goodyear Tire Centers, Tire America, National Tire Wholesale, and Vakuum Vulk U.S., Inc.
- *Transmission Services.* AAMCO Transmissions, Cottman Transmissions, Lee Myles Transmissions, Interstate Transmissions, Mr. Transmission, and many more.
- *Tune-Up Shops.* Precision Tune, Sparks Tune Up (subsidiary of MAACO), Tunex, and Acc-U-Tune.
- *Miscellaneous Products and Services.* Harley-Davison (motorcycle sales and services); Truckstops Corporation of America (franchised full-service truckstop facility); and Fantasy Coachworks (automotive accessories).

Beauty and Health. This type also has several categories, ranging from cosmetics and skin care to tanning parlors. Some of them are:

- *Body Wrapping.* The Body Wrap and Sun Wrap.
- *Cosmetics and Skin Care.* "i" Natural Cosmetics, Christine Valmy Skin Care Salon, Syd Simons Cosmetics, Judith Sans Internationale, and Nails 'n Lashes.
- *Hair Care.* HairCrafters, Command Performance, Great Expectations, Fantastic Sam's, and Hair Performers.
- *Opticians and Optical Services.* Pearle Vision Centers, American Vision Centers, and NuVision.
- *Suntanning Parlors.* Eurotan International and Sun Studio.
- *Weight Control.* NutriSystem Weight Loss Centers, Diet Center, and Physicians Weight Loss Centers.
- *Miscellaneous Beauty and Health.* Great Earth Vitamin Stores and Kwit Smoking Centers.

Beverages. This could be listed under food franchises, but the IFA gives this its own category. Coca-Cola, Pepsi-Cola, and all the major cola and soft drink companies franchise their bottling operations and have for many decades.

Bookstores. Few bookstores are franchised, but Little Professor Book Centers have specialized in family-oriented, full-service bookstores.

Business Services. An increasingly popular type of franchise, certainly with the franchise companies, these are available for many business and professional services. They do not include advertising or printing franchises. Here are the major categories and some companies offering franchises in each:

- *Accounting and Consulting.* These provide bookkeeping, accounting, income tax, and general assistance to the small- to medium-size business and professional practice. General Business Services, Comprehensive Accounting, E-Z Keep, and Marcoin Business Services.
- *Business Brokers.* These firms serve as finders and sellers of businesses for sale. VR Business Brokers, Business Investment Group, and Allied Business Brokers.
- *Credit and Collection Services.* Credit Clinic, Corporate Recovery Services, and American Lenders.
- *Temporary Personnel Agencies.* Manpower Temporary Services, Norrell Temporary Services, and Personnel Pool America.
- *Miscellaneous Business Services.* Mail Boxes Etc., USA, Telecheck Services, The Headquarters Companies, Property Damage Appraisers, Deliverex, and Mail Sort.

Children's Services. This is a small category of franchisors offering educational and development services for children; one of these is Gymboree Corporation.

Clothing, Shoes, and Accessories. Athlete's Foot Marketing, Le Sportsac, T-shirts Plus, Knapp Retail Shoe Store, Gingiss Formalwear, and so forth.

Computer Stores and Services. ComputerLand, Entré Computer Center, MicroAge Computer Store, Computer Maintenance Service, Computer Tutor, Computer Scholar Learning Centers, and Software City.

Construction: Materials, Service, and Remodeling. A very large category, this covers a range of product and service franchises, including hardware and home improvement, building materials, energy, prefabricated housing, remodeling, and similar franchises:

- *Building Materials.* Lumberyards, such as Beaver Lumber Company.
- *Energy Products and Services.* It includes solar energy and energy conservation firms, such as American Energy Managers, Energy Doctor, and Doctor Fix-It.
- *Prefabricated Housing.* Log homes, cedar homes, modular homes, and the like, such as Lincoln Log Homes, Lindal Cedar Homes, Mill Craft Building Systems, and Ryan Homes.
- *Remodeling.* Mr. Build and Mister Renovator.
- *Miscellaneous.* B-Dry System (waterproofing); House Master of America (home inspection service); Eldorado Stone (precast stone products); and The Linc Corporation (heating and air-conditioning services).

Dental Clinics. More and more, hard-pressed dentists are turning to franchise operations in shopping malls and the like to increase their business. Dwight Dental Care, DentaHealth, Dentalworks, and Omnidentrix Dental Centers.

Drugstores. Medicine Shoppe International and The Medicine Stores are two examples of pharmacy franchises that compete with Rexall and similar licensed dealerships.

Educational Products and Services. These include everything from dance studios to modeling schools and adult training institutes, such as John Robert Powers, Arthur Murray, Barbizon School of Modeling, Success Motivation Institute (SMI) Intl., and Mary Moppet's Day Care. The latter is not included among children's services because it is not specifically geared toward improving the child's life, but rather the parents' through professional day-care facilities.

Electronic Stores. Radio Shack is the largest and best known of these.

Employment Agencies and Search Firms. Snelling & Snelling, Dunhill Personnel System, Bryant Bureau, Career Blazers, Acme Personnel Service, Management Recruiters, and many more.

Exercise and Fitness Centers. Elaine Powers Figure Salon, Jazzercise, Body Design by Gilda, and Aerobic Fitness & Diet Center.

Florist Shops. This category does not include services such as Teleflora or FTD; they are not franchises. It does include Conroy's and Flowerama of America, Inc.

Food. The food category, of course, is the largest single category, and has huge subdivisions, with fast food leading the pack.

- *Baked Goods.* Baked goods is a relatively small category, with several good companies involved, such as Pepperidge Farm, Bun Masters, Grandma Lee's, and the Original Great American Chocolate Chip Cookie Co., Inc.
- *Candy, Nuts, Fruits, and Confections.* Karmelkorn Shoppes, Jo-Ann's Nut House/Chez Chocolat, The Corn Popper, Morrow's Nut House, and Galerie Au Chocolate.
- *Cheese and Special Foods.* Swiss Colony and Hickory Farms of Ohio.
- *Donuts.* Dunkin' Donuts, Mister Donut, Spudnuts, Jolly Pirate Donuts and Coffee, Donut Inn, and Donutland.
- *Grocery and Convenience Stores.* Convenient Food Mart, 7-Eleven Food Stores, Jr. Food Mart, Dairy Mart Convenience Stores, Inc., and Piggly-Wiggly Food Stores.
- *Ice Cream.* Baskin-Robbins 31 Flavors, Swensen's Ice Cream Parlour, Häagen-Dazs, Bresler's 33 Flavors, Carvel Corporation, Dairy Queen, Tastee-Freez, I Can't Believe It's Yogurt, and Mister Softee, Inc.
- *Manufacturers and Suppliers.* A small category of food wholesalers and distributors, including Canteen Corporation, a food-service and vending operation.
- *Recreation and Public Concessions.* Concessionaire at public and outdoor facilities; Atlantic Concessions is one example.

Gift Shops. Cutlery World and The Love Store.

Hardware and Home Improvement. Coast to Coast Services, Dominion Hardware, Color Your World, and St. Clair Paint and Wallpaper.

Home Furnishings—Retail. This category, too, has several divisions:

- *Art and Picture Framing.* Frame Factory, The Great Frame Up, and Deck The Walls.
- *Bed and Bath.* Bathtique International, Nettle Creek, and Scandia Down.
- *Interior Decorating.* Decorating Den, Pier 1 Imports, Spring Crest Drapery Centers, and G. Fried Carpetland.
- *Furniture and Furniture Stripping.* The Work Bench, Dip 'N' Strip, and Naked Furniture.

Income Tax Services. H&R Block, Triple Check Income Tax Service, and Econotax.

Insurance. These either operate as or provide services to independent insurance agents. Systems VII, Insurance World, and Pridemark.

Laundry and Dry Cleaning. One Hour Martinizing Dry Cleaning, King Koin Laundry Center, and Martin Franchises, Inc.

Lawn and Garden Services. Lawn Doctor, Inc., Lawn-A-Mat, Spring Green, and The Weed Man.

Liquor and Wine. Foremost Liquor Stores, Ernie's Wines and Liquors, and M.G.M. Liquor Warehouse.

Machinery. Machinery Wholesalers Corporation.

Maintenance, Cleaning, and Sanitation. This has several subdivisions for easy reference:

- *Carpet, Upholstery, Drapery, and Ceilings.* Duraclean International, Servicemaster, Rainbow Intl., Chem-Dry Carpet Cleaning, and Stanley Steemer.
- *Exterior Washing.* Sparkle Wash and Jiffiwash.
- *Maid Services.* Servicemaster, Mini-Maid, Merry Maids, and The Maids International.
- *Porcelain Repair.* Perma Ceram Enterprises, Porcelite International, and Gnu Tub.
- *Home Repairs.* Dial One International and College Students Painting Co.
- *Sewer and Drain Cleaning.* Roto-Rooter, Mr. Rooter, and Rescue Industries.

Medical Services. These include home health and nursing care services as well as physicians' offices. Nursefinders, Homecall, Inc., and Alpha Nurses.

Motels and Hotels. Holiday Inns, Best Western, Quality Inn, TraveLodge, Sheraton, and many more well-known names.

Pet Shops. Doktor Pet Care Centers (veterinary services) and Petland (pet shop).

Photography Services and Supplies. These include photofinishing, videotaping services, photography studios, camera shops, and the like. One Hour Photo, Inc., Chroma Copy Franchising of America, Video Data Services, and Photo Logo.

Printing Services. Printing, business cards, and photocopying franchises are included. Sir Speedy, Postal Instant Press, Business Cards Tomorrow, Inc., Kwik-Kopy, Quik Print, Alphagraphics Print Shops of the Future, and many more.

Real-Estate Sales. This category includes real-estate sales, property management, do-it-yourself home-seller services, and so forth. Coldwell Banker, Century 21, Help-U-Sell, Better Homes Realty, ERA (Electronic Realty Associates), Prime PM, and so on.

Recreation and Amusements. Kampgrounds of America (KOA), Putt-Putt Golf and Games, and Corner Pocket.

Rentals—Tools, Equipment, Supplies. Taylor Rental Center, Nationwide General Rental, A to Z Rental Centers, National Video, and Remco Enterprises.

Restaurants—Fast-Food. This category is divided into numerous small categories to show the incredible variety of fast-food and sit-down restaurant franchises available.

- *Delicatessens.* Mr. Dunderbak's and Big Top Deli.
- *Ethnic Fast Foods.* Manchu Wok, Quick Wok, and Mew Meiji Take Out (Japanese).
- *Fish and Chips.* Long John Silver's Seafood Shoppes, Skippers, and London Fish & Chips.
- *Fried Chicken.* Kentucky Fried Chicken, Church's Fried Chicken, Popeye's Famous Fried Chicken, Chicken Delight, Lee's Famous Country Recipe, and Bojangles of America.
- *Hamburgers.* McDonald's, Burger King, Wendy's, Jack in the Box, and Fatburger.
- *Mexican.* Taco Bell, Taco John's, Taco Time, and Pepe's Mexican Restaurants.
- *Pizza.* Domino's Pizza, Pizza Hut, Pizza Inn, Godfather's Pizza, and Shakey's Pizza Restaurant.
- *Salads, Sandwiches, and Potatoes.* Schlotzsky's, Jan Drake's Garden Cafe.
- *Submarine Sandwiches.* Subway Sandwiches, Blimpie, and Mr. Submarine.
- *Miscellaneous.* Arby's Roast Beef, A&W Root Beer, Orange Julius, and Dogs and Suds.

Restaurants—Family-Style.

- *Coffee Shop.* Huddle House, Dobbs House, and Copper Penny Family Coffee Shops.
- *Dinner-Style.* Benihana and Dosanko.
- *Italian.* Boston Pizza and Noble Roman's Pizza.
- *Pancakes.* International House of Pancakes and Village Inn Pancake House.
- *Steakhouse.* Ponderosa Steakhouse, Bonanza Family Restaurants, and Sizzler Restaurants.
- *Miscellaneous.* Big Boy Restaurants, Hardee's Restaurants, Gino's, Roy Rogers, Perkins, and Howard Johnson's.

Sales—Equipment and Supplies. National Equipment Finders, Inc.

Security Services and Products. Sonitrol, Alliance Security Systems, and Rampart Security Systems.

Stereo, Record, Video, and Audio Stores. Curtis Mathes, Team Electronics, Sounds Easy, and Sam the Record Man.

Storage Facilities. Miniwarehouses and homeowner storage services. Your Attic, Inc.

Stores—General Merchandise. Variety stores, such as Ben Franklin Stores, Inc., and Coast to Coast.

Travel Agencies. International Tours, Uniglobe Travel, Empress Travel, and Travel Agents International.

Video Rental Stores. Video Connection, Video Cross Roads, Video Biz, and so on.

Water Conditioning. Culligan and Rainsoft.

Miscellaneous Products and Services. These include a wide range of services, such as the following: packing and shipping services (Pack 'N' Ship); job and school résumé preparation (Best Resume Service); private buying service (United Consumers Club); financial services (Family Financial Planning); and many more.

From this extensive list, you may find a type of business to your liking. You may have had jobs in one or more of those businesses, or you may have had training in high schools, colleges, or vocational-technical institutes that matches the required skills. One of them may fit a hobby you would like to turn into a paying proposition. Or one may simply represent a lifelong dream you wish to pursue.

Your qualifications to own and operate a successful franchise are not dependent on these factors alone, however. Your success depends on many other personal factors, too. Chapter 2 helps you explore your strengths and weaknesses, your goals and desires, and your short- and long-term objectives so you can decide whether you are ready to own—and succeed in—a franchise of your own.

2

Are You Ready to Own a Franchise?

One of the main reasons people cite for buying a franchise is that their old job or profession doesn't fit them anymore. Could this be your reason, too? Maybe your job isn't delivering the financial rewards you want. Maybe it isn't giving you any sort of satisfaction. Maybe you hate commuting, or you don't like the way your job separates you from your family. Maybe you've decided you no longer like detail work. (Or perhaps you've been begging for more detail work and can't get it.) Possibly you find the industry itself displeasing. Or you firmly believe the company has taken a wrong turn since the new chairman arrived—a turn that won't be good for your future. Maybe the signs are already there: You're being dumped from your corner office to one with no window. Maybe you're in a job that causes you to get your hands dirty, and you've had enough. (Or maybe you wish you could do something with your hands!) Maybe you like your job, but would rather do it for yourself than for someone else. There are as many reasons for leaving jobs as there are people working, or more.

Even people who have no job, like those below, opt out of what they're doing and begin franchising. Maybe you fit one of these categories:

• Self-employed businesspeople or professionals staying in the same field. These people want the recognition, "legitimacy," and competitive edge a "brand-name" franchise can give them. This is very prevalent in the real-estate business, in which the vast majority of franchises are sold to independent realtors and local or regional real-estate broker chains.

• Homemakers and unemployed spouses who buy a party-plan franchise or sell a franchised line of goods from their homes.

• Investors and syndicates that hire professional management or pay the franchisor to manage their outlets. (Perhaps you'd like to form one; or maybe you've been asked by a friend or business acquaintance to invest in his.)

• Existing franchisees expanding their successful operations.

No matter which of these categories you come from, in order to be successful, you'll share the same goal with all the franchise owners from all the backgrounds—profit.

You may find this a big change from your former goals. Suppose you were a salaried professional. Your goals may have been to please your boss, obtain a promotion, get a raise, achieve professional recognition, and so forth. In your own business, you might be tempted to place too much emphasis on your public image—or private one—and not enough on the cash accounts.

Or perhaps you were a production manager; your goal was to get products out the door. Other people determined how much you could spend to do it. In your own franchise, you may tend, because of your professional background, to be too concerned about producing the hamburgers and controlling their quality and not concerned enough about keeping your costs and overhead down.

But these kinds of goals become secondary when you own a franchise. The bottom line becomes practically an object of veneration. That's why businesspeople with "bottom-line" backgrounds—directors of sales and marketing, for example—often find owning a franchise easier than do people from backgrounds that emphasize other aspects of working life, such as job enrichment.

But whatever your working background, you will have taken from it— and given to it—certain characteristics that may be of more or less use to you in your own franchise. Here are some of the questions people from various business backgrounds might ask themselves. Try them on yourself and answer honestly. If you know what your major tendencies were, you can use them or counter them to provide the best all-round attitude to achieve your own franchise success.

(Hint: A successful franchisee will very likely display traits from all the job types in varying degrees, whether learned on the job or on his own. Think about how your liabilities may also be an asset, and think about training yourself in assets from other disciplines. Use these short analyses to jog your own thoughts.)

Your Professional Self

Are you or were you, or were you trained to be, a(n):

Manager or executive? Do you know how to get your hands dirty? That is, can you do what needs to be done, from sweeping the floor to delivering pizzas if need be?

Often managers from large companies are used to having staffs at their beck and call. A pitfall for you, if you're from this type of background, may be to load your business with employees, a sure way to create overhead and eat into your profits. Evaluate whether you actually can lend a hand as well as a brain.

(The asset side? You have no trouble handling responsibility, a bugbear for many would-be business owners.)

Salaried employee? Can you face the responsibility of making decisions that directly determine the success or failure of your business?

Often salaried employees have no decision-making experience, and have relied for years on others to make decisions and take responsibility. In a franchise, the buck stops where the owner stands. That's you. Do you really welcome this?

(If you can continue to do a job for its own sake, however, that will help tide you over the slow times in your own business. An asset for you.)

Wage earner? Have you worked by the clock and by the hour?

You may never have had to worry about giving the boss advice, or taking responsibility for anything other than your own set of tasks.

Now can you accept that you must make practically all of the decisions? Can you learn to delegate authority instead of taking orders or having work assigned to you?

(You will have an easier time than some, perhaps, in taking direction from the franchisor. An asset.)

Self-employed person? Can you accept the franchisor's authority under the agreement you will sign?

Self-employed businesspeople most often trip up over their responsibilities to the franchise company.

Can you accept the franchisor's supervision and your financial and reporting obligations to the franchise company? If you come to resent the franchisor's authority, it may lead to serious trouble on both sides.

(On the other hand, you may be able to view the franchisor's authority as a source of blessed relief, giving you a "responsibility vacation" and husbanding your underlying strength. Work this into an asset.)

Homemaker/unemployed spouse? Can you translate your experience in managing a household into useful ways to manage a franchise?

For these people, accepting the routines that accompany working outside the home can be stressful.

Can you accept the need for training? Can you interact with employees and customers in an adult-to-adult manner instead of a parent-to-child relationship?

(In your personal role, you've also had "buck-stops-here" experience. An asset.)

Salesperson? Can you accept that, while you will probably still be selling to some extent, you will now be primarily managing a business, making decisions, and accepting responsibility?

The temptation for sales professionals is to sell at the expense of the myriad other aspects of running a business, especially managing people.

Can you avoid the trap of selling yourself too well to your employees and customers alike, letting them take advantage of you and bombarding your bottom line?

(Naturally, your sales experience will always come in handy too. An asset.)

Teacher? Can you, like homemakers, make the transition from talking down to people dependent upon you to speaking on a level to your equals— whether the franchisor or your customers?

The temptation for teachers is to pass on knowledge, often bypassing the cash drawer in the process.

Can you accept that any teaching you engage in will be limited to training your own staff? You can suggest things to customers, but you can't give them a failing grade if they reject your advice, nor can you afford to act that way.

(Your facility at explaining is, however, a significant asset.)

Artist or crafts worker? Can you accept the fact that your creativity is limited by the requirements of the franchisor's product or service?

The temptation to be a free spirit is a danger, and may outweigh the desire to make a large income.

Can you balance your desires for aesthetic perfection with the necessities of the bottom line? Can you sometimes accept things that are less than aesthetically pleasing to keep your business running?

(Your essential insight is a great asset, however, if you use it with restraint.)

No matter which category you fit into, there's a lot more exploring you'd better do before you commit substantial financial resources and a large hunk of your time and energy to buying a franchise. Remember that many new franchisees fail because they were simply not cut out for the line of business they chose. Many fail simply because they went into what appeared to be the easiest and most profitable business in the short term. But by far the most failures happen because franchisees fail to know their own minds.

Spending the time in the beginning to seek out the franchise that's a perfect fit can save you months of hard work and disappointment, not to mention financial loss. That is not to say you will not have to work hard or face periodic disappointments and trouble, but overall, you will feel better and probably make more money if you enjoy working in your franchise's field of endeavor.

In any case, you may even be prevented from making a wrong decision by knowledgeable franchise marketing directors. They will carefully consider whether you are cut out for their business before they sign an agreement with you. Remember, when you visit them or they visit you—and these visits are very likely to occur before an agreement is signed—you get a chance to evaluate each other. Franchisors would be unwise to let someone with little real interest or ability buy a franchise; they know from experience that way leads to disgruntled franchisees, lowered profits, and heightened managerial problems for franchisee and franchisor alike. After you see how to plumb your own depths, you'll see how deeply the franchisor can—and should— plumb them with you.

(In fact, if the franchise company does not insist on a thorough investigation of your business and work experience, personal and credit history, psychological makeup, and financial standing, there is something wrong. A franchisor who makes a cursory examination of your application is likely to be a fast-buck artist—and the one making the fast bucks will be him, not you.)

So save effort and disappointment all around. Conduct a thorough evaluation of yourself, and then present yourself to the franchisor. You'll have a better chance of succeeding from the start.

Keep in mind that people do the strangest things for the strangest reasons. Any behaviorist, from Sigmund Freud to Allen Funt, will tell you so. That's fine if you're talking about buying shirts or even spending your vacation. But if you're talking about spending the rest of your life—or even a good portion of it—you'd do best to make sure the reasons are not strange, at least to you. (They can be strange to someone else. That's fine. But you're the one who has to bear the burden.)

To sum it up, you owe it to yourself to evaluate your own motivation, background, goals, business experience and acumen, and family relationships. Do it ruthlessly, and don't worry ahead of time about what you think you may find. There are no right or wrong answers to self-knowledge. There is just the inestimable advantage of knowing whether you are truly suited to become a successful franchisee.

Almost 20 Questions

You know where you've been, your business background, and "industrial strengths." You have identified the pitfalls your profession may make you prone to; you have honestly determined whether you can overcome them or even turn them into assets. Now it's time to see if you have what it takes to succeed in franchising.

Be as upbeat as possible when answering. Avoid doing this self-evaluation to be hypercritical of yourself, or to *prevent* yourself from ever owning a franchise. Avoid giving answers someone else might give for you; ignore the little voices that sound like your mother, your spouse, your best friend. Answer the questions with an aim to discovering whether owning a franchise is really the answer to your business future.

1. Why do you want to own a franchise? What are the real reasons you want to stop doing what you are doing and make an important change in your life-style and career?
2. How do you feel about money, making money, having lots of money, and being financially secure and independently wealthy?
3. Do you consider owning a franchise an end in itself?
4. In a corporate or institutional situation, have you ever been characterized as a maverick, a dreamer, an oddball, a misfit, or a malcontent? Do you feel lost among the legions of coworkers or out of place in the corporate world?
5. Do you enjoy hard work even if that work does not necessarily result in immediate rewards?
6. How self-reliant are you? Do you wait for others to take the initiative? Do you need the approval of others and lots of emotional and mental support before you make a decision, start a task, or make a change in your life?
7. Are you a risk taker? Are you willing to bet your time, your energy, your brainpower, and a goodly portion of your money on a venture that has a better than even chance of *success?*
8. Do you take real pleasure—find true enjoyment—in running the show, being on your own?
9. Do you honestly accept responsibility for your actions? Or when things go wrong, do you blame others? On the other hand, can you honestly accept credit when you cause things to go well?
10. Do you enjoy thinking up new ideas and putting them into action, even if you risk failure?
11. Are you the type of person who does more than you have to do?
12. Are you an enthusiastic type of person with a positive outlook on life?
13. Do you work effectively with other people? Do you know how to smooth ruffled feathers, calm an angry person, satisfy a disgruntled customer?
14. Although you are ambitious, enthusiastic, and strong-willed, can you follow the formula, organization, and requirements of the franchisor?

15. Can you deal with stacks of tedious, repetitious, monotonous, boring paperwork, and tend to a thousand picky details, and still keep up a reasonably positive outlook?
16. Do you like to show or teach other people how to do things?
17. Do you enjoy *multitasking,* the ability to handle many chores in tandem, which franchising requires?
18. Are you willing to accept the help of others?
19. Do you have the determination to get what you want and go after it without doubt or hesitation?

Now that you've answered for yourself, here's some insight, from the franchising point of view, into what each answer might mean to your success. Remember that these are simply possible answers to the questions; they may not be yours. Use them as guidelines and food for thought.

1. *Why do you want to own a franchise? What are the real reasons you want to stop doing what you are doing and make an important change in your life-style and career?*

• To be my own boss and own my own business. Does this ring true to you? Probe further. Do you simply not like your current boss (this might change with a change of bosses), or do you strongly prefer running things, giving directions, managing people, and making decisions?

• To change careers. Be aware that owning a franchise is much more than changing careers. If you are going from employment to self-employment, you are changing everything—your home life, working hours, family relationships, self-image, social status, and free time. If you could change careers and do anything you want to do, would you still prefer owning a franchise and being out on your own? Or do you think that the career of your choice would be working in a different, better job for someone else—perhaps as chief executive officer of a major corporation, or becoming the top commercial artist in a graphics studio? Could your desire for career change be either a desire to advance in your present field or to change fields while still performing as an employee?

• To escape a dead-end job. If someone came to you tomorrow and offered you the job of your choice, would you abandon the idea of a franchise and take it? Or are you completely dedicated to going on your own?

• To gain prestige in your community and increase your social standing. Owning a franchise may lead to those things. But often you spend so much time with a franchise you have little time to participate in community affairs and civic groups. Your social standing may even suffer, at least temporarily. It may take some time to build community prestige—time that will be added to your initially long working hours. Could you achieve this goal simply by doing volunteer work and keeping your current job?

• To make more money. Are you willing to devote the long hours, the hard work, and the smart work that owning your own business requires to make more money? Making more money with a franchise than you do now in a job carries far more risks under normal circumstances. Are you willing to take those risks?

Most people who end up in their own franchise have at least several, if not all, of these motivations to a greater or lesser degree. But it appears that the owners who are most successful have as their primary motivation making more money. Only that motivation—followed by effort, dedication, and smart thinking—puts the odds of success firmly in your favor.

All of the other motivations carry their own limitations. The desire to be your own boss and own a business is easy to fulfill. Yet if you do not have an equally strong urge to make money, you can end up owning a business that *loses* money, or earns just enough for you to scrape by. Remember that hundreds of thousands of businesses make little or no money and go out of business each year. Many of their owners were "light" on the money motivation, having one of the others as their single greatest motivator. Survival, owning a business, proving something to themselves, changing careers, or any of the other motivators probably took precedence over making money.

2. *How do you feel about money, making money, having lots of money, and being financially secure and independently wealthy?*

What was your instant reaction to that question? Something like "Oh, it's a sin to get rich." Or "I'll be a bad person if I make a lot of money." Or "Money is the root of all evil, isn't it?"

Was your reaction one of these, or any of the many other negative thoughts one might have about money? Despite Norman Vincent Peale, Og Mandino, Albert Lowry, and many other successful and wealthy men and women who teach that achieving prosperity, wealth, and abundance are good and worthy goals, many people still believe they are "bad" if they have a lot of money.

Yet the evidence is to the contrary. The wealthiest people often turn out to be the most generous, giving far more than they need to give if they merely wanted tax deductions. They often are the most interesting, lively, entertaining, informed, upbeat people around. Who do you think would be interesting to have as a dinner-table companion—your neighbor who never made a dime and spends most of his time complaining about not having enough money? Or someone like Norman Vincent Peale, who has lived an encyclopedia of stories, most with happy, prosperous endings?

Many successful and wealthy people started with nothing—or even with a pile of debts—and learned how to do many things, profiting at the same time. They travel to interesting places, meet other successful and interesting people, enjoy the pleasures life has to offer, and most of all, they never stop learning. They have or developed open, inquisitive, searching minds and continously seek out better, more efficient, and effective ways to achieve their primary goal: to make more money. So they can continue to live abundantly and have interesting experiences, pleasures, things, and results.

If this does not describe you—if your reaction was similar to the first negative bunch of answers—don't despair. Work on your attitude adjustment before you sign up for your franchise. Repeat positive statements about money over and over; read financial success stories and convince yourself that money is not the root of all evil.

When you begin to believe it (you don't have to believe it perfectly just yet), begin to think seriously about your franchise. After your first few successes, you'll have proof enough that money is not the root of all evil. In fact, it's the root of your prosperous future—and that's good.

3. *Do you consider owning a franchise an end in itself?*

Once you own a franchise, will you be satisfied? If so, then owning a franchise is your primary motivation. This may lead to an emotional involvement with the *franchise* itself, rather than the object of the franchise—making a profit. Further, if your franchise does not do well, you might feel as if *you* are a failure, rather than just feeling that your business has failed.

A better point of view is to consider a franchise just a convenient and easier method of reaching your primary goal: making more money. With that attitude, you cannot become hopelessly devoted to the franchise. You can make the franchise succeed. Then you might even consider selling it to buy a different one, or multiples, or none—whatever you feel will best help you attain your profit goals without unnecessary and unhealthy emotional attachment. Save the emotional investments for your family, friends, and pets, not your business.

4. *In a corporate or institutional situation, have you ever been characterized as a maverick, a dreamer, an oddball, a misfit, or a malcontent? Do you feel lost among the legions of coworkers or out of place in the corporate world?*

If you feel this way, you have a better than average chance of making it on your own; most successful people in business for themselves characterize themselves this way.

But beware. If you believe you carry these attributes to their extremes, perhaps you would feel constrained by owning a franchise. Seek help from people who know you well to decide whether you have a moderate or extreme number of these characteristics; but rely on your own judgment in the end.

Owning a franchise requires that you follow the business format and formula of the franchise company. Success in a particular business often does not allow for much monkeying around with the methodology. Still, a successful franchisee needs to have at least a healthy dollop of independent thinking. Ask yourself: When I work for someone else, do I prefer to be given a task and then left alone to accomplish it, no matter how long it takes or how much research and decision making I've got to do to come up with the answer? Can I accept and ask for help when I'm stuck?

If you answer yes to both questions, your maverick attributes are probably in healthy balance and you can succeed in franchising.

5. *Do you enjoy hard work even if that work does not necessarily result in immediate rewards?*

Some franchises, particularly the cash businesses, do provide immediate rewards. But many others do not. They may take a year or more to build up so that you are receiving lots of positive feedback from customers and lots of money as well. Buying a franchise may also require you to go fairly heavily into debt to get started, and you may feel that you are working for the bank or your investors instead of yourself. If you think waiting for the big payoff would be too much to take, you should orient your thinking to a franchise with low startup costs and high up-front rewards. This would consist of a small fast-food franchise or any business that deals primarily in cash receipts.

Even with these, naturally some of that cash will be earmarked for bills and for reinvesting in the business. But just seeing the cash flow through is helpful to some people in keeping their interest and enthusiasm perking.

6. *How self-reliant are you? Do you wait for others to take the initiative? Do you need the approval of others and lots of emotional and mental support before you make a decision, start a task, or make a change in your life?*

The more self-reliant you are, the more likely that you can handle the slings and arrows sure to come your way as you start up a franchise.

7. *Are you a risk taker? Are you willing to bet your time, your energy, your brainpower, and a goodly portion of your money on a venture that has a better than even chance of success?*

If you want guarantees of success, or a guaranteed level of income, or a guaranteed low-hassle enterprise, then a franchise is not for you. If you can handle a moderate level of risk, can cope with fluctuating income at least in the beginning, and are willing to take the good with the bad, then you'll probably do well with a franchise. By and large, they succeed more often than fail. But there is, to be sure, some risk.

To be doubly certain, rate yourself on this risk scale:

Avoids all risk: An example of this is the classic bureaucrat, the person who cannot handle any risk at all, the person who performs most productively and successfully when he is in a secure cradle-to-grave job. Is that you? Now? In the past? Would you like to change?

Takes any risk: This is the classic gambler, the person willing to take any risk at all at any odds for any reward simply for the thrill of the gamble.

(1) Do you spend days and nights at the track? (2) Or just go occasion-

ally for fun? (3) Do you think business is a gamble? (4) Or a calculated risk? If you've answered questions two and four yes, you are likely to be a successful franchisee. If, on the other hand, you've answered yes to questions one and three, watch out. You may be a gambler. Save the thrills for your leisure time; don't let them interfere with the workings of your business.

Will take odds of three-to-one or calculated risks: The classic entrepreneur likes three-to-one odds for success. These people, who love big risks for big rewards, may not find owning a franchise very exciting. In fact, this kind of person is usually better at starting the franchise company itself and making it into a gigantic success. The late Ray A. Kroc, who built McDonald's into an empire, was like this, as was Conrad Hilton of Hilton Hotels.

Does this story describe your attitude? If so, you might be best advised to develop a franchise, not buy one. Or if you are willing to accept the constraints, buy one and use it as a means to the financial freedom to eventually cut loose on your own. You can successfully own a franchise if you dispassionately view it as a learning and growing experience.

Likes at least even money: The classic franchise owner is someone who is an independent thinker and wants to be in business on his own. He believes in profit, but has decided he needs help getting started. He believes in himself and in his decision. With a franchise, he will get odds a bit better than an entrepreneur's—but life will be a whole lot less certain than a bureaucrat's. The most successful franchisees are those who are comfortable with a moderate amount of risk, for substantial financial rewards, and are willing to seek help getting those rewards.

8. *Do you take real pleasure—find true enjoyment—in running the show, being on your own?*

If you prefer others to carry the load, if you always follow the crowd instead of leading it or going your own way, if you do not like telling others what to do, you may not make a good franchise owner—unless, of course, the franchise is a one-person operation. And there are, indeed, several of those. In what fields? Health and exercise, sales of personal and home products, and candy-flower-singing telegrams to name a few.

9. *Do you honestly accept responsibility for your actions? Or when things go wrong, do you blame others? On the other hand, can you honestly accept credit when you cause things to go well?*

If you blame others for your difficulties ("My parents hate me, my boss doesn't like me, the economy is too poor for me to succeed, my spouse doesn't want me to succeed," and so on), then you are likely to have trouble managing a franchise. You will find yourself saddled with employee discontent (they will catch it from you), poor customer relations (they too will catch attitude flu from you), and, very likely, serious disagreements with the franchisor.

Accepting responsibility means taking a clear view of what you do right and wrong, and then saying to yourself and others, "Well, I was wrong. What's done is done; now let me see how I can correct what needs correcting and improve on what I am doing right."

Owning a franchise will also require you to accept the responsibility for what your employees do. An employee may spill a soft drink on a customer, but you may be the one who has to apologize, offer to pay to clean the person's clothes, and make other types of restitution. Can you do this without blaming the employee, but gently correcting the action instead?

Be careful too that you aren't a member of the magical mystery tour who thinks that all things that go wrong are his own fault, and anything that goes well does so by magic. This sort of attitude flu is just as damaging in the long run. It will eat into your self-confidence, if it hasn't already. So be sure to take credit, as well as responsibility, where it's due.

10. *Do you enjoy thinking up new ideas and putting them into action, even if you risk failure?*

Although you need to follow the franchisor's basic formula, you will find owning a franchise gives you plenty of leeway to create new ways to increase your business, save money, improve management, improve customer relations, reduce overhead, and so forth. And the more creative and inventive you are—within the franchisor's guidelines—the more involved you may become, if you like to act creatively. In many franchises, however, where the formula is standard, there may not be as much need for new ideas and creative thinking as you would like.

11. *Are you the type of person who does more than you have to do?*

If you are willing to take an extra step to help someone else, to make your store looks better, to finish a major task, you are better prepared to succeed with a franchise than is a clock-watcher or a person who does the absolute minimum to get by.

12. *Are you an enthusiastic type of person with a positive outlook on life?*

This does not mean you have to be a cheerleader. It means that if you can maintain a reasonable level of enthusiasm despite hard work and adversity, you will find it easier to keep yourself, your family, and your employees moving steadily toward your goals.

13. *Do you work effectively with other people? Do you know how to smooth ruffled feathers, calm an angry person, satisfy a disgruntled customer?*

Not only will you find this a very useful skill in running a franchise, but you'd find its opposite—excitability in yourself—would be a hindrance. Develop your calm, cool, and collected capabilities if you want to go out on your own.

14. *Although you are ambitious, enthusiastic, and strong-willed, can you follow the formula, organization, and requirements of the franchisor?*

If you can temper your desire to do it your own way and run the business according to the formula and advice of the franchise company, you will find it much easier to succeed. Many surveys of successful franchisees show that they obtain the best results by following closely the franchisor's formula and taking advantage of the benefits and opportunities—special discounts, group purchase plans, and so on—a franchisor offers.

15. *Can you deal with stacks of tedious, repetitious, monotonous, boring paperwork, and tend to a thousand picky details, and still keep up a reasonably positive outlook?*

Owning a franchise involves filling out dozens of forms—franchisor reports, income tax forms, withholding tax forms, loan applications, W-2 forms, unemployment compensation reports, and more—and they are all time-consuming and deadly dull. But despite these monotonous tasks, you still need to be able to keep your ultimate goals in sight and keep moving toward them.

16. *Do you like to show or teach other people how to do things?*

In most types of franchises you might run, you will have employees and they will have to be trained. You may experience rapid employee turnover, especially in restaurants and fast-food businesses, and you may have to train and retrain frequently. If you do not like to train others, you will need to have someone else available to do it. But if you were ever a *successful* amateur sports coach, seminar leader, or teacher who really enjoyed what you were doing, you will find you'll enjoy training employees too.

17. *Do you enjoy* multitasking, *the ability to handle many chores in tandem, which franchising requires?*

Consider the following tasks you will have to do when you own a franchise. Have you ever done them before? If not, do you honestly think you could enjoy them, or at least do them effectively?

• Hiring others to do a paid job. Even if you have never hired anyone, have you ever chosen someone from a group of applicants to be part of a team, committee, club, and so on? While not the same thing as hiring and firing, even these experiences help.

• Managing the work of employees or other people. Parents certainly have done this with their children. Have you ever captained a sports team or run a club committee or community affairs group?

• Bookkeeping, filing tax returns, writing cash-flow statements, developing monthly budgets, or other accounting procedures. Unfortunately, many people do not like doing these financial tasks. But knowing how to read and grasp these statements and forms is the best way for you to keep your finger on the financial pulse of your operation. Fortunately, you can hire an accountant, and the franchise company provides forms to make the job easier.

• Selling or marketing products or services. Even if you have no more experience selling than helping your kids sell Girl Scout cookies, did you like doing it? *Could* you like doing it?

• Dealing with angry or upset customers. Have you ever served as a peacemaker among colleagues, smoothed the ruffled feathers of neighbors and coworkers, perhaps angry parents at a Little League game? Are you the Great Mediator in your family?

• Meeting deadlines, making products, or performing services. Experience might include completing reports on time, meeting quotas on a job, even getting the kids off to school on time every day, and so on.

No doubt one or more of these activities didn't strike you as pleasant. Further delve into your ability to do it by applying this question to each of those activities: How do you feel when you *must* do any of the tasks described above?

• Calm, poised, and ready to take on a new challenge? This is a feeling few people manage. But it's certainly desirable. Luckily, unless you have true antipathy for most tasks, it can be learned.

• Somewhat nervous? This is a far more common, yet still normal, reaction to doing something new, unfamiliar, or even somewhat unlikable. It can be overcome, or used to your advantage, the way actors use preperformance "butterflies" to enhance their onstage energy.

• Overwhelmed, panicky, and actually physically ill? This may be an unnecessary overreaction brought on by dire fears of failure. If you feel this way about any of the common tasks required by a franchise operation, you have several choices.

First, you can learn better ways to deal with the situation. Practice relaxation techniques. Ask yourself what is the worst that can happen if you do the unpleasant task.

Second, you can hire someone else to do it for you. But you may not be able to do that right away. Can you handle it until then? Or get a source of free help, a spouse or child?

Third, and really no alternative at all, you can avoid owning a franchise. Then, of course, you would have let your fear defeat you.

On the other hand, ignoring fear can also get you into trouble. A modicum of fear is not only natural, but instinctual and good. Fear makes you jump out of the way of an oncoming bus. If you convince yourself you must always be fearless and ignore signs when you have every right to be afraid, you could do yourself grave harm. If you saw that the income of your franchise had been steadily falling for several months and blissfully ignored the decline, you would be acting without fear, but without good sense either. A modicum of healthy fear would encourage you to study your operation to find out why your income was falling and what you should do about it.

18. *Are you willing to accept the help of others?*

Many people feel badly about asking others for help. They want to be able to tell the world they did it on their own. But franchisors have a lot to offer—training, advertising support, management training, location assistance, and so on—and only foolish people would turn down help they are paying good money to obtain.

19. *Do you have the determination to get what you want and go after it without doubt or hesitation?*

Succeeding with a franchise requires a combination of a one-track mind aiming at your goal and an open mind willing to find the best methods of reaching it.

Notice that none of these questions has dealt with your education. Education, particularly in professional service franchises (accounting services, dental clinics, medical services, and so on), may be necessary to *work* in those businesses, but they are not necessary for you to *own* successful professional service franchises. (There are exceptions to this; in some states, you must be a dentist, for instance, to own a dental franchise; you cannot be an office manager and hire the dentists to work for you. But these instances are relatively few in the huge world of franchising, and generally limited to licensed professions.)

Conrad Hilton did not have a master's degree in hotel management, but he founded companies that own or manage hundreds of millions of dollars worth of hotels. Formal education—college degrees, graduate study, and so on—can actually hamper you if you have adopted an academic turn of mind, and have become dedicated to the ideal, rather than the real. At best, experience shows, formal education beyond high school is a neutral factor in franchise success. Practical experience, short-term training provided by the franchisor, and a degree from the school of hard knocks are all more important.

Your Family's Feelings and Reactions

Although you alone can determine whether you are ready and able to succeed in franchising, don't leave your family out of the process. Many couples buy a franchise together, sharing the decision. It is especially helpful if each person brings strengths and personal traits that complement or enhance the other person's, or even compensate for a spouse's weaknesses. Having a personal shortcoming is nothing to be ashamed of, and relying on a spouse or partner to shore up that part of the business only makes good business sense. In short, although you may have to *seem* like all things to all people when you buy a franchise, realistically you will do some things better than others. It is only smart business to allow your spouse to contribute his or her strengths where they are needed.

If you do plan to work with your spouse, you should both go through the self-evaluation exercises. Compare and contrast your responses and share your feelings about each other's perceptions. If your preceptions of yourself differ markedly from your spouse's view of you, and vice versa, discuss the differences. Both of you probably have a lot to learn about yourselves and your relationship. You may even find hidden strengths, talents, and desires.

If your spouse does not plan to be directly involved, determine his or her reactions and feelings nonetheless. Remember that spouses are bound to be somewhat concerned and afraid of such a big step. Buying a franchise concerns the immediate future of your family's finances, it disrupts well-established working schedules and living patterns, it may disrupt family routines (who's going to take Johnny to the orthodontist on Thursday afternoon if you have to make donuts at 3 P.M.?), and so forth.

Ask your spouse his or her feelings about many things at various stages in the game.

• Ask for his or her feelings about buying a franchise as soon as you begin to seriously consider the idea.

• Ask your spouse to review your answers in the above self-evaluations and ask for his or her reactions to your responses. Most of us have a blind spot or two about certain personality traits—both good ones and bad ones— yet our spouses know them like the back of their hands. Listen to your spouse and trust his or her opinions because your spouse will have your best interests at heart and may be able to bring to light not only some shortcomings, but many strengths you may be unaware of.

• Ask your spouse about his or her feelings about the type of franchise you want to buy. He or she may remind you of a health condition or a personal trait that could prevent you from doing some part of the required work.

• Ask your spouse to help you evaluate the franchise company. He or she may be more objective: You may have "presold" yourself on a particular company.

• Ask your spouse how the long hours likely to be required of you may bother him or her and discuss the adjustments to your family life that may occur.

• Most important, ask your spouse whether he or she will help you with the franchise if it becomes necessary. It is highly likely your spouse will have to work in the store, keep the books, pay the business bills, make deliveries, count inventory, handle disgruntled employees, pick up supplies, or perform a dozen other major or minor tasks on occasion. Get straight on both sides whether you expect this help, whether it will be resented, and so on. Remind yourself and your spouse of Murphy's Law. Like it or not, when one member of the family owns a business, in some sense, all members do.

• Finally, talk to your children and find out their attitudes toward your buying a franchise. If it is an ice cream or pizza franchise, they may jump for joy—at first. But they may soon tire of the sight, smell, or mention of fast food. Children do, however, tend to be supportive of parents who want to buy a franchise, despite the parents' wildest fears. Especially today, kids are no dopes; they, too, understand the potential for greater family income and even prestige. They may even be concerned for your happiness!

So don't automatically join the legions of disgruntled parents who fail to buy a franchise because of vague fears of shortchanging the kids. These people *think* their children will not like their being away at all hours. They *think* the kids will hate to work with their parents in the store. They *fear* not spending enough time with their kids.

Remember that children grow up very rapidly, and as they grow, they tend to spend less and less time with you. It is unwise to avoid buying a franchise because you think it will harm your children. Ask them. Discuss all the factors with them objectively. Show them the benefits (more money for college, guaranteed summer jobs, more responsibility for them as they grow older) and the drawbacks (perhaps less time with you, perhaps less money to spend at first, and so on).

Most kids will agree with you. But even if they don't, you have the final decision. To make it, balance short-term inconvenience against long-term rewards and then decide if it is still right for you.

What the Franchisor Will Investigate About You

If, after completing your self-examination, you decide you are ready, willing, and able to own your own franchise, you have one more examination to pass—the franchisor's. Before letting you buy in, a reputable franchisor will begin to investigate you and how worthy you are to represent that company before the public.

The franchisor will probably investigate the following:

• Business experience in or related to the franchisor's field, including your employment record. If you have been employed, your previous employers may be interviewed; if you're self-employed, the franchisor will probably visit your current place of business and talk with current clients or customers. If you are unemployed or a homemaker, the franchisor will probably go to greater lengths to evaluate your potential; you can help by providing all the supporting evidence you can muster.

• Your own and your spouse's financial situation, including wage and salary records, tax returns (if self-employed), bank statements, profit and loss statements, savings and checking accounts, net worth statements, and bank credit rating.

• Spouse's and family's attitude toward your buying the franchise and toward the franchise company itself. The franchisor will want to know if they approve of the franchise, whether they will provide the moral and emotional support you need, and whether they believe in you and your success.

• Credit rating and history. The franchisor will run at least one or two credit checks on your record, and probably make calls to your principal creditors to discuss your creditworthiness and payment record. The company will probably want to interview your personal banker or financial planner.

• Psychological profile. You may be required to provide a psychological profile so the franchisor can evaluate better whether you have the temperament its operation will demand of you. The franchisor will particularly want to know whether you can maintain the uniformity of approach and follow the system the franchisor has established. The franchisor will explore your motivation and your emotional, mental, intellectual, and social makeup. It may do this through questionnaires and/or personal interviews or by interviews by a third party, for instance, an industrial psychologist.

• Managerial ability. The franchisor must know whether you can handle people in the types of situations you will face. If you have managed 5,000 autoworkers, that does not mean you can handle half a dozen teenagers in a fast-food place—although it would bode well. The franchisor wants to make sure your managerial skills—developed or latent—can adapt to its requirements. The franchisor may do this by putting you into a mock business situation or by preliminary training sessions.

Figure 2-1 is a sample prospect information form. Franchise companies use this one or one like it to obtain basic information from you. It is no more complicated than many credit applications, and it serves as the basis from which a franchise company will begin its investigation of you, your finances, and your business background.

The Intimidation Scam

These are the major avenues of evaluation reputable franchisors follow. However, some less-than-reputable franchisors may use a so-called investigation to rush you or intimidate you into acting rashly. Avoid being pressured. Just because you are being investigated is no reason you can't investigate the investigator. Indeed, you must. Chapter 3 will show you how to do this, for any franchisor.

Second, do not get trapped into the belief that the investigation is a series of "tests," and if you are a good boy or girl and pass the tests, you will be "accepted." Don't put your self-image on the line with a franchisor; whether or not you can make a deal with one particular franchisor does not

Figure 2-1. A sample franchisor evaluation report for prospective franchisees.

CONFIDENTIAL EVALUATION REPORT

Note: The information contained herein will assist _____Corporation to determine if you are qualified
to become a _____ Franchisee. THIS CONFIDENTIAL INFORMATION IS NOT A CONTRACT!

PERSONAL INFORMATION

Name _____ _____ May we contact you at below numbers?
Address _____ Home # ( ) _____ Yes ☐ No ☐
City/State/Zip _____ Work # ( ) _____ Yes ☐ No ☐
Names & ages of dependents _____
Spouse's occupation: _____
Describe any physical disabilities or limitations _____
HOME: Own _____ Rent _____ House _____ Apartment _____ Other _____

EDUCATION	NAME & LOCATION	YEAR COMPLETED	MAJOR
High School			
College			
Other			

Describe any experience in related field _____

BUSINESS

Present Employer _____ From _____ / _____ To _____ / _____
Address _____ City/State/Zip _____
Supervisor's Name _____ Business Phone No. _____
Job Responsibilities _____

PREVIOUS BUSINESS EXPERIENCE

Firm Name _____ From _____ / _____ To _____ / _____
Address _____ City/State/Zip _____
Supervisor's Name _____ Business Phone No. _____
Job Responsibilities _____
Type of business _____ Why you left? _____
Firm Name _____ From _____ / _____ To _____ / _____
Address _____ City/State/Zip _____
Supervisor's Name _____ Business Phone No. _____
Job Responsibilities _____
Type of business _____ Why you left? _____

PERSONAL FINANCIAL STATEMENT

ASSETS

Cash in Banks-See Schedule A _____ $ _____
Stocks & Bonds-See Schedule B _____ $ _____
Real Estate-See Schedule C _____ $ _____
Autos (Year-Make) _____ $ _____
Other Assets (describe):
   1. _____ $ _____
   2. _____ $ _____
   3. _____ $ _____
   4. _____ $ _____
   5. _____ $ _____
                                                    TOTAL ASSETS $ _____

LIABILITIES

Notes Payable _____ $ _____

Home Mortgage (monthly payment:$) _____ $ _____

Other Liabilities (describe): $ _____

   1. _____ $ _____

   2. _____ $ _____

   3. _____ $ _____

   4. _____ $ _____

   5. _____ $ _____

                        TOTAL LIABILITIES $ _____

     NET WORTH (Total assets minus total liabilities) $ _____

SCHEDULE A–CASH IN BANKS

Bank Name/Location/Cash Balance _____

_____ $ _____

_____ $ _____

_____ $ _____

SCHEDULE B–STOCKS & BONDS

No. of Shares Amt. of Bonds	Description	Name of Owner(s)	Current Market Value (estimated)

ANNUAL INCOME

Salary _____ $ _____

Salary (Spouse) _____ $ _____

Securities Income _____ $ _____

Rental _____ $ _____

Other Income (describe):

   1. _____ $ _____

   2. _____ $ _____

   3. _____ $ _____

   4. _____ $ _____

                           TOTAL INCOME $ _____

ANNUAL EXPENDITURES

Real Estate Payment(s) _____ $ _____

Rent _____ $ _____

Income Taxes _____ $ _____

Insurance Premiums _____ $ _____

Property Taxes _____ $ _____

Other (describe)—include installment payments other than real estate:

   1. _____ $ _____

   2. _____ $ _____

   3. _____ $ _____

   4. _____ $ _____

                 TOTAL EXPENDITURES $ _____

SCHEDULE C-REAL ESTATE

Complete Property Address	Name of Owner(s)	Current Market Value (estimated)

GENERAL INFORMATION

How were you introduced to _____ ?

_____ Customer _____ Friends _____ Advertising

If Advertising, which publication? _____

What area would you prefer for a _____ Franchise? _____

_____ Alternate area? _____

Why would you like to become associated with our organization? _____

Any other facts about yourself you'd like us to know: _____

APPLICANT PLEASE READ AND SIGN

It is understood that the purpose of this questionnaire is for information only, and it is in no way binding upon either _____ Corporation or the applicant. It is, however, understood that the information supplied herein by the applicant is, to the best of his knowledge and ability, true and that _____ Corporation relies on this fact in **assessing** the desirability and qualifications of the applicant.

Submitted this _____ Day of _____ 19 _____

By _____

Signature of Applicant

FOR OFFICE USE ONLY

SIGNED _____

MAIL TO:

determine your self-worth. If you are not accepted, it means only that you do not fit into that franchisor's standard profile. Frankly, not fitting into a franchisor's mold could easily mean that you would do better with a different franchisor, or even in your own business. Evaluate the possibility of other franchisors or beginning your own venture. It is possible that you have exhibited too much motivation and too little awe of the franchisor's authority to suit him, characteristics sure to hold you in good stead in your own business.

Facing Fear of Franchising

Through all of this self-examination, and into the franchisor's examination of you, no matter how friendly and benign, you will probably suffer from some fear. Are you doing the right thing? What if you fail? Cold feet, in short.

While fear of franchising hasn't a catchy name, like agoraphobia (fear of going outside; literally fear of the marketplace), it is just as real. Like any phobia, it can be overcome. But first you have to recognize it. When the subject of franchising comes up, do you give voice to statements such as these?

- "It's too expensive."
- "Someone else will be running my life anyway."
- "What if no one helps me? What if the franchisor leaves me high and dry?"
- "There's too much legal business involved."
- "Suppose I don't like it; then what?"

Any thoughts that have a "what if" or a "too much" in them are likely to be expressions of fear.

You can turn the fears into concerns, however, simply by adding the solutions. "What if no one helps me? What if the franchisor leaves me high and dry?

"Then, I'll either use my contract, my lawyer, and my association to help me make him provide service, or I will sell my franchise to someone else for a profit, or I will make up the franchisor's deficiencies with strengths of my own," and so on.

Frankly, even after you've run your own business successfully for long periods, the pressure may one day begin to build. Terror reigns! You may face sleepless nights, queasy feelings in your stomach, or moments of blind panic and frozen indecision.

But just like the night terrors of childhood, such fears are mostly imaginary. You can banish them by picking the nugget of healthy concern out of them and dealing with it.

What constitutes concern rather than fear? Your responsibility for paying your employees is a concern—as long as you plan ways to achieve it when the subject comes up. Your responsibilities to the franchisor are concerns—as long as you plan ways to meet them. Government regulations are a concern—as long as you put time aside to deal with them, either by meeting them or fighting them legally.

Most of us have turned fear into concern at one time or another. But if you are among the rare few who have been completely sheltered all their lives, you might have trouble running a franchise. While franchisors try to provide a cushion you can fall back on, they won't offer support indefinitely. In the end, you've still got to make it (mostly) on your own.

Of course, most franchisees find that, once they've turned the corner to success, their fears and concerns are more than adequately compensated for by the joy and exhilaration of being their own boss and even more important, making more money than they ever had before.

The benefits of overcoming fear and becoming a franchisee can be enormous: more income; greater social status; better community standing; far more relative freedom of time and movement; better chance to save for retirement; more long-term financial security; increased personal wealth; increased opportunity to make more money by investing in other franchises or money-making opportunities; better ability to provide for your spouse, children, and extended family; personal satisfactions; and much more.

So recognize fear and plan for its demise. Once you know the size and shape of the beast, you're better armed to tackle it, and win.

3
Sizing Up
the Golden Goose

Once you have decided you are definitely a candidate for franchise success, you can begin your search for the right franchise. You probably already have a pretty good idea of the field you'd like to work in, possibly tempered by your self-evaluation. At this point, you've probably narrowed the field down to one industry, or even to a few specific companies.

Now you can start investigating them.

Preliminary Research

First, of course, you'll need to understand the nature of the industry in which you want to buy a franchise. How do you learn this? The government prints material that will help you; find the Department of Commerce and Bureau of Census publications about your industry. These publications probably won't be on the shelf at your local public library. Instead, look for the federal depository library near you. It will usually be found in a large city or university library.

Once you've found the library that houses these publications (and the only way to do it is to call around and ask; there is no formula), ask the reference librarian to help you find exactly what you need; he will have the names and catalog numbers of these useful publications handy. Then read the publications, looking for the following information:

1. Current (or latest) size of your industry in dollars and number of businesses involved
2. Growth rates over the past several years
3. Projected growth rates for the next several years

If it appears that the industry is stagnant or in decline, beware. Do further research. You will probably find it difficult for your franchise to grow and prosper in an industry that has already peaked out.

Even if your preliminary reading gives you good news, it will be worth it in the long run to read other sources as well. Some are:

- Standard & Poor's reports, both on industry segments and individual companies.
- Back issues of *The Wall Street Journal*.
- *Business Week*.
- *Forbes* and other business magazines.
- Frost & Sullivan's Predicast indexes. These indexes are arranged by company name and by Standard Industrial Classification (SIC) code. The SIC code is a very valuable number and can save you many hours of searching for information.

The Thomas Register of Manufacturers will also be useful. This provides lists of the major vendors in a wide variety of industries; yours is very likely among them.

While reading all this material, how do you determine whether the industry's future is bright or dim? There's no surefire way, of course. Even industries showing great past growth and with great projections for future growth could suddenly take a turn for the worse. So you'll have to trust your instincts in the end. But back yourself up with knowledge. Check industries you're interested in for these economic characteristics that *might* mean trouble:

- The industry has filled its current market; that is, the need for its product is more than amply filled by one or more companies.
- More than half of the companies in the industry experienced no growth last year or even reported their first losses. (Be careful to balance this against evidence of poor management of those specific companies, rather than taking it automatically as an industry trend.)
- A large number of companies in the industry have very unbalanced debt/income ratios.
- There have been two or more "spectacular" failures recently.
- There has been a slump in the industry's stock prices, and brokers are predicting that it will continue, even with a rise in the industry overall.
- There has been a "spike" in stock prices, indicating profit taking by people who think, or know, the industry is about to go under.
- Federal regulations concerning abuses by the industry have recently been, or look as if they will soon be, restrictively tightened, making it difficult for you to gain any profits.

Information About Franchises

Your research into your industry in general will include statistics, information, and predictions about both franchise and nonfranchise corporations. Once you've decided that your industry at large is a good prospect, you'll need information about specific companies in the industry, the franchisors. Luckily, that, too, can be easily and readily found. The Commerce Department publishes *Franchising in the Economy,* the leading annual publication of general information and statistics about franchising in general and prospects for growth and change among various types of franchises. It is available from the Superintendent of Documents, U.S. Government Printing Office, Washington, D.C. 20402, or from district Commerce Department offices. It is often available for use at local libraries. To order a copy, use the government stock number, which is 003-008-00189-1. The price for the paperback version is about $2.50, but check this before ordering.

Another valuable book that contains listings of names, addresses, and basic information about hundreds of franchises is the *Franchise Opportunities Handbook,* U.S. Department of Commerce, stock number 003-008-00191-2. It is also available from the Superintendent of Documents. The cost fluctuates each year, so call and find out what the current price is before you order. This handbook lists more than 1,100 franchises, and discusses their operations, the investment required, business history, and financial and training help given. It provides a list of government agencies that can help you as well.

A nongovernment body also offers a useful tool. Each year, the International Franchise Association publishes its *Directory of Membership*. This includes a guide to investigating individual franchisors, called "Investigate Before Investing," and lists the basic information about all of its members, divided into industry-based categories, much like those in Chapter 1 of this book.

By reviewing these listings and the information they contain, you can narrow your choice of business and then create what is called in negotiations a "short list" of possible franchise choices. For example, you may want to buy a muffler franchise, but you may conclude that there are so many muffler franchises now that it would be very difficult to find one that offered the growth potential you want. But you still want an automotive service franchise. Looking through the directories, you see that the market for automobile detailing and cleaning services seems to offer more opportunity. That's amenable to you, so you decide that you'll give it a further look. Your "short list" contains three names of auto-cleaning franchises and one for auto detailing.

Approach all these materials with an open mind. Perhaps, even if one type of franchise is out of your financial range, a similar one will fit your budget and still give you a chance to make plenty of money.

How to Investigate a Franchisor

Once you have narrowed your choices down to between two and four potential franchise companies, begin to investigate them. Follow the first and foremost rule in investigating a franchisor: *Take control.*

When you first approach a franchisor, you may feel that you are on the spot. You may feel uneasy when you first contact the franchisor's marketing manager because you know the company is going to want to know all about you, your business background, and your financial support. Divulging the intimate details of your bank accounts to anyone but the IRS is a sensitive matter, and in your concern over what the franchisor wants, you may overlook your right to investigate before buying a franchise.

But logically and rightly, you must be more concerned about the franchisor's financial strength and ability to survive than it is about yours. The franchisor is not, after all, banking its entire future on your application, while you probably are betting a good deal of yours on its company. At the very least, you are betting a good deal of your time, money, energy, and effort on the franchise.

Investigating a franchisor is not a simple, easy, or quick task. It requires research, discussion, and thought as well as a strong dose of emotional reaction, instinct, and intuition. Most of all, it requires that you ask questions.

Initially, you will ask for the franchisor's packet of information about the firm's offering. It may contain various reports, sometimes very exciting photographs, a few testimonials. Some franchisors even send along records or cassette tapes explaining their organization. They usually include a preliminary questionnaire for you to complete.

You'll have to answer the franchisor's questions sooner or later. But you'd do best to get the franchisor to answer your questions first.

Below is an extensive checklist of questions you can use to take control of the negotiations. Supplement it with additional questions of your own if you like. But be sure every franchisor you are interested in satisfactorily answers at least these 45. This may not be easy. Franchisors wish to use their time as efficiently as possible, and writing answers to your questions will make them spend their time on you, before you've spent much time on them.

Do not allow yourself to be put off or teased out of asking. Reputable franchisors will be glad that you are investigating them as thoroughly as they are investigating you, and will cooperate in the end.

Sizing Up the Golden Goose:
45 Essential Questions

Some franchisors will try to get you to hunt for the answers to these questions in the fine print of their own documents, prospectuses, or contracts. It will be easier for you, however, and much clearer, if you can get the marketing manager or other knowledgeable official to write out the answers to these questions for you in full.

When you get the answers, double-check them with other available sources of information: the franchisor's bank, attorney, or accountant; current franchisees; the Better Business Bureau. Confirm and reconfirm whenever possible. After all, your prosperous future depends on it in great part.

About the Franchise Company

1. What is the exact type and line of business in which the franchisor is engaged?
2. What is the corporate structure and business organization of the franchise company? For instance, is it a subsidiary of a parent company?
3. If it is a subsidiary of a parent company,
   A. What other businesses does the parent company own and operate?
   B. Does it now or has it ever *franchised* any other type of business?
   C. Will any of these compete or conflict with your franchise?
   D. If the franchisor has other subsidiaries that compete with your franchise, how does the franchisor plan for *you* to succeed?
4. May you examine *audited* financial statements of the franchisor since the year before it began offering franchises? (Remember: Figures don't lie, but liars figure.) If you may not, why not? This had better be a more than plausible answer.
5. How long has the franchisor been in business, both as a company and as a franchise company?
6. A. What is the franchisor's reputation among other franchisors in the same industry?
   B. What is its reputation among competing *franchisees* in your area?
7. A. What is the franchisor's credit rating with local and national credit rating organizations, such as Dun & Bradstreet?
   B. Can you obtain a copy of the franchisor's latest Dun & Bradstreet rating or a report from a stock rating service, such as Standard & Poor's or Moody's? (You may find the stock rating

services in your local library, or get them from your stockbroker, if the franchisor is listed on a public stock exchange.)

8. What is the size of the franchisor: in number of franchises, in assets and liabilities, in net worth, and so on?

9. A. How many franchisees of the same company are now located in your territory, city, county, metropolitan region, and state?

   B. How many franchisees does the company plan to add during the next 12 months, 3 years, 5 years, 10 years?

   C. How are you expected to compete with other franchisees with the same franchise company?

10. A. How many independently owned franchises are there and how many company-owned? Obtain accurate verification.

    B. How many franchises are owned by company officers *and* members of their extended families—spouses, children, cousins, uncles and aunts, grandparents, and so on—or corporations, partnerships, or proprietorships controlled by them?

About the Management

11. Who are the principal officers, directors, partners, managers, and investors in the franchise company? If the company is a public company, who controls the largest blocks of various classes of stock?

12. How much experience and with whom does each of the top managers—executives and department heads—have in franchising and in the industry?

13. What were the precise positions each of these managers and executives held during the past ten years? (Check out their claims with their previous employers.)

14. Have any of the top managers gone bankrupt during the past 14 years? (This includes any filing under Chapters 7, 11, and 13 of the bankruptcy code.)

15. Has any company in which they were managers or partners gone bankrupt while they held their previous positions in that firm?

16. Have any of the managers, principal officers, directors, partners, and so on been involved in criminal suits or civil litigation within the past five years? (This should include even those proceedings in which they were officers or representatives of another company.)

17. Have any of these people been involved in any criminal or civil proceedings with allegations of fraud, embezzlement, misappropriation of property, unfair trade practices, restraint of trade, or similar situations?

18. A. What was the disposition of each of those legal proceedings?

    B. If any are pending now, what is the opinion of the franchisor's counsel (lawyer or attorney) concerning the merits of these actions? Have your own lawyer review these cases. What's his opinion?

19. Have any of the officers, managers, partners, and so on ever been convicted of a felony or misdemeanor for criminal activity or held liable in a final judgment in a civil suit for any of the above actions—that is, fraud, embezzlement, and so on?

20. How successful have the management's previous companies been?

21. How experienced and successful has each manager, officer, executive, partner, or director been in franchising specifically and in the industry at large?

22. What is the reputation of each of the top managers, executives, partners, officers, and directors in the industry and among other franchise companies and franchisees in the same or a similar line of business?

About Products and Services

23. What are the exact products and services the franchisor offers nationwide? Are there any differences in those marketed in your territory and why?

24. Are product sales seasonal (ice cream, snowshoes) or year-round?

25. A. How long have the products been on the market?
    B. Are they out of date now, or are they likely to become unfashionable at a later date?
    C. Are they scheduled to be replaced by new products?
    D. How often does the product line change, why, and according to what schedule?
    E. How do these changes affect the franchisor's short- and long-term marketing plans?
    F. Is any product that is integral to the franchise either untried, not market-tested, in development, speculative, or a fad or gimmick?

26. If the franchise offers services, what exactly does the franchisee have to do to provide those services to customers? (Repeat the questions in 25 A-F, substituting *service* for *product*.)

27. Does the franchisee's income depend on learning a specialty trade?

28. A. What is the basic consumer demand for the products or services?
    B. What are the short- and long-term prospects for consumer demand for the franchisor's goods and services?
    C. On what foundations of fact or expertise are the franchisor's market projections based?

29. A. What is the source (manufacturer, vendor, provider, originator, and so on) of the product or service?

       B. Does the franchisor manufacture any of the products used by the franchisee? If so, where and for how long? Under what discount structure are the products sold to the franchisee?

30. What are the financial condition and long-term prospects for the manufacturer or vendor of products and services used by the franchisee?

31. How reliable is the manufacturer or vendor in meeting production and delivery schedules?

32. A. Who sets the price you must pay for products?

       B. Are these prices competitive with what is available to similar, nonfranchised businesses? (Get confirmation.)

       C. Are the suggested retail prices you may charge for products and services competitive and likely to be profitable for you?

33. What is the competition, and what are its products, services, and pricing?

34. A. Must the products or services meet government standards (health regulations, zoning codes, Food and Drug Administration guidelines, and so on)?

       B. Do the products and services now meet all standards and regulations, and what proof is there of their compliance?

       C. Are there federal or state restrictions on how the products or services are used, offered, sold, and so on?

35. Are there any product warranties or guarantees for which the franchisee becomes responsible when he buys the franchise and/or when the franchisee begins to sell to the public? Are such liabilities also assumed by the franchisor? Or will you have to agree to "hold harmless" the franchisor, assuming all liability yourself?

36. A. Who offers the warranties or guarantees—the franchisor or the franchisee? And who backs them up?

       B. Who pays for the cost of warranty or guarantee service, repair, and/or replacement?

37. What is the franchisor's reputation and track record on the quality of its products, customer satisfaction, and fulfillment of warranty or guarantee requirements?

38. Is any product or service protected by copyright, trademark, patent, or other legal protection?

39. A. Does your franchise give you the right to use all of these protected products, services, trademarks, logos, and so on?

       B. Are there any restrictions on your use of these?

40. Can you buy your products, services, supplies, and so on from any vendors other than those approved by the franchisor?

41. A. If so, which products *must* you buy from the franchisor, in what quantities, and how often?

B. How much inventory of the franchisor's approved, recommended, or required products must you carry, in what form,
   and for how long?

42. Is the franchise likely to have a short "shelf life" in terms of
    customers growing older, moving away, and so on?

43. A. Is a celebrity or well-known person involved in marketing the
       franchise and/or the products?

    B. If so, does the celebrity have a finanical interest in the franchise
       company? How is the celebrity compensated?

    C. What impact on the franchise and its products and services
       would occur if the celebrity or spokesperson withdrew his or her
       support?

44. What is the reputation of the products and services among the
    consuming public, other franchisees with the same license, and
    competing franchisees or businesses?

45. What objective measurements prove that the products and services
    meet or exceed the franchise company's stated quality requirements?

Once you've got the answers to these questions, you'll have a clearer
picture of the strength and staying power of the franchise (or a few
franchises) you might like to own. But there's more information you'll need
before making a commitment. Next, ask for the franchisor's disclosure
statement, which it must file with the Federal Trade Commission.

The Federal Disclosure Rule

Although the federal disclosure document and the contract will provide a lot
of information, they may be given to you—perfectly legally—too late for you
to do a serious investigation. Under the federal rule, the disclosure statement
need only be shown to you *ten* days before the signing of a contract. (The
contract, which may contain very useful information, need be given to you
only five days before you sign it.)

Since late 1979, the FTC has required that every franchisor present a
complete and accurate disclosure statement to each prospective franchisee
before a contract is signed. You must receive a copy of this statement:

1. At least ten business days (not including weekends or *national*
   holidays) before a contract is signed; or

2. At the first *personal meeting* between a franchisor, a franchise company representative, or a franchise broker (a franchise broker is
   anyone or any business *not* directly employed by the franchisor that
   sells you a franchise); or

3. Ten business days before you pay either the franchisor or a broker any money, even a small binder or deposit.

There are some sticky bureaucratic interpretations, however, that define what the first personal meeting really is. The rule itself defines a personal meeting as a face-to-face meeting between you and a franchisor or—and this is an essential point—a franchise broker. In this case, he is considered the franchisor.

The personal meeting does not, of course, include any telephone conversations or mail correspondence. The FTC uses four measurements to determine when a face-to-face meeting has *not* taken place; then the prospect would not have to receive the disclosure statement.

First, it is not a face-to-face, or personal, meeting if the franchisor states or clearly indicates before or at the beginning of the meeting that he is not prepared to discuss the sale of the franchise during this session.

Second, it is a not a personal meeting if you, the prospect, asked for or initiated the meeting rather than the franchisor's doing so.

Third, it is not a personal meeting if it is limited to a brief and general discussion.

And fourth, it may not be a personal meeting if no earnings claims were discussed.

When is a meeting not a meeting? When it meets any of these requirements for not being one, naturally. The FTC considers these conditions to be rules of thumb. The agency also advises franchise companies to use common sense in their face-to-face meetings.

If you do have a personal meeting under these guidelines and do receive a disclosure statement, it will be divided into these parts:

- *The basic disclosure document,* including information about the franchisor, the franchisor's business, and the franchise agreement's terms.
- *The earnings-claim document,* discussing actual, potential, or promised earnings claims.
- *The franchise agreement.* This is the detailed franchise contract, and a copy must be included in the statement.

20 Basic Disclosure Categories

The basic document includes 20 categories of information. Much of this information is general and does not necessarily include the depth of detail you need to make a wise decision—but you have used, or will use, the 45 questions to flesh it out. Legally, the disclosure statement must include:

1. Identification of the franchisor's company.
2. Business experience of the franchisor's directors and top managers (usually members of the board of directors, president, vice presidents, treasurer, and corporate secretary). Often these are not the crucial operational staff people, so dig deeper to find out the backgrounds of the general manager, the purchasing manager, the district sales managers, and the like. These people will have a significant effect on how your experience turns out, and are not necessarily included in the documents.
3. The franchisor's or franchise company's business experience.
4. History of litigation (current and past) against the franchisor, its directors, and top managers.
5. History of bankruptcy of the franchisor, its directors, and top managers.
6. Franchise description.
7. Money payment required by the franchisor of the franchisee to buy, obtain, or begin the operation.
8. Expenses—royalties, advertising fees, management fees, and so on—to be paid by the franchisee to the franchisor on a continuing and/or regular basis.
9. A list of people and businesses—the franchisor or any of its affiliates—with whom you as franchisee must do business. (To get more detail about this, probe to find out the specifics of how much product you must buy, how often, when, at what cost, and so on.)
10. Any capital assets (real estate, equipment, fixtures, signage, and so on), services, supplies, inventories, and so forth that the franchisor requires you to buy, lease, rent, or use. And a list of people or companies from whom you must buy, lease, rent, or obtain the above.
11. Any fees or considerations—commissions, royalties, and so forth— paid to the franchisor by someone else, such as a broker, if you buy the franchise from the broker.
12. Description of the financial assistance a franchisor offers to a franchisee. (Probe deeper and get information about interest rates on loans, amortization schedules, monthly payments, and so forth.)
13. Any restrictions the franchise company places on you in how you conduct or operate your franchise.
14. Any required personal participation; that is, the franchisor must disclose whether and how often you must personally manage the franchise.
15. Circumstances and terms under which the agreement may be canceled, terminated, or renewed by either you or the franchisor.

16. Statistical data on the number of franchises and the rate of termina-
tions. (Dig deeper into why, where, when, and how these termina-
tions have taken place during the past five years.)
17. A franchisor's right to choose or approve a location for the franchise, if the franchisor wishes to exercise that right. This may not be
as important in some professional or service franchises, but would
be in food and product franchises.
18. The training programs offered by the franchisor for your benefit.
19. Any celebrity involvement with the franchisor.
20. The franchisor's financial information.

Within these areas, there are numerous loopholes through which a
franchisor can avoid giving significant details. It is up to you to plug them.
Use the 45 questions, and keep your wits about you. When in doubt, ask,
ask, and ask again.

State Disclosure Laws

Although the federal rule sets a standard, at least 21 states and some
municipalities have their own franchise laws and regulations. As long as these
disclosure rules are tougher than the federal rule, franchisors operating in
those places must comply with the tougher regulations. The federal rule,
however, "preempts" those portions of state or local regulations that are
weaker than the federal rule. Thus a franchise company must always comply
with the most stringent disclosure requirements. Some states use a form
called the Uniform Franchise Offering Circular (UFOC), and the FTC
accepts the UFOC in those states where it is used.

The most common additional state regulations include: requiring a
bond or escrow account from the franchisor; registration of the franchisor's
salespeople; regulation of financing arrangements; regulation of how a
franchisor terminates or cancels an agreement; and even regulation of
contract provisions.

The states with their own disclosure rules and regulations include:
Arkansas, California, Connecticut, Delaware, Florida, Hawaii, Illinois, Indiana, Maryland, Michigan, Minnesota, Nebraska, New Jersey, New York,
North Dakota, Oregon, Rhode Island, South Dakota, Virginia, Washington,
and Wisconsin. See the Appendix at the back of the book for more details and
the addresses of each state's franchise regulatory agency.

Because ten days is not much time to do all the verification even a very
well executed disclosure statement calls for, create your own disclosure

statement—if not a better, more accurate document—long before you are given the one the franchisor provides by law. From the answers you got from research and the 45 questions, fill out these categories:

• *Who is the franchisor?* First, exactly what company offers the franchise and what is its history? Is it a new franchise, a division of a larger firm, or a subsidiary of a corporation; a partnership, a sole proprietorship, or a corporation? What is its reputation? Ask people who already own the franchise what it's like to work with the company. Getting critical replies from several people in different locations is a bad sign.

Talk—in person—to at least three franchisors *not* suggested or made available by the franchise company. Make sure they are in different locations, serve different demographic areas, and have been in business for different lengths of time.

• *What are the franchisor's financial status and credit rating?* The firm must disclose a great deal of financial information under federal and local laws. Much of it will be available in the company's annual report; ask for this report now, if you haven't already.

Most franchises are public companies—that is, they sell stock—so this information must be available. Some are not, however, and they may provide you with less complete material. Use whatever you can obtain. Study it thoroughly, with the help of your accountant if you do not understand what the numbers mean. If the franchisor sends the disclosure along with the reports, all the better. Some do.

Check the firm's Dun & Bradstreet rating either through D&B or Standard & Poor's, Moody's, or similar reports in the local library. If you have a stockbroker or know one, ask him to help you find information on a given company. Stockbrokers, financial planners, and the like also have access to computerized data bases "laypeople" do not; information obtained this way can be very helpful.

Check with the Better Business Bureau in the franchisor's headquarters city. Check with a credit collection bureau in the headquarters city. You may have to have a business name or be a corporate entity to obtain this information. If you aren't yet incorporated and do not yet have a dba (doing business as) certificate of your own, perhaps your accountant or lawyer could help. It may cost you between $100 and $200 for these reports. But crucial information that saved you from improperly investing thousands of dollars would be worth it. Naturally, you will have limited your field down to one or two possible companies before you begin to take these expensive steps.

• *Who are the franchisor's officers and top executives?* Determine their backgrounds; make sure you get more detailed information than a half-page résumé. Ask for professional references and follow them up. Ask how long the top people have been in the field, where they worked before, and what their positions—and far more important, their *responsibilities*—were. Titles often mean little. Talk to their former bosses to double-check their claims, but be aware they may not have parted on the best terms with their former employers. Ascertain as best you can whether the former boss or the subject of your investigation was "at fault," if fault there was, during the parting.

• *How many franchises are in operation at the present time?* How many are company-owned, and how many are owned by independents like yourself? Verify the franchisor's claims. How many franchises are there in your area already, where are they located, and does that mean the best locations are already taken?

• *What is the legal status of the franchisor's trademarks, copyrights, patents?* How many and what kind are claimed? Double-check patent numbers with the nearest U.S. Patent Office or federal depository of patent information. Ask for proof of trademarks and copyrights, if these are essential to the business. How long do these have to run before the item becomes public domain? Patents are good for only 17 years. Copyrights filed before 1984 are good for 28 years and an extension of 28 more years; copyrights filed after 1983 are good for the life of the copyright owner plus 50 years.

If the franchisor's success is based on a patent about to expire, be cautious: Some other company is probably ready to pounce on the market as soon as that happens.

• *What role does a big-name sponsor play in the franchise?* Does the sponsor have an active financial interest, does he help promote the franchise, is his name likely to have lasting value as opposed to being a flash in the pan? Remember that celebrity names do not guarantee the success of any franchise. In fact, they might even be a hindrance. For instance, a franchise based on a country music star's name might not sell fast food well on the posh East Side of Manhattan, although it does fine in Nashville. Weigh the value of celebrity ownership or endorsement.

• *Is the franchisor, or are its managers, directors, officers, or celebrity sponsor or spokesperson, in any difficulties that could affect the franchisor's continuation, especially lawsuits?* Have they been involved in lawsuits in the recent past? If they have, what effect did each lawsuit have on the franchisor, its financial status, and its future ability to continue in business?

• *Have any of these people been convicted of felonies or assessed civil penalties?* When, what was the offense (embezzlement, fraud, restraint of trade, unfair practices, misappropriation of property, and so on are particularly onerous), and what were the results?

If you find that filling in these blanks, based on the questionnaire information, sets off little bells in your head, dig deeper until you get a satisfactory answer, good or bad. Investigating a poor-quality franchisor can be like peeling an onion; by the time you've peeled away all the blemished layers, you may find there is no substance left. Unless you do so, however, you may be left with tears in your eyes and little else.

Overcoming the Hocus-Pocus of Profit Projections

During the past three or four years, franchisors have been increasingly reluctant to give out firm figures concerning how much income—gross or net—their franchisees can expect to make. In some cases, they have good reason; they've been taken to court or otherwise harassed by people who wrongly took their estimates as guarantees.

So in the initial packet of information you received, income or profit projections may be missing or given in very round terms, indeed. It might say only, "You'll make more money than the average postal worker" or "Certainly, income will surpass the national average for all working people with red hair." More and more franchisors will not disclose any financial projections at all until they must show you the required disclosure statement.

Don't expect any firm, dollar-amount profit projections at all after your first contact with the franchisor. Since anyone can write a company for its initial franchise material, it's to the company's benefit not to give out projections in the first packet. If the figures are terrific, they might hear from a lot of goof-offs who care nothing for the product or service in question, but are simply dazzled by the dollars. If income appears to be on the low side, they might lose a lot of potentially good businesspeople who would balance several factors a little further down the line in the process and make good, profitable franchisees.

Expect to receive financial projections only when you have shown you are a very serious potential buyer.

When you get them, keep this is mind: You must be able to make from the franchise the profits you need to maintain or improve your life-style through reasonable effort on your part and the franchisor's. It is a very bad idea to buy a franchise and take a giant step backward in income, assets, family life-style, and other measurements of prosperity. There's no getting around the fact that running your own business is hard work. If it doesn't pay off, you'll be dissatisfied very, very soon.

No matter how badly you want to be your own boss, you want to be sure the payoff will at least equal the pay check from the boss you left behind. If it won't, look for another opportunity. If you cannot now afford the investment for such an opportunity, consider building up your assets and capital until you can afford it.

When you're talking about your own business, don't just "settle."

A Basic Benchmark for Profit

Once you've got your own requirements covered, make sure the business will not only give you adequate income, but a good rate of return on your investment in it.

A good basic benchmark for the amount of profit a given franchise should return is this: The projected return on your *total* investment should be greater—preferably much greater—than the amount you could earn on the same amount of money invested in a more secure manner. Put simply, if you determine you can earn a better return on your money by investing in a certificate of deposit, why in the world should you buy a franchise and work long hours for low pay? The answer, of course, is that you should not because the chance of losing all or a significant portion of your investment in a franchise is much greater than the chance of losing your interest and principal on a certificate of deposit obtained from a stable bank or financial institution. And you'll have wasted time and effort besides.

A rule of thumb is this: If you can buy a practically invulnerable treasury bill (T-bill) that pays percent interest or more, a franchise investment should certainly return at least 16 to 24 percent and preferably more. In short, your working investment should offer you a return of two to three times more than a nonworking investment for the same amount. Remember too that the return must be on your *total* investment, and that includes many factors: the value of your own and your family's time; your capital expenditures; the cost of your corporate capital (that is, the interest you pay on any loans); and other variables. These "hidden costs" of investing in a franchise will be discussed in detail in Chapter 6.

Beware of Impossible Promises

Be realistic when you do see the company's financial projections. Naturally, income and profit will bear some relation to the initial investment. If you choose a franchise that requires a total investment of only $5,000, don't expect to reap a quarter-million-dollar-a-year windfall. If you pay $100,000 for your franchise, on the other hand, that figure might not be out of line if you do a good job and the local economy favors you.

Recently, a Florida-based company was accused by the FTC of falsely promising in advertisements that franchisees selling the company's car tune-up parts could earn $150,000 a year full-time and $50,000 a year part-time from an initial investment of only $14,000 for inventory. The ad also claimed the investment was risk-free because the company would reimburse failed distributors. According to the FTC, many distributors lost their investments, yet the franchisor refused to pay them back. Worse, the FTC charged the company with paying some distributors to tell prospects they were successful. The franchisor also listed as successful franchisees people who had never bought the franchises.

So when you receive profit projections be sure they are at least logical and not works of fiction. Use the above rule of thumb to decide, as well as your own good sense. Remember, there is no such thing as a free lunch—or a caviar lunch at hot dog prices, for that matter.

If the franchisor is a new company, the projections will not be based on a track record, and will therefore be more difficult to read properly. Often, new franchisors will give you projections based on the returns they receive from a pilot store. These projections will probably be far too optimistic because a model or pilot store is run as well as any store may ever be run.

For an established outfit, however, the projections should tell you which stores they were based on, or if they are an average from all stores. The projections should state in which year, very specifically, they were developed. This will allow you to take into account the general economy at the time, to determine whether the franchise you are considering did well in a sagging economy or badly in a booming one or vice versa. Of course, you hope you'll boom right along through thick and thin, but only complete figures can help you decide if you might.

Consider too whether the projection was made during a boom time in that industry, while you may be buying in a less favorable, more depressed, or more competitive climate for the same franchise.

Also attempt to get projections from other franchisors in the same or similar fields. If you haven't done so already, hire an accountant to compare them. Ask him, with the information you give him, to draw up what he feels are reasonable projections for an operation like the one you're considering.

Make sure you know the geographic areas used in the projections. If the profit estimates for a surfboard store in Hawaii are slumping, how much worse will your North Dakota location be? Of course, you're unlikely to be dealing with hypothetical goods, and no franchisor in its right mind would offer a franchise for surfboards in North Dakota. The truth will be more subtle, so you'll have to be a bit more canny when you deal with projections.

Also consider these factors used in the franchisor's projections:

- Each franchise's length of time in business. A franchisor could use only successful franchises that have established themselves over three to five years in prime locations. A franchisor should use a range of new, old, and medium-age franchises in various types of locations (malls, strip shopping centers, downtown areas, and so on).
- Each franchise's territory protection.
- Each franchise's type and quality of management—owned and managed by the company or by independent franchisees.
- The total number of franchises used in the projection.
- Type of accounting systems used by the sample franchises.

For instance, the franchisor may expect you to collect payment for goods electronically—directly from the customer's bank account through your electronic cash register, and its projections may be based on this fact. But if you live in the Northeast, beware. Studies have shown that in the Northeast, customers are particularly resistant to this form of payment, preferring credit cards and paper checks. If you were forced to use electronics, you might lose business.

Another document you should receive from the franchisor before any money changes hands is a profit and loss statement of the parent company. This will help your accountant determine if the profit projections for the franchisees hold water.

And be very cautious of any franchisor that does not want you to talk to a random sample of other franchisees! Make personal inquiries and visit any existing *independent* franchisees in your region or within what you consider a reasonable traveling distance.

Is The Franchisor's Truth Your Truth?

Before deciding that the bottom line—the projected profits—suits your financial and psychological requirements, dig deeper still. Yearly profits of $50,000 can look pretty grand at first glance. But then you realize you'll be on your feet alone 12 hours a day, 7 days a week, 52 weeks a year to make it. Suddenly, you figure, if you want to live to enjoy it, you'll have to take $18,000 out of that to hire a helper, pay Social Security taxes for the helper, and so on. Does the $32,000 remaining strike you as the income you want and expect on your investment of time and capital? If it still does, then go ahead and further study the projections. If it does not, consider investigating until you find a franchise that lets you take out the $50,000 after paying your help. Remember, though, that could increase your investment costs.

How often does this happen? Here's a composite example of several recent experiences:

A prospective franchisee recently decided to investigate a sandwich-shop opportunity. The initial projection was for an annual income of about $50,000 if the franchisee and spouse managed the shop. Then, as the investigation proceeded, it was revealed that a delivery person had to be paid $96 a week in cash out of that same $50,000. And if the shop got busy, or the spouse did not or could not work that week, an assistant would have to be paid $225 per week—out of the same profit. That could easily whittle the profit down to less than $34,000 per year, yet the owner would still have to plan on working 7 A.M. to 5 P.M., 6 days a week, 50 weeks a year. This potential franchisee withdrew. Why? He was already earning more than $40,000 a year in a white-collar job. He had his weekends free. And he could continue in that vein without dipping into his savings account or tying up his credit. Although the person was very tired of working at the white-collar job and wanted badly to own a business, it became clear that the sandwich-shop franchise—at least that one—was not the answer for him. If he had been earning far less—say, $25,000—it might have been a different story.

Although franchisors are reluctant to give out profit projections, you can—with the right efforts—discover what the real bottom line will be before you put down your hard-earned cash.

Face-to-Face: What to Expect in a Personal Meeting

Beyond these federal regulations, the first face-to-face meeting with the franchisor's top sales executive may well be the most crucial stage in buying a franchise. This face-to-face meeting will create first impressions—yours and the franchisor's—that may be hard to change later.

Before the meeting, sit down, review the results of your investigation to date, evaluate any material you have received from the franchisor, and think through the possible questions the franchisor may ask you. And determine any pertinent questions you have about the franchise, saving the most difficult ones for last. Plan to get answers to questions on the checklist for which you have had no answers so far.

Visualize how you wish to act and the image you want to convey. In short, have a brief practice session with yourself.

If it is a personal meeting, under the FTC rules of thumb, the franchisor will be legally required to show you the firm's disclosure statement, which contains all of the fine print about your duties and obligations as a franchisee for this firm. But unless you have obtained the disclosure statement before this face-to-face meeting, now is not the time or place to discuss its contents, nor the contents of a contract. You will be at a disadvantage, so take it home. Closely examine the statement with your lawyer and accountant first and then ask questions and go over details at a later meeting. The contract and agreement are discussed in detail in Chapter 5.

You can best use this first "face-to-face" as a way to get a feel for the franchisor's attitudes toward franchisees. Find out about the franchisor's background and the personal and professional backgrounds of the company's principals, particularly the franchise sales executive with whom you are meeting—especially if the person you're meeting with was not included in your research of the 45 questions.

Once you have your answers, and as you seek more, establish the foundation for a cooperative and mutually beneficial relationship. The importance of this cannot be stressed too much. Do not assume an adversarial attitude, but a friendly, interrogative one. Building a solid relationship with the franchise company is discussed more thoroughly in Chapter 10.

On the Hot Seat: Be Prepared for Your Own Disclosure

The franchisor is, needless to say, doing much the same thing you are: forming lasting impressions, finding out answers to his questions. What can he ask you during this meeting? Here are several categories of information the franchisor will want to know more details about:

• *Personal character.* Expect the franchisor to ask subtle or not so subtle questions about your friends, relations, business associates, club and society memberships, and so forth.

• *Health.* The franchisor plans to grant a 5-, 10-, or even 20-year license to you, with options for renewal, and he wants to know that you are in reasonably good health. If you have had medical problems but have recovered, you may be smart to reply to the franchisor's question that you will submit a doctor's letter attesting to your good health. But *do not* have such a letter with you and hurriedly hand it over to him. You will appear to be overly anxious, and this may make the franchisor nervous.

• *Stability.* The franchisor will likely ask you questions about how long you have owned your home, lived in the same town, been married to the same spouse, and so on. He may even try to see how well you can take a joke or respond to criticism. He will want to know how well you stand up under pressure; he may try to cause some so he can see for himself.

• *Financial standing.* You will have to submit detailed, written personal and business financial statements, but during the meeting the franchisor will probe to see what type of investments or savings you have, the amount of equity you have in your home, your ability to obtain money from family or friendly backers, and so forth. Of course, a good credit rating is important, and it is a good idea, when you first look into franchising, to obtain a copy of the latest credit report on file so you can correct any errors, or plan on how to counter any less favorable information it contains.

• *Management ability.* If you do not have a background in sales, marketing, or management, you may be asked questions to determine your attitudes toward supervising employees, dealing with suppliers, handling customer relations—all of the things you must do to run your operation successfully. An intelligent, informed, and up-to-date attitude toward these questions will stand you in good stead.

• *Devotion to the task.* If you are not wealthy and cannot afford to hire professional management, you will have to run the business yourself. That takes longer hours and more "brain work" than a nine-to-five job, and the franchisor will undoubtedly try to determine your desire to put in the hours and work necessary to succeed. Franchise sales executives often work 50 to 60 hours a week, and they may not look on it kindly if you see your franchise as a way to do less, not more, work. Retail stores, for example, are almost always open from 9 A.M. to 6 P.M., five or six days a week; they may be open even longer on at least one weekday, and there may be a weekend opening as well. Fast-food restaurants may be open 18 hours or more a day, and you may need to be on call, if not actually present, most of that time.

Of course, you should have determined whether you were willing to work harder and longer before you reached the first meeting.

• *Family attitudes*. The franchisor is fully aware that his business requires long hours and puts extra strain on family life, so he will be keenly interested in how your spouse and children view your buying the franchise. If your spouse is unhappy or very anxious—beyond a healthy and a normal apprehension of doing something new—the franchisor will be able to tell in your reaction to his probing questions. In any case, going into a franchise without the enthusiastic support of your spouse and children may not be a good idea; they are likely to be some of your first partners or employees, and they share the burdens and the risks with you. If they don't do so willingly, it will tell on the bottom line.

So important are these relationships, in fact, that the franchisor may ask that your spouse attend either the first, or certainly a later, meeting with you. Naturally, you may ask if you can bring your spouse with you to the first meeting to demonstrate his or her support. This will be especially important if you will be partners or share the management and workload.

• *Team attitudes*. The franchisor is looking not only for someone with the persistence to succeed over a long period of time, but for someone willing to cooperate and follow the franchisor's rules and regulations regarding the management of the franchise.

• *Education and experience*. The franchisor probably will not care whether you have advanced or graduate college degrees. He will care about your business experience. Education level is near the bottom of the list of required attributes, generally, unless the products you handle are very technical. Even then, few computer-store franchisees knew much about computers before they started. Certainly, most had no academic knowledge of computer science.

Beyond asking questions, the franchisor will very closely study one final aspect:

• *Personal presentation*. This includes your appearance, your dress, your posture, your personal habits, your gestures, your speech, practically every move or comment you make. The franchisor wants to know whether you present yourself in a manner consistent with the image the firm wants to present to the public. Your personal presentation will do more at the first "face-to-face" to determine your success in obtaining the franchise than almost any other factor. Money, character, health, family support, and emotional stability will not be enough if you do not present the image the franchisor is looking for. The desired image varies from franchise to franchise: Midas Mufflers needs different kinds of people than Nettle Creek Bed and Bath Shop. Yet the executive you meet will be looking for the *sine qua non* of his ideal franchisee nonetheless.

To put your best face forward, do your homework. Plan your possible responses to the areas of questioning outlined above. You may also want to bring your attorney or accountant with you to the first meeting or surely a subsequent one, so he can ask technical questions and jot down notes of key points needed to advise you. Do not, however, spring a gaggle of experts on the franchisor unannounced. Let him know who is coming; it's only polite, and besides, he may need to line up a similar technical expert to save his time hunting for answers someone else can better provide.

Above all, don't regard the first meeting with fear and trepidation. In many respects, it's like meeting your financée's family *after* the engagement has been announced. You'll be a little bit nervous and feel like a specimen in a jar. But you'll also know, if you too have gotten answers to your questions, that you are in control of this situation, in control of your future. You can afford to be polite and enthusiastic. You can lay the foundation for a long, friendly, and profitable relationship—once all the details are worked out.

4

Location, Location, Location

In the real-estate business, the first words you hear about investing successfully are almost always "location, location, location." For home-based franchises, such as cleaning and decorating services, location may not be all-important in the same way, but you'll still need to be located where you can easily serve a substantial part of your customer base. For other types of franchises, certainly all of the fast-food, automotive, and retail-store franchises, location is indeed paramount.

How can this be? Isn't there a McDonald's or Burger King on almost every corner, the way it used to be with gas stations? Won't putting a similar franchise, or any franchise, nearby ensure that you profit?

Not at all. Here's how one computer-store franchise, which we'll call CompuOutlet for convenience, failed in less than two months; it will show you just how important location really is.

The CompuOutlet franchise was located in a new, excitingly designed, although very small, strip shopping center. The location's apparent key advantages were: closeness to a major interstate highway interchange; closeness to a small but rapidly growing area of offices and light industry; inexpensive lease terms; and an area of good potential residential growth.

Looks pretty good so far, doesn't it? Look again and look deeper.

In addition to the plus factors, and ultimately more important, the strip center was next door to a very large and stable slum; few computer buyers were likely to come from that area, and others moving into the area were likely to avoid the strip center as well because of the nearby "taint of poverty."

The predicted residential growth wasn't likely to help, either. While it was not slum expansion, the growth was in retirement villages; no matter how upscale, and these were not particularly, the elderly do not buy computer equipment.

What about traffic from the office park? Several competitors selling small business computers already inhabited some of those offices. And, while there were other potential customers within a five-mile radius, they were served already by computer stores in their own areas. The traffic that passed the location did not deliver customers either; the major highway carried the elderly on their shopping rounds and the potential customers only on the way to and from work. Mixed with the nearby slum neighborhood and four fast-food restaurants catering to the low-income segment of the market, these factors made it practically impossible for a computer store to succeed.

In the long run (or in the short run, in such exemplary cases as CompuOutlet), location may be more important than almost all other factors, including financing, inventory control, merchandising, even sweat and toil. Location can mean the difference between success and failure, of course. But it can also mean the difference between small success achieved with back-breaking work and major success achieved with relative ease.

Understand What "Location" Really Means

Location, which can also be described by the words *site, facility, factory, premises, outlet,* and *storefront,* is the physical place of business of your franchise. The franchisor is very likely to prefer one location over the several others; he probably has experience bearing out his suggestions. Here, briefly, are the four possibilities for most retail franchises (with the exception of home-based franchises or manufacturing operations):

• *Suburban outlets.* These are found in predominantly residential areas located outside of a central downtown area. Franchises located in suburbs get most of their customers from the surrounding residential developments and subdivisions. Franchise operations are usually located in a storefront in a strip shopping plaza or small shopping center, often anchored by a large grocery store and a drugstore. But a very great number of suburban franchises are free-standing, occupying their own building along a major highway or main road.

• *Shopping center.* This includes any large shopping center, shopping mall, or regional mall with dozens of stores, and hundreds or thousands of parking spaces. Generally, it is anchored by two or more major department stores. These centers are usually located near the intersections of major highways and may be meant to serve a large geographical area. Regional malls in rural locations may serve areas as large as 1,000 square miles. In suburbs, they may serve as few as three or four communities.

• *Downtown shopping area.* These are clusters of both major and minor established retail shops in the downtown area of a major urban center. Major retailers and department stores often have their flagship operations here, and these are often surrounded by dozens of small retail operations. In recent years, city governments have been closing these areas to traffic and creating open-air "urban malls." Whether they are "malled" or not, these areas depend heavily on pedestrian traffic to generate walk-in sales. More and more, too, this type includes completely renovated downtown areas such as South Street Seaport in lower Manhattan, Harborplace in Baltimore, and Faneuil Hall in Boston, which combine retail shopping, food, and entertainment into a complete "experience."

• *Neighborhood shopping locations.* Generally consisting of small, usually strip-type areas, they may also be large buildings housing only two or three stores. The neighborhood shopping locations are more and more being dominated by all-night convenience stores rather than mom-and-pop groceries. The other tenants are generally very small retail stores, possibly a two-chair hairdresser or barber or a self-service laundry. These are located in or very close to residential neighborhoods. These differ from suburban locations in that they have far fewer stores and depend almost entirely on walk-in or drive-in traffic from the nearby homes. Locating in one of these was one of the critical mistakes made by the CompuOutlet franchisee.

A Critical Concept

Beyond the type of area in which you will place your franchise, location also has another, perhaps more crucial, meaning. That is its meaning of *territory*. In franchising, territory is defined as the geographic area or region in which your facility or operation *must* be located or in which you may operate.

The territory you're entitled to will be defined by numerous legal and contractual requirements of the franchisor. Most prescribe the area in which you can place a franchise outlet, although, by law, they can not limit how you market your franchise. You can advertise anywhere you want to in order to gain customers, but it is usually self-defeating to compete too far outside your territory as defined by the franchisor.

Franchisors use the concept of territory for several reasons. First, they can offer more franchises to more prospective franchisees. Second, they can obtain more franchise fees and royalty payments, increasing their own income. Third, they can make their products or services available to more potential customers. Fourth—and the main advantage for the potential franchisee—they can protect you from competition from *within* the same company.

A common misconception is that a territory protects you from *all* competition. A territory granted you by a franchise company does *not* protect you from competitors. Just because you have an exclusive Biggie Burger franchise for Flat River, Wyoming, does not mean Burger King, Arby's,

Wendy's, and a dozen other restaurants will not attack the same market. In fact, if you are first and you are successful, you can rest assured that plenty of competition will open next door and across the street in short order.

The best locations in the country for franchises—high family income, high disposable income, highly motivated shoppers—are now or soon will be inundated with competition for many types of franchise operations, many of them offering products or services similar to yours. The least you can do to protect yourself is make sure you won't have competition from within your own company.

Know Your Territory

In the musical *The Music Man,* Professor Harold Hill's fellow salesmen advise him that you need to know your territory. Hill sure knew his; he sold a whole community on a boy's band he had no intention of forming. He originally had no intention of delivering the instruments, either. But there was a factor he had ignored. He fell in love with the town's attractive young librarian, and it was very nearly his downfall. He went straight, however, and turned it into his salvation. Good thing: He was about to give franchising a bad name.

You won't be getting into anything so dramatic. In any case, traveling sales franchises are few and far between. But you will need to understand your territory. First, of course, you want to know how territory is defined. Next you'll want to know all about the word *exclusive.* It is defined differently by different franchise companies. Ask for an explanation, in writing, of what the "exclusive" in your territory really means.

And don't ignore this even if it seems a moot point. You may be the first Wally Widget franchisee in Houston, Texas. Right now, exclusivity may not seem important. But it will be important when, a few years later, there are 50 Wally Widgets, 35 Bobby Widgets, and 27 Rent-a-Widgets, all trying to carve a profit from the same small neighborhoods.

Consider this real-life example of the potential for trouble.

Along a five-mile stretch of highway on the Gold Coast of south Florida, near Fort Lauderdale, are: three McDonald's; three Burger Kings (one of them brand new and right next door to an established McDonald's); two Kentucky Fried Chickens (one brand new and literally cheek-by-jowl to the new Burger King and older McDonald's); one Arby's Roast Beef; two Wendy's; three Denny's Restaurants; three Wag's Restaurants; one Sizzler Steakhouse; one former national ribs restaurant chain location; one Dairy Queen; and at least 30 local or regional fast-food chain outlets. The permanent population this stretch serves is just 100,000 people, although during the four-month tourist season, this number more than doubles.

If the overall national economy slows, and the expansion of franchised outlets continues to grow faster than the national economy, the competiton among similar types of franchises and between franchises and independent small businesses will intensify. These conditions make securing a firm commitment to a truly exclusive territory very important. You certainly do not want to be competing against another franchisee in your own company or, worse, against a company-owned outlet. In this Gold Coast area, that's extremely likely.

The Population Pitfall

In these cases of several franchisees of the same company operating close together, the franchisor probably defined the territory merely in terms of *total* local population, rather than specifying physical boundaries for each outlet.

But as you will see in more graphic detail below, you must put that population figure into meaningful terms, and you'll want the franchisor to do it for you, or at least agree to it.

Here's an example of how one franchisee recently fell into the Population Pit.

A young man with a yen to strike out on his own purchased from a national franchisor an exclusive territory of 25,000 people. Unfortunately, he had failed to find out who those 25,000 people really were. It turned out that few of those people had a real need for a maid service. Yet his maid service franchise already had stiff competiton from two other national franchises, several private housecleaning and home-maintenance services, and a large local population of independent cleaning women who had traditionally provided far more services—laundry, ironing, shopping, and so on—at a much lower cost. Needless to say, that maid service operator was struggling to survive and was begging the franchisor to expand his territory—at a lower price—into more suburban, more affluent neighborhoods where two working spouses abounded, making a potentially greater need for an upscale maid service.

Here's an analysis of the specific difficulties the maid service operator faced:

First, the competition was well established and offered services at a very low price, slicing profit margins to the bone from the beginning.

Second, the population mix was poor: mostly low- to middle-income elderly who had no history of using maid services and were unlikely to pay for it and young married couples with children in which the mother did not work or worked only part-time. Indeed, many of these women looked to the maid services to provide part-time employment for them.

Third, the total number of potential clients was small compared to the number of available competing services. A "territory" of 25,000 people would have, at best, a maximum of 12,500 households. And considering the demographics—households that do not want or cannot afford a maid service, households in which the spouse stays home and cleans, households in which both people are retired and in relatively good health, and so forth—the actual number of potential customers was very low.

Thus, the maid service operator's only choice was to try to reach potential customers through marketing and promotion. Yet the advertising rates for the local newspapers and weekly shoppers were high. And the portions of their circulations that reached his potential customers were very low; upscale clients generally throw away the "throwaways."

Clearly, the operator was in a bind. To maintain good growth over a period of time, he would need to add new services, such as carpet and drapery cleaning, and promote the heck out of them in expensive ways—handouts, flyers, discount coupons, telephone solicitation during his own evenings, and so on. All this would cut into his profit margin further, and he could not charge higher prices to make up for it. He would be bucking established pricing for similar services offered by competition fully aware of the difficulties he faced, if not sharing them. His only hope was in talking the franchisor into granting him the adjacent, more lucrative territory at a cut-rate fee. But the franchisor had that targeted for another franchisee—so it looked like a long shot. The young man had fallen into the Population Pit; his pleas for a ladder were falling on deaf ears.

If you don't want to fall into a similar trap, be sure the "exclusive" territory offered by the franchise company really includes an adequate base of customers.

The maid service's view of "exclusive" is common in service franchises, and it can be devastating if the franchisor has not profiled the areas to your benefit and ignores the national advertising that can help you gain recognition and referrals. Or it can be helpful if franchisees from adjoining territories work together to pass on referrals.

Fast-food and most other retail franchises do not have these restrictions; they can serve customers from anywhere. Often, to avoid conflict, the franchise company will coordinate advertising campaigns to benefit all franchises in an area and prevent overlapping media coverage and competing marketing efforts. But they may retain the right to restrict the type of marketing you do within your area.

Wide-open Territory

If a territory is not exclusive, and many are not, it means anyone with the same franchise can compete with you in any area. And sometimes, a franchise company may reserve the right to open a competing, company-owned store

Figure 4-1. Checklist for defining territories.

1. How does the franchise company define *territory?* Geographically? By population? By household income? By age of residents? By purchasing motivation? A combination?
2. Does the franchisor offer "exclusive" territories?
3. If a territory is not exclusive, are there any limitations on what other franchisees with the same company can do within the same territory?
4. If it is supposed to be exclusive, what written, contractual assurances are there that the territory is exclusive?
5. For how long—five years, length of contract, and so on—is the territory exclusive?
6. In an area where no franchises yet exist, do you have the right to choose the geographic area and the location for your business or service within the territory?
7. What is the franchise company's policy about the freedom to do business as guaranteed by antitrust laws? (Pass this one by your attorney.)
8. How well does the franchisor protect your "exclusive" territory? Be sure to ask several current franchisees about the day-to-day impact.
9. In "virgin" territory, do you have the right of first refusal to expand within that territory or buy the rights to open franchises in adjoining territories, regions, or areas *before* the company offers or sells them to other people?
10. Within a region or metropolitan area in which some franchises sold by the same franchisor already exist, what guarantees does the company offer that they will not encroach on your territory?
11. Does the franchisor support or sponsor a plan to share referrals among franchises with limited territories in the same areas?
12. What are the exact geographical boundaries of your territory?
13. What is the physical quality and character of the neighborhoods within your territory?
14. How close to your operation, physically, will the next franchisee's store or location be? In the oil business, unscrupulous drillers have been known to locate oil wells near territory boundaries and drill a well at an angle into another company's producing wells. They simply steal the oil from the other company while it is still in the ground. If another franchisee can place a store on your boundary line, he could inadvertently or deliberately siphon off your customers.
15. When will the nearest "competing" location from within the same franchise be established in a neighboring or adjoining territory? What impact does the franchisor expect it to have on your potential growth and the advertising plans you both have?
16. Can the franchisor enlarge or divide up your territory if the population within the geographic boundaries grows? What are the company's policies and procedures for dealing with population growth—and more important, decline—within your territory?
17. Are you protected not only from population decline but also from a deterioration or other serious change for the worse in the character of the territory? That is, if this happens, can or will the franchisor enlarge your territory or provide other short- or long-term relief?
18. Can you lose part of the territory if you fail to meet quotas, specified royalty payments, or projected growth rates?

19. For what other reasons, if any, can you lose part or all of your territory and your exclusive rights within that area?
20. Does the franchise company have the right to establish new franchises under different names in the same or a similar line of business within your territory?
21. Does a subsidiary or parent of the franchise company have the right to establish new franchises in the same general line of business within your territory?
22. In nonexclusive territories, does the franchisor take any steps that, in effect, establish an exclusive or limited territory that benefits other franchisees?

within your territory. It may be defined in the agreement or contract as the franchisor's right to open a "model," "pilot," "demonstration store," or "training center" in your territory. The result could be the same—stiff competition for you.

Use the checklist of questions in Figure 4-1 to determine everything a franchisor's "exclusive" territory means to you.

The territory and exclusivity provisions are usually spelled out in the franchise agreement, and it is important for your attorney and advisors to review these clauses and get precise written answers to these questions. Besides the franchisor's name, your territory is probably the single most valuable consideration you license when you obtain a franchise.

How Franchisors Help Find Locations

Fortunately, most franchise companies go out of their way to help you find the best location and to protect your location. They realize that both your long-term interests and theirs are served through a mutually beneficial relationship. Actually, helping a potential franchisee find the best possible location at the best possible price, along with building a store or fixing up a storefront, are among any franchisor's key responsibilities in the franchisor-franchisee relationship.

Factors that make a site a good one will vary according to each type of franchise; a good site for a Midas Muffler Shop may be lousy for a ComputerLand or a Nettle Creek Shop. Different franchises appeal to customers with different tastes and different "demographics" and "psychographics." These are the personal characteristics, attitudes, and preferences of the individuals and families living in the area in which you want to locate a franchise.

The better and more established franchise companies have developed very precise and scientifically selected locations in which they want franchise operations located. Their staffs include marketing specialists who study census, demographic, and psychographic information about the best poten-

Figure 4-2. Checklist of key questions about location.

1. Who will be responsible for finding the exact location of the franchise outlet?
2. Has the franchise company studied the market potential in your proposed location, or theirs?
3. Do you have to buy or lease the outlet? Do you have to sublease the facility from the franchisor? How much in prepaid capital fees do you have to pay?
4. Does the franchisor provide specifications for the physical layout of the building and the grounds on which it sits? Are these included as part of the franchise fee, or if they are extra, are you to pay them up front? Finance them? Take them out of operating expenses?
5. Under what circumstances and in what ways can you change the specifications for your location?
6. What is the current population of the territory, and what are the demographics? What are the growth trends for the next five years likely to be? What evidence is available to support those growth projections?
7. Who will arrange the purchase or lease of the land, building, storefront, or outlet?
8. What are the terms, conditions, and duration of any leases and subleases likely to be? Can the franchisor provide a sample commercial lease and suggested changes you can bargain for?
9. Will the term for any lease or sublease be the same as that for the franchise agreement?
10. Is the cost of finding, acquiring or leasing, building, or refurbishing a location included in the franchise fee? If not, how much will it cost, and who must provide the financing?
11. If the franchisee must arrange for a lease and any construction, will the franchisor provide any assistance? If so, what kind of assistance—financial or otherwise—will this include?
12. Are there any local zoning or planning restrictions or variances required, and who is responsible for making sure your location conforms to these ordinances and regulations?
13. Has the franchisor compared your location and territory to those of other existing franchises or those of competitive franchises? If so, how does yours stack up?
14. What plans for new highway development might affect your territory during the next five years?
15. Will the franchisor relax your quotas, reduce your royalty rate, or give other considerations if highway construction significantly and adversely affects your operation?
16. What are the licenses and building permits required to build or refurbish your location?
17. What traffic counts and evaluations of traffic quality are available, from whom, and how recently were they completed?
18. What direct and indirect competition for your franchise exists within your territory and adjoining territories?
19. If the franchisor specifies a certain site, how was it determined and on what factors was the decision based? What is the quality—as related to the franchise—of the neighborhood and nearby business establishments? Do they match the quality and image sought by the franchisor?

20. How do the plans for your site compare with the appearance or location of existing sites? (If your site is to be very different, ask why.)

---

tial areas for franchises. Then the franchisor's real-estate specialists seek out available sites—vacant land, shopping centers under construction, empty storefronts, and so on—within those targeted areas. In the best franchises, the staff continually updates and refines the information.

Often a new franchisor will limit its efforts to one region first and then expand as the regional franchises succeed. The marketing and location staff expand their efforts as the expansion planning proceeds. So in some cases, a franchisor may be able to offer you, practically on a platter, a choice of well-researched and available locations within your territory. But you won't get it for a blue-plate-special price.

To be sure you are getting the right franchise for the right location at the right price, you will have to know how the franchisor plans to handle your locations. Figure 4-2 outlines the questions to ask him.

Franchisors' Help with Real Estate

Franchisors may help negotiate the purchase or lease of your land or building. They may help arrange with a contractor to build the facility, and with the owner/developer to lease it to you. If you are locating in an existing center or mall, the franchise company may lease a storefront and sublet it to you on the same terms as or on better terms than you could obtain for yourself.

The franchisor may even provide plans for your store that are already approved by local government agencies such as the fire department and building code authorities. But the catch is, the franchisor may require you to stick rigidly to those plans and only those plans, even if you have strong preferences of your own. Fast-food franchises, of course, most often require franchisees to build their buildings according to set plans, put up the required signage, and install the required equipment in a certain way.

Then again, a franchisor does not have to do any of these things. It can place the whole burden of doing market research, finding a suitable location, leasing or buying the space, laying out the interior, fixing up the exterior, even building a new structure, on your shoulders. You must determine what the franchisor will do to help you find the best available location and then make sure these steps are put into the agreement in writing.

Franchisors' Deepening Real-Estate Involvement

Lately, many franchisors have found it expedient to find and offer to you a specific location. More and more often, the franchisor *owns* the site and the building on it. One estimate is that fully 35 percent of all franchisors are heavily involved in the real estate of their franchisees.

These franchisors constantly look for good locations, buy or lease the land, build a facility that reflects their format, and lease the structure to a franchisee. They often build a structure *before* a franchisee has bought it, looking for a buyer as they build. Franchisors are doing this for several reasons. First, in many areas of the country, good, inexpensive business space is becoming harder to find. So they buy the land while it is still inexpensive and reap the capital gains—a very good way to build wealth—when they put a building on it.

Second, a franchise with an existing building is more valuable and can garner a higher franchise fee than a franchise without a building or facility ready to go. If franchisors sell a franchise and no facility is available, they may have to wait a while for the franchise fee to be paid. The fee will be lower as well, and they relinquish some control over the location and construction.

Third, franchise companies are protecting themselves from franchisees who buy a franchise, take advantage of the franchisor's help to get started, and then terminate the agreement and strike out as independent competitors. Without owning the land and/or the building or holding the lease, the franchise company could easily end up with a very bad bargain.

This has happened frequently. Here's a hypothetical example of one such instance.

WomanSport, a ladies' casual-clothing franchisor, bought name sportswear at large volume discounts. The franchisor then resold the goods to the franchisees. In a short time, a few of these franchisees got together, found out the franchisor's supplier, and pooled their resources to buy large lots of the clothing at the same price the franchisor got—and more cheaply than the franchisor sold it to them. Because the franchisor did not control the land and the buildings in which the turncoat franchisees were located, its only recourse was to sue the former franchisees to force them to pay—a long, arduous, and expensive process. If the franchisor had owned the land or controlled the lease, however, it would have needed only to give the franchisees eviction notices and have them removed. Although in most states, residential leases are weighted in favor of the tenant, it is not so in commercial leases. These are almost always heavily in favor of the landlord.

All this is not to say that the franchisor is always the aggrieved party, at least not so clearly. There are franchisors who use their ownership of lease or land to wipe out a franchisee's investment, for cause or not. Usually, this happens in slow-growing franchises in which franchisees cannot meet required royalty payments for one reason or another: Perhaps they have borrowed heavily to open their franchise and are using the fees to pay back loans instead; or they are using them to meet operating expenses during a cash-flow crunch; or any of a number of other reasons. In these cases, franchisors who own the land, building, or lease have been known to bring "unlawful detainer" actions that force the franchisees to forfeit huge sums of prepaid capital expenses and fees. The franchisee loses the business and his up-front capital investment.

Some of this is honest recouping of losses and prestige, of course, by the franchisors. But there have been reports that some less scrupulous franchisors have sold franchises for the same locations as many as 15 times. This can be very lucrative for the franchise company and is a much faster way to make money than collecting royalties. For example, a franchise company could lease a small piece of land on a long-term lease for a few hundred or a few thousand dollars a month. The franchisor then borrows the money to build a $200,000 building, depreciating the building and deducting the interest on the loan. Then it collects up to $250,000 or more in prepaid capital fees from the franchisee and charges a monthly rental of $2,000 or more plus annual increases. A franchisor could easily net $200,000 from the up-front fees, and net a nifty profit on the monthly rental as well as collecting royalty payments.

And if the franchisee defaults on either the rent or royalty payments, the franchise company takes possession of the premises and starts all over again with a new franchisee. Furthermore, the franchisee has few legal cards to play. Most courts give the property back to the franchisor *before* they consider any of the franchisee's claims against the company for fraud, violation of antitrust or fair-trade laws, deceit, and so forth. This means the franchisee forfeits the prepaid capital fees and loses his livelihood; it also makes it practically impossible for the franchisee to raise enough money to fight the franchisor in court.

As a franchisee, you must protect yourself against such actions. How? Obtain a franchise from a company that does not insist you lease or buy your location from it or its real-estate subsidiaries. But be aware that franchisors may own or control real estate through separate corporations. Make sure you know who owns or controls the property you lease or buy. If you decide you do want to buy a franchise from a company that controls the land, add provisions for royalty grace periods to the agreement; this will protect you from being thrown out instantly during a slow period.

The Buy-Back Bugaboo

In addition to getting involved with real estate, franchise companies may buy back franchises for various reasons, although they almost always resell them rather than operate them. Recent Commerce Department figures show that during 1983, about 550 outlets were purchased by franchisors from franchisees, but almost 1,100 were converted from company to private ownership. The Commerce Department reported that the trend between 1975 and 1983 was an increase in the conversion of company-owned to franchisee-owned outlets. Most buybacks were temporary, with permanent company ownership playing a relatively small part in the decision to buy back.

But, as always, look at the other possibilities behind the raw figures. A franchisor may sell off several relatively weak franchises, yet keep the most profitable ones. It is known that company-owned units generally make more money than individually owned ones. The franchisor may also sell franchises to groups of investors or tax shelter syndicates, some of the principals of which could be the franchisor's own executives or directors. The franchisor may buy up all of the franchises within an urban area, making its lines of management, communication, supply, marketing, advertising, promotion, and distribution more efficient and less costly. But it may then sell a lot of rural or suburban franchises that face increased costs because they are so far apart. When you seek to buy a franchise, determine whether the one you are offered is a previously owned one, a company-owned one, or a new one. If it is an existing franchise, determine why its status is changing to make sure you are not being shortchanged.

Beware, too, if you buy a franchise that the franchisor quickly offers to buy back. Find out what is going on in your area to create such interest. You may find something beneficial is on the drawing boards—a new housing development, factory, or whatever nearby—which would make it of benefit to you to keep it.

On the other hand, if you do want to sell, you may find the agreement gives the franchisor the first right of refusal, even an exclusive option to buy back the franchise or the right to approve or disapprove of the party to whom you wish to sell. Indeed, these possibilities are ones to check before you buy; negotiate for yourself the right to sell your franchise to anyone you choose. This may be impossible—after all, the franchisor does have a legitimate interest in who will run the shop after you—but try to get as close to that position as you can.

Few franchisors abuse their involvement in franchise real estate, or unfairly try to steal away their franchisees' investments. Still, there are pitfalls for you in the trend toward franchisors' owning their own outlets and the land under yours, and the trend is growing stronger.

The best way to protect yourself from these potential problems is to buy your business from a franchisor that doesn't buy or lease real estate for you and owns no company stores, or maybe just one for demonstration at headquarters. These are generally the smaller franchisors. The many larger franchisors that do this do, however, offer other advantages, not the least of which is the license to use their highly visible, often well-regarded name. You will, as always, have to weigh the risks against the advantages.

Finding Your Own Location

If the franchisor is involved in your real estate, it should have information available to assure you the site it has selected for you, or the territory it is selling you, is the right one for your potential success. If you are responsible for your own site selection and/or preparation, the franchisor should be able to provide information to help you make a sound choice. If it doesn't, of course, you'll have to dig out the information for yourself. Luckily, it is more time-consuming than difficult. So if your franchisor does not provide the information in these categories, gather information according to the categories that follow to work it up for yourself.

Traffic Counts

This is the estimated number of cars and/or pedestrians who pass by your store each day. If the franchisor cannot provide this information, follow the directions at the end of "Traffic Quality," below.

Traffic Quality

More important in competitive franchises than the amount of traffic is its "quality," that is, the likelihood that a relatively high percentage of passersby will stop and shop at your store. For example, the traffic count in a shopping mall will probably be very high. At that location, the traffic quality for Pizza Hut will probably be very high—most shoppers like to eat lunch or a snack. But the traffic quality for an Entré Computer Center, which sells small computers to businessmen, would probably be lower. Why? Because shopping malls are most often frequented by women and children and far less often by businessmen. A shopping mall may actively discourage the kind of traffic a small-business-computer store may seek.

If you must develop traffic count and quality information for yourself, excellent sources include local and state traffic or transportation departments. They keep records of traffic counts and often can help with information about the "quality" of traffic. They should also know current and future plans for road improvements in or near your area. For example, they could tell you whether a new highway will bypass a shopping mall or a new exit ramp will be built specifically to serve that mall. Such information is crucial to making successful decisions about site location. Also helpful would be city, county, regional, and state land-use and environmental-planning departments and zoning and planning departments as well as the franchise company's own planning department.

Local Business Conditions

Is the area growing or declining? Is the area changing from rural to suburban, or farm to industrial? Industrial to commercial, or residential to commercial? Is it changing from one-family residential to apartments and multifamily? Is the area in general getting more or less prosperous? Older or younger? More urban? How many competitors are there in your area? What are the prospects for the future?

On your own, you can get help with this from:

• *Chambers of commerce.* The local chamber represents the cream of local businesses, and it should have plentiful information about the current state of employment, industries, service businesses, educational institutions, and medical institutions in the community. You can use this information to discern some basic psychographic patterns. For example, if chamber information shows your town to be dominated by a private university, it is likely the psychographics of your customers will be far different than those of a town dominated by several declining steel mills. You should also obtain historical records so you can compare a profile of your community's recent (20-year) past with its present and projected future.

• *Local businesspeople.* If you have a good relationship with any local businesspeople, have a conversation with several to determine how local business conditions shape up for the near future. They will be the first to feel the effects of any economic slowdown and hear the rumors of any major plant closings or expansions.

• *Other franchisees.* If your chosen franchise company has other franchises in the area, of course, your task should be much easier. You can go, perhaps with an introduction from the franchisor's regional representative, to visit the other franchisees and discuss with them how local business conditions have affected them as well as many other topics.

• *Premises' vacancies.* The franchisor may have some idea about where vacancies exist in key areas, such as shopping malls or highway strips that meet some or all of the preferred site criteria.

You can also get help with this facet of site selection from:

• *Local, regional, and state zoning and planning departments.* They often have completed much of the research you seek, and their research is often more up-to-date than a census report that is prepared only once every ten years. They will, of course, know the zoning and building restrictions on any site on which you want to place a franchise. They may also be responsible for approving your application to erect signs on or outside your store. They also should know the geographical direction for future growth and development in the area.

They will know the vacancy rate for retail establishments; make sure you know whether a large number of vacancies means a growing area is temporarily overbuilt or is declining.

• *Realtors and developers.* If you want to locate in shopping malls or centers, commercial realtors and developers should have available a lot of demographic data about the families and people who live or will live near their properties. They will also know about any future development in the area long before it becomes general knowledge. Be aware, of course, that some realtors and developers will try to sell you on their location instead of providing objective information. To separate the wheat from the chaff, always double-check, perhaps with a competitor, any information they provide.

• *Banks and financial institutions.* Banks work with developers far in advance of construction, and even if they can't give you specifics, they often provide accurate general information on the direction for growth.

Accessibility

Another key factor will be how easily customers can get to your store. Having a fast-food franchise on a major highway may be great, but what if there is a median divider and no traffic signals and no left turns allowed for half a mile in either direction? You will lose half of your potential customer base. This information would also make an initial traffic count fairly meaningless.

Here again, local zoning boards can help, and the locality's traffic control coordinator or department of transportation can tell you if any changes are going to be made in the structure of local roadways.

If you are locating in a shopping mall, this sort of traffic count won't help. But do spend some time at the location you have in mind to make sure it is not tucked around a corner completely out of traffic flow. Count passersby and note what sort of people they are; traffic counts of musclemen and mountaineers won't help a lingerie shop.

Customer Profiles

The franchisor's sales representative should have readily available a customer profile. This should include basic demographic information about the ages, income, and spending habits of the market you are trying to reach. For instance, the franchise you are buying might be interested in people fitting the following customer profile:

Middle-class couples ages 25 to 45 with children ages 4 and up. Family income should exceed $20,000 per year. Most of them should own their own homes, and aspire to or live what is known as a "yuppie" life-style, with preferences for designer clothes, "natural" foods, high-quality educational and recreational experiences for their children and themselves.

The franchisor should provide satisfactory proof that the territory it proposes to sell you does, in fact, contain enough of the targeted customers for you to be successful. Beware the Population Pit, however, and be sure that your location, whether chosen by the franchisor or by you, is accessible and desirable to the target customers.

Of course, the customer profile will vary from one type of franchise to another. It may even vary within a single franchise company. Why? Because the franchisor may be trying to distinguish itself from others in its field not by carving out a single market, but by catering to several. For instance, although Wendy's competes with McDonald's, Wendy's menu, sit-down atmosphere, salad bar, potato dinners, and so on are aimed at a different type of person than a McDonald's patron. Its advertising campaigns also reflect this difference in customer preference: McDonald's largely appeals to a teenage and working-class audience, while Wendy's emphasizes slightly more choices for middle-class families eating out together. Nonetheless, it is possible for McDonald's, in a given location, to compete for the Wendy's market; such a franchise outlet would be inclined to market more meal-type offerings, such as the chicken and fish specialties, than a strictly teenage McDonald's would.

If the franchisor does not offer a customer profile, you'll have to work up your own. This, too, is more time-consuming than difficult if you know how to go about it. Here is the method that works for professional market researchers:

Determine the kind of information you need. The information you need to develop a customer profile for a given area would include:

- Total population
- Age groups represented (singles, young marrieds with/without children, couples with teenage children, empty-nesters, retirees)
- Number of children (total and per household)
- Family income
- Education
- Types of employment (main ones in community)
- Mobility
- Ethnic groups represented
- Marital status
- School enrollment
- Industry in which adults are employed

- Type of housing (apartments, single-family homes, and so on)
- Property values

This information is readily available; the best and most complete source of demographic data is also free. The local federal depository library (usually either a main city library or a college or university library) should have complete Census Bureau data for your area either printed or on microfilm. The Census Bureau divides the country first into SMSAs (Standard Metropolitan Statistical Areas) and then into census tracts and blocks within census tracts. Dozens of categories of information, as shown in Figure 4-3, are given in these records.

All of these are demographic factors. But psychographic factors—lifestyle and attitudes—will also affect the success of your franchise, so it will help to know a bit about them, even if your franchisor does not.

Modern psychographic research techniques show that people who share the same demographics often have vastly different buying preferences and attitudes. One person living in a $75,000 home, with two kids and a nonworking wife, may be a 35-year-old purchasing manager who loves light beer, professional football on TV, and virtually never eats out. Another 35-year-old who lives next door in a similar house may be a policeman who makes the same salary as the purchasing manager, is unmarried, loves opera, eats out often, and drinks imported wine.

This sort of information is more difficult to obtain than demographic data. Often large advertisers use sophisticated market research techniques, from measuring pulse rates of advertising viewers to calculating how wide the pupils of subjects open when they're exposed to the ads. This takes quite a bit of capital and is probably overkill where your franchise is concerned. You can draw up quite a helpful psychographic profile of your intended market simply by thoughtfully "walking around."

Visit the supermarkets and observe what foods people buy. What cars are prevalent and popular in the neighborhood? Is the community heavily represented on local cultural committees? Or on sports boards? Or both? Is involvement with public schools significant? Are there private day schools in the area? What is the nature of the local industry? Is it likely to employ people with college backgrounds? High school? How well are the homes kept up? Is there an active high-society component? Is it a resort or beach community? Do the people dress up or dress casually compared to people in nearby towns?

Here's an example of two neighboring communities where a franchisee might like to locate an ice cream shop:

Fort Lauderdale, Florida, is both a resort town and a big city. Local residents dress up—they're going to work in business offices downtown.

Figure 4-3. Census information variables.

Household Income, 1979:
Less than $5,000
$ 5,000 to 9,999
$10,000 to 14,999
$15,000 to 19,999
$20,000 to 24,999
$25,000 to 29,999
$30,000 to 34,999
$35,000 to 39,999
$40,000 to 49,999
$50,000 to 74,999
$75,000 or more
Less than $15,000
$50,000 or more

Total Aggregate Income, 1979 ($000)
Aggregate Household Income ($000)
Median Income
Average Income
Aggregate Family Income ($000)
Median Income
Average Income

Occupation (employed civilians, age 16+):
White-Collar—Total
Managerial, Professional—Total
Executive, Admin., Managerial
Professional Specialty Occupations
Technical, Sales, Admin. Support
Blue-Collar—Total
Precision Production, Craft, Repair
Operators, Fabricators, Laborers
Service
Farming, Forestry, Fishing

Industry (employed civilians, age 16+):
Agriculture, Forestry, Fishing, Mining
Construction
Manufacturing
Transportation
Communications, Other Public Utilities
Wholesale Trade
Retail Trade
Finance, Insurance, Real Estate
Services
Public Administration

School Enrollment (age 3 and over):
Nursery School
Kindergarten Through Grade 8
High School
College

Private Schools—Nursery
K—8
High School
College

Educational Attainment (age 25 and over):
Did Not Finish High School
Finished High School Only
Completed 1 to 3 Years of College
Completed 4 or More Years of College

Employment Status (age 16 and over):
Male: in Labor Force—Total
Armed Forces
Civilian-Total
Employed
Unemployed
Not in Labor Force

Female: in Labor Force—Total
Armed Forces
Civilian—Total
Employed
Unemployed
Not in Labor Force

Families Without a Worker
Average Income, 1979
Families with 1 Worker
Average Income, 1979
Families with 2 or More Workers
Average Income, 1979

Mothers (age 16+) in Labor Force:
With Children Under 6
With Children 6 to 17 only
Mothers (age 16+) Not in Labor Force:
With Children Under 6
With Children 6 to 17 Only

Number of Housing Units—Total
  Owner-Occupied
  Renter-Occupied
  Vacant: for Year-Round Use
          for Seasonal or Migratory Use

Characteristics of Occupied Units:
  Type of Structure: 1 Unit, Detached
                      1 Unit, Attached
                      Multi-Unit
                      Mobile Home, etc.

  Age of Structure: Built 1975 to 3/80
                     1970 to 1974
                     1960 to 1969
                     1940 to 1959
                     Before 1940

Householder Moved in: 1979 to 3/80
                       1975 to 1978
                       1970 to 1974
                       1950 to 1969
                       Before 1950

Number of Bedrooms: 0 or 1
                     2
                     3 or More

Number of Bathrooms: 1 Complete Only
                      1½ or More

Cars/Vans/Pickups Avail. to Household:
  None
  1
  2
  3 or More
Average Property Value (owner-occ. units)

Average Monthly Rent (renter-occ. units)

Mortgage Status (owner-occupied units):
  Units with Mortgage
  Units Not Mortgaged

Characteristics of Owner-Occupied Units:

  Type of Structure: 1 Unit, Detached
                      1 Unit, Attached
                      Multi-Unit
                      Mobile Home, etc.

  Age of Structure: Built 1975 to 3/80
                     1970 to 1974
                     1960 to 1969
                     1940 to 1959
                     Before 1940

  Householder Moved in: 1979 to 3/80
                         1975 to 1978
                         1970 to 1974
                         1950 to 1969
                         Before 1950

  Number of Bedrooms: 0 or 1
                       2
                       3 or More

  Number of Bathrooms: 1 Complete Only
                        1½ or More

Heating Fuel in Occupied Units:
  Home Heating: Utility Gas
                 Electricity
                 Oil, Kerosene, etc.
                 Other Fuel

  Water Heating: Utility Gas
                  Electricity
                  Oil, Kerosene, etc.
                  Other Fuel
Air Conditioning (Year-round housing units):
  Central System
  Individual Room Unit(s)

Characteristic

Population	Race: White
Number of Households	Black
Number of Families	American Indian, Eskimo, Aleut
	Asian, Pacific Islander
Sex: Male	Other
Female	Spanish Origin: Mexican
	Puerto Rican
Age Groups: Total 0 to 5	Cuban
6 to 13	Other Spanish Origin
14 to 17	Not of Spanish Origin
18 to 24	
25 to 34	Marital Status (age 15 and over):
35 to 44	Male: Single, Never Married
45 to 54	Married, Not Separated
55 to 64	Separated
65 and over	Widowed
Male 0 to 5	Divorced
6 to 13	Female: Single, Never Married
14 to 17	Married, Not Separated
18 to 24	Separated
25 to 34	Widowed
35 to 44	Divorced
45 to 54	
55 to 64	Number of Households with: 1 Person
65 and over	2 Persons
Female 0 to 5	3 Persons
6 to 13	4 Persons
14 to 17	5 Persons
18 to 24	6 or More
25 to 34	
35 to 44	Group-Quarters (Nonhousehold) Population:
45 to 54	Total
55 to 64	Inmates of Institutions:
65 and over	Mental Hospitals
	Homes for the Aged
Mobility (age 5 and over):	Other Institutions
Lived in Same House in 1975	Others:
Lived in Different House—Total	In College Dormitories
In Same County	In Other Group Quarters
In Different County, Same State	
In Different State	
Abroad	

Visitors dress in Hawaiian shirts and shorts. Your success here would depend on knowing which of those constituencies you would be serving.

If you were planning on serving the tourist crowd, you might opt for a site where you could keep the overhead down (to cope with seasonality), and which you could decorate in a tropical manner. You might adjust the ice cream flavors accordingly—lime sherbet, mango ice cream, and so on. And you wouldn't want tablecloths.

In downtown Fort Lauderdale, however, you might indeed want tablecloths. You'd want air conditioning. You might want to have some tropical treats, but standard favorites such as Rocky Road might be more popular. You could assume more overhead, as the business would not be so seasonal, and you could raise prices accordingly.

Just a few miles up the road is Delray Beach, and it offers still other demographics and psychographics. While it is "beachy" too, most of the residents are year-rounders, seeking the casual life-style. There are few resort hotels. A visit to a real-estate office will turn up realtors in madras shorts rather than pin-striped or even khaki suits. The local supermarkets carry extensive lines of health foods compared to the Fort Lauderdale outlets of the same chains. The most popular cars are converted Marathon taxicabs, BMWs, and small Mercedes; locals in Lauderdale prefer Cadillacs and larger Mercedes or Mercedes lookalikes—in short, more formal cars.

In Delray Beach, an ice cream store featuring tropical flavors and truly weird ones—cinnamon or even parsley—would work. You'd want to keep the overhead down even though the place is not as seasonal as its neighbor; people in Delray Beach are not conspicuous consumers and might be intimidated by a place that looked too sleek. Plus, they just don't like to spend money, except on "investments."

Stay on Target

Now that you know what sites are available to you in your target area, and who your target customers are, you'll need to know precisely where they congregate so you can pick the best possible location of those available.

If you have lived in an area for a long time, you generally know where certain types of people live. To more precisely analyze where your target population lives, compare your customer profile to the Census Bureau data. Also compare it to any information you have gathered from other sources that tends to contradict the census. Neighborhoods do change, often rapidly, and you cannot trust census data without checking to make sure they are still accurate.

Obtain a large map of the area you are considering. Block off areas

Table 4-1. Customer profile/census tract analysis.

Profile/Census Tract	Customer Profile	Tract 100	Tract 101
Population	10,000	15,123	12,542
Ethnic background	75% white	85% white	65% white
	15% black	12% black	33% black
	10% Asian	3% Asian	2% Asian
Age range	25-45	35-55	20-45
Household income	$25,000 & up	$26,500	$17,750
Children per family	1.5 min.	2.5	3.4
Number employed/family	1.4 min.	1.7	1.1

corresponding to the areas defined by the census reports. Locate your potential sites within each area. Next, create a table for each area listing in one column your customer profile and in the others the information contained in the census reports. Then, you can easily compare these factors in each area, and decide which might be best from the customer standpoint. (Remember, you'll have to weigh the traffic factors into a final decision as well as price of site and other variables.)

Here's how to create your customer profile table for each potential site.

Down the left-hand column, list the census variables you want to consider. Across the top of the page, in the first column, put the information you know about your targeted customer profile. Across the rest of the top, put the census tract numbers. Then, fill in the columns with information from each census tract report or summary. Table 4-1 above provides an example of a customer profile table.

In the example, Tract 100, while not perfect—the population may be too big for you to handle—could be a far better location for your franchise than Tract 101. Comparing several tracts for most of the census variables should give you a very clear picture of where you should locate your franchise.

But don't forget the psychographics either. After you've narrowed the choices along demographic lines, do some more "walking around." In the above example, Tract 101 might still be included in your possible sites if your franchise is designed to appeal to the low end of the income scale, or predominantly to minority groups.

Before you settle on a specific site, and after you've narrowed down your list, there are still several things to do. You'll need to:

1. Find the nature and location of the existing and potential competition. Using the census map or a local street map, identify where the competition is located. Be sure to include both direct and indirect competition. If you want to buy an athletic-shoe franchise, direct competition will be any other athletic-shoe franchise, including those of the same franchise company. Indirect competition would include other types of shoe stores, athletic sportswear and sporting goods stores, and department stores. Weigh the impact any of these will have on your franchise.
2. Outline the traffic volumes and major traffic thoroughfares with information from the franchisor and the local traffic departments.
3. Shade in areas zoned for your type of franchise business, using information from the zoning board (from which you should have been able to get a detailed zoning map).

When you are finished, you should be able to clearly see a range of potential sites within the census tract in which you might want to locate your franchise. Just because there is a lot of competition in one area doesn't mean you should not locate a franchise there. You must take other factors into account, especially traffic counts, growth patterns and potential, population density, and so on. It may be, too, that the competition does not actually provide what the people really want; perhaps the people want to buy $100 running shoes and $250 exercise outfits and all that is available are $15 tennis shoes and $10 shorts.

Next you'll need to find available sites within that area. Local newspaper and weekly shopper ads do not usually offer the best commercial real-estate bargains. Your franchise company, of course, may already have a local realtor available to help you. And you will need to work from the franchisor's specifications on the size, shape, dimensions, and layout of the store or outlet. Frankly, instead of going to a local commercial real-estate broker and asking to see his listings, it would be better to enlist the aid of a broker to act on your behalf. Tell the broker what you want, and request that he not show you any sites that do not fit those specifications. Further, if there are fees involved, consider offering to pay them, rather than having the seller or landlord pay them. This will put the broker on your payroll, and you may even be able to negotiate a reduction in the commission. If there is a cobroker, you will probably have to pay all of that fee, however.

The advantages of hiring a broker are:

• *You can keep your name—and particularly the franchise company's name— out of the search.* McDonald's does not announce to the world it wants to buy or lease land. The price would skyrocket. No, smart franchisors work through brokers to keep the price reasonable. So can franchisees.

• *You can save a lot of time and frustration.* The broker knows the market thoroughly and should quickly recognize whether a lot or parcel meets your specifications.

• *You can avoid negotiating from weakness.* If you try to conduct face-to-face negotiations with a selling broker, you will almost always lose. In the professions, there is an unwritten law called the "Professional-to-Professional" Respect Rule. It means that one professional treats another professional of the same type—lawyers, accountants, doctors, brokers, and so on—on equal terms. Possibly this is because each professional knows the other one will eventually have a chance to do him a favor or a disservice, depending on how he has been treated in the past. You, however, they don't expect ever to see again, so there is a tendency not to treat you quite as well as an insider. Thus negotiations between brokers often result in far better terms for you.

Recheck Details

Although you should have done this as you went along, before you sign a lease or hand over any money, be sure to review the trends in your area. You will probably sign a three- to five-year lease, if not longer, with options to renew. You must make sure the winds of change are blowing at your back and not into your face.

And make sure you are personally happy with the location. You will have to work there, often and for long hours. If you have a strong inkling that anything about a particular site will rankle, look again. Consider whether you simply have generalized cold feet—which isn't unusual—or a true gut feeling that the location is not for you.

Armed with this arsenal of well-analyzed information, you will be ready to choose an excellent location, whether you're going to open a Hot Dog Den or a Den for Doggies.

5

Franchise Contracts: Small Print Can Lead to Big Trouble

No two franchise contracts are alike. That's reasonable because most franchises deal with different lines of business, each of which has individual attributes. Running an auto muffler shop creates different obligations—for both the franchisor and the franchisee—than running a fast-food restaurant.

Each franchisor will have a preprinted standard contract that includes all of the legal protections the franchisor wants to preserve for *itself*. Unless protections for you, the franchisee, are required by law or custom, they will not be included in a standard contract. You may not believe that is fair, but it is clear that the franchisor has the right to place written, binding obligations on your purchase of a franchise. After all, the franchisor is risking its name and reputation, and, at least in the beginning, some of its money on you. Requiring you to fulfill certain obligations to protect the franchise itself is not out of line, and a franchisor would be foolish not to do it.

However, although each franchise has a standard contract, that does not mean it is like the Ten Commandments. Any provision in any contract can be negotiated and changed with the mutual agreement of the involved parties. When you and the franchisor are ready to close the deal, however, expect to be "encouraged" to sign the standard contract without making any changes. Don't do it. Take as your motto, *"I never sign a document I have not changed."* You will thereby prevent yourself from succumbing to a temptation to be a nice guy—and get yourself in trouble while you're at it. Do not be hurried. Be sure your attorney and your accountant review the contract. Discuss with them its provisions and the obligations it places on you to perform certain functions, and determine areas for negotiation in which you can make changes to your benefit. A one-sided contract is hardly a contract at all; it is more like an agreement to participate in indentured servitude.

Most franchisors know you will want to renegotiate many provisions in their standard contract and will be willing to do so. Some will make changes with little or no pressure from you; others will require tough negotiations to make key changes. If you are a desirable franchisee, the franchisor will be willing to go an extra step to get your name on the dotted line.

The Ties That Bind

Although all franchise contracts differ, all of them also include common clauses governing the standard rights and obligations of both the franchisor and the franchisee. Of course, the franchisee promises to do more than the franchisor. Here briefly are the uniform provisions a franchisee is usually expected to live up to:

- You pay an initial fee and the company gives you the right or a license to use its trademark, business format, or process.
- You agree to pay royalties and additional fees, often a percentage based on gross income, on a periodic basis.
- You agree to follow the franchise company's standards for setting up and maintaining your franchise premises.
- You agree to follow the franchisor's quality-control standards and to purchase goods, supplies, equipment, and products according to those standards.
- You agree to provide periodic financial statements, often monthly, on forms specified by the franchisor.
- You agree to submit an audited balance sheet each year.
- You agree to keep in force required insurance coverages.
- You agree to give the franchisor the right of first refusal when you want to sell the business. You also give the franchisor the right to approve the purchaser. (As mentioned before, you may want to get rid of that right of approval. Or at least pin it down. Such language as "Franchisor cannot reasonably refuse" your potential buyer can lead to discord; what does "reasonable" mean? Pin it down unless you want to risk a court battle at a later date.)

Now the contract is not completely in favor of the franchisor, no matter how it looks at first. Franchise companies do agree to do certain things to benefit you and your franchise. In most contracts:

- The franchisor promises to train you—but often at your own expense.
- The franchisor promises to loan you an operations manual, but usually

requires you to follow it to the letter. And the operations manual remains the property of the franchisor. This means you cannot legally "borrow" from it to set up on your own or loan it to a friend to use in setting up an independent business.

- The franchisor promises to help you get your franchise started.
- The franchisor often promises to run advertising and marketing campaigns in your area.
- Depending on the type of franchise, the franchisor may give you an exclusive territory.
- The franchisor may promise to use its best efforts to make sure you receive wholesale discounts on the purchase of products, goods, supplies, equipment, and services.

Be Specific

Franchise contracts, like artichokes, must be peeled clause by clause until you get to the heart of the matter. Franchise contracts tend to have the looser leaves—the easy clauses dealing with site selection and exclusive territories—on the outside, or in the beginning of the contract. To reach the heart of the matter—the sticky clauses that give the franchisor the right to take away your franchise—you'll have to read through "leaves" of legalese to the end of the contract. These "leaves" deal with franchise termination, noncompetition, right of first refusal, and similarly controversial issues.

In negotiating a franchise contract, the franchisee begins at a severe disadvantage. As a potential franchisee, you may want something—often very badly—only the franchisor can give. But your best hope of amending the contract to protect your interests is simple: Be as specific as you possibly can be in each contract clause. Make sure every extravagant verbal promise made by the franchisor's sales representative is reduced to writing and is included in the contract. Make sure you understand each sentence, each requirement, each obligation you incur, and each obligation the franchisor incurs. After you sign the contract, you will not be able, without great difficulty and expense, to claim that you did not understand the contract and that, therefore, the franchisor took advantage of you. Make sure each clause is written in clear, easily understood English.

Make sure your accountant and your attorney carefully review the contract, and bring one or both of them to the negotiation session. In fact, it is often a good idea to have someone else, possibly your attorney, do the face-to-face negotiations with you. Actors, authors, players of professional sports, major corporations, labor unions, and other smart people and organizations with a lot on the line all use representatives to negotiate for them. Why shouldn't you, especially if you plan to spend tens of thousands of dollars obtaining a franchise? The answer is, of course, that you should.

Clause for Concern

In a standard franchise contract, there are often more than 20 essential clauses you need to study and, if possible, negotiate to your advantage. Rather than letting your eyes glaze and mind go blank at the prospect, wake yourself up to the task by considering it a game, with each clause an "inning." Like the manager of a baseball team, you will develop strategy and tactics to win each inning, changing those as the game goes along.

You may question whether all of this is necessary. "Can't I trust the franchisor to do right by me without dotting every *i* and crossing every *t*?" you wonder. The answer is that most franchisors will do right by you, according to their definition. However, their definition is not likely to coincide with your definition of what is "right." And the only way to know exactly what each side means—and to reach a meeting of the minds about it—is to put it in writing.

To begin planning your strategy, read the discussions below. Included are brief descriptions of what each of the crucial 25 clauses is likely to include and advice on how you may turn them to your advantage. Use this information to prepare yourself for what you will find when you receive a real franchise contract.

Clauses for Alarm: Which Fine Print to Read and Why

Clause 1: Term of contract. Franchise contracts may be granted for almost any period, from as short as one year to as long as the franchisee and his inheritors live. The usual *initial* term is 5, 10, or 15 years, with a five-year renewal option.

Of course, it is to the franchisor's advantage to keep the term relatively short, and to your advantage to make it as long as possible. Why? With a short term, the franchisor keeps you on a short string and may get the opportunity to sell again a fully functioning franchise, into which you've put at least a couple of years of backbreaking startup work, if you do not renew. During the early years, you are liable to run up the greatest costs and reap the lowest profits. With a longer term, you are far more likely to gain the greater profits of the smoother operation you'll achieve through experience, and you may reap the long-term capital appreciation when you decide to sell out.

Clause 2: Contract renewal. This states that, given certain conditions, the franchise company gives you an option to renew the contract. The franchisor usually includes a provision that you cannot be in default on any royalty or fee payments as a condition of renewal. The renewal clause also limits the territory included in the renewal to the same territory granted in the original agreement. And it may force you to exercise your right to renew—and execute the new contract (also often called a *license agreement*) at least 180 days (six months) before the current contract expires. You should make several changes. You should:

- Limit the default provision to allow you to be in arrears for the current month's royalty payments when the contract comes up.
- Limit the same provision so that it does *not* include any royalties or fees involved in a dispute or arbitration proceeding between you and the franchisor.
- Get an option to expand your territory under the renewal clause.
- Reduce the timing of the renewal to between 60 and 90 days before the contract expires.

Clause 3: Location selection. If you are responsible for finding the location, the standard clause usually gives you 90 days after the signing of the contract to find a suitable location acceptable to the franchisor. It will state that your choice of location must meet the franchisor's standard site policies, and require you to submit the location to the franchisor for its approval. The clause may also include a promise that the franchisor will help you select the site, but it will probably be very short on specifics.

About the only help this clause will offer you will not be any help at all; it may be a phrase that promises that "such approval will not be unreasonably withheld." However, if the franchisor does arbitrarily turn down your choice of locations, you have to sue—and win. That takes months or years. You would already have paid your franchise fees, and yet you couldn't get started. Again, the word *reasonable* must be further pinned down. More than one person has learned very expensively that the "unreasonably withheld" clause is largely meaningless and offers no protection to the franchisee whatever. In fact, it is a universal escape hatch for the franchisor.

To amend this clause to your advantage, first extend the length of time you have to find a good location to 150 to 180 days. Second, make part of the contract the franchisor's *exact* standard location policies. Third, make even the extended time period further contingent on your ability to obtain any required zoning variances or other changes. In effect, the clock would stop while you were getting any extraordinary zoning permissions and variances. Fourth, make the franchisor list exactly the kind of assistance it will provide in finding a site. Refer to Chapter 4 for a list of information and assistance—demographic studies, market research, referrals to real-estate brokers and developers, traffic counts, and so on—you can choose to require the franchisor to provide.

Clause 4: Territory and exclusivity. This clause defines the geographic boundaries of your territory and whether and to what extent that territory is exclusive. If a contract does not spell out exclusivity, it is *not* exclusive. How much protected territory you receive varies widely from franchise to franchise. You may be buying a fast-food franchise that gives you as little territory as a one-mile radius, or you may buy a franchise that gives you an entire state or region. Often the territory is defined by census tract boundaries, streets and roads, geographic or marketing boundaries, or a radius extending in a straight line out a certain number of miles from your premises.

In this clause, the franchise company promises not to appoint another franchisee within that territory, and often adds that a competing facility will not be located within a certain number of miles from your own. To strengthen this for yourself, include very specific real boundaries, such as streets or census tracts. And if no other franchisees adjoin your territory, negotiate your own "right of first refusal" to expand into the unoccupied territories. This means that if a prospect wants to buy the territory next to yours, you would have the right to buy it before it was offered to him.

Clause 5: Lease approval. In retail franchising, the franchisor usually reserves the right to approve any lease, sublease, or other tenant-landlord relationship you establish. You must submit the lease or similar contract to the franchisor before you sign it. There may be little you can do about this requirement, but you can use your acquiescence to it as leverage for other points you want to win.

As noted in Chapter 4, however, more and more often the franchise company will act as your landlord, and may use this leverage to make sure you do not default on any rent, royalty, or fee payments. To protect yourself, legally separate the lease issue and payment of rent from the payment of fees and royalties, so that the franchisor cannot terminate your franchise for nonpayment of rent or other charges related to a lease or landlord-tenant relationship. Be careful too if the landlord is a separate subsidiary of a holding company that also owns the franchisor or vice versa. Such arrangements would enable the franchisor to come at you from both sides with the same results for it: It wins.

Make sure any commercial lease offered by the franchisor is made part of the franchise agreement, and negotiate its clauses separately. In Chapter 7, negotiating the terms of a commercial lease is discussed in more detail.

Clause 6: Franchise fees—initial and cash requirements. This should spell out, in precise detail, the initial franchise fee and cash requirements you must pay—and when and in what form—to complete your purchase of the franchise. The franchisor is likely to want the lion's share up front. Give it to him the way he wants it only if you are a sheep.

Renowned negotiations expert Gerard I. Neirenberg advises that you operate from the following assumption: There is no deal until money changes hands.

This advice will help you retain leverage so you can get what the franchisor has promised, when it was promised. How? Consider down payments as an object lesson.

Frequently a franchisor wants a large bundle of cash—often called a binder, a down payment, good faith payment, and so on—*before* a contract is signed to "hold" the franchise for you. If you deliver this, money has changed hands. Even though you may be told you can get your money back, it isn't likely to be easy. The franchisor may drag its heels refunding your money. It may be using its hold on that money to force you to complete a deal that, the harder you look, looks too hard to swallow. And besides (and this is a shout) MONEY HAS CHANGED HANDS. As far as the franchisor is concerned, there is a deal, contract or no, and it will be up to you—and hard for you—to prove there isn't. You have lost all the leverage over the franchisor you ever had, that is, cash.

Instead, arrange to have the franchisor get its money as you get its help. Don't deliver *any* money until you have signed a contract. And then include in it an installment payment schedule under which you pay the fees, other required costs, and prepaid capital requirements as the franchisor provides assistance and services and you move toward a grand opening.

The types of fees that should be spelled out in this clause include:

- Initial franchise fee and exactly what you receive in exchange, such as the right to use the trademarks, patents and copyrights, training, location selection assistance, startup advertising and promotion expenses, and so on.
- Training fees—such as your own transportation, room and board, training materials and manuals—that are not included in the initial fee.
- Additional charges or fees for bookkeeping, accounting, and computer services, both startup and continuing.
- Additional startup charges for advertising and promoting a grand opening and up to a month beyond.
- Payments for equipment, supplies, startup inventory, signage, and furniture required to open your franchise or to be acquired from the franchisor. Remember that you do *not* have to acquire anything from the franchisor. Your equipment, supplies, and so on need only meet the franchisor's quality standards.

Make sure the details of each—amounts, financing arrangements, payment schedules, and so on—are written into the contract. Remember that different phrases commonly used in franchise contracts mean different things to different franchisors. These phrases include: *cash required, initial investment, initial cash required, investment, down payment, equity investment, prepaid capital investment, capital fees, franchise fee, license fee, initial costs*, or similar terms. Make sure the exact definitions of these phrases are spelled out.

Fortunately, despite what franchisors want you to believe, every fee and charge is negotiable under certain circumstances. It is well known, for example, that someone buying two, three, or more territories receives significant discounts over any received by a franchisee buying just one franchise. The up-front fees and charges give you an opportunity to negotiate reductions in cost, better payment terms and financing arrangements, or to accept the fees pretty much as stated in exchange for winning the bargain on other clauses that may be more meaningful to you.

In negotiations, the rule of thumb is that he who quotes price first loses the negotiation. Why? Once you quote a price, you have nowhere to go but down. This would indicate that franchisors would have no place to go but down, since they almost always quote price first. They know this, however, and are prepared to hang very tough on the fees they charge. You, however, must approach the negotiations viewing the quoted franchise fees as a starting point only; be prepared to obtain concessions from the franchise company on this point or any other points you can.

All of the costs of opening a franchise and doing business are discussed in Chapter 6.

Clause 7: Royalties or regular fees. A standard contract spells out when (usually by the tenth of the following month) and how much (a percentage of gross income) you pay the company as royalty fees. You may also be expected to pay an additional advertising fee or monthly assessment. A franchisor may charge interest on overdue royalty payments. Royalties vary from as low as one percent to as high as 12 or 15 percent of gross, and advertising fees range from as low as a few dollars a month to 10 percent of gross income.

Before you reach this stage, you should have already compared the franchisor's royalty rates and advertising charges to those of others in the same industry. Some franchisors offer low franchise fees, but charge relatively high royalties. It appears to be a bad idea to trade a lower up-front fee for a higher royalty because, if and when your business slows, you may find the higher royalty wipes out your profit margin.

You may be able to negotiate volume discounts and pay a smaller percentage as your gross income increases or if you operate more than one or two franchises.

The same clause may require you to send in a "complete and accurate written statement" giving the month's receipts and a royalty calculation form. The franchisor may require you to use its forms for these statements and calculations.

Clause 8: Advertising policies. This may be divided into several subclauses and spells out the responsibilities of both the franchisor and the franchisee to advertise and promote the franchise. And it may mention an advertising committee, composed of representatives of the franchisor and franchisees that is charged with developing ad and promotional campaigns and giving them to the franchisees. The franchisor usually agrees to spend the fees for national and regional ads and promotion. The kicker comes when the contract states that the fees may be "allocated on a reasonable basis." This means the franchisor may retain the right to decide how much money is spent to advertise in your territory.

The "reasonable" spending of ad fees has long been a sore point among franchisees. Many have complained that they do not receive advertising support commensurate with their payments of advertising fees. This is not a problem with the largest franchises with tens of millions to spend each year on national television, but it becomes a serious problem for a small franchise company with franchises scattered around the country. Such a firm will find it hard to buy air time economically in major markets, so it often just gives its local franchisees advertising slicks or packaged advertising materials without helping them find and choose the best media in their territory.

Be as specific as possible in the contract so that the franchisor will allocate to your territory ad dollars at least equal to your contribution. Have the contract describe the exact types of advertising and promotional campaigns the franchisor will offer to benefit you.

One protection you should not overlook is a guarantee that the franchise company will not have any right, claim, or interest in the ad fees or the advertising fund. This means too that the franchisor cannot benefit from setting up its own advertising agency and accepting payments from its advertising fund. During 1985, several large franchisors got into trouble for alledgedly shifting ad fees to their general operating revenues.

In the same or accompanying clause, an advertising committee is charged with managing the ad fund, selecting advertising agencies, approving ad campaigns, and settling conflicts over the expenditure of ad dollars. Often the committee is made up of two franchisor reps and three franchisees.

A common kicker clause, often added to the end of the ad committee or fund phrases, forces you to accept *all* coupons or discount promotions offered by the franchisor or the committee. As discussed in Chapter 1, heavy coupon promotions can seriously harm your profit margins and increase your royalty payments. Change this clause to make acceptance of coupons optional under certain conditions. Of course, this clause does not override any state laws that prohibit sweepstakes, lotteries, or promotional giveaways.

In addition to the ad fee paid into the companywide fund, the contract may require you to spend a certain additional percentage of your gross income on local advertising and promotional campaigns. And worse, the clause may allow the franchisor to project your first year's gross sales and require you to spend a percentage of that figure on local ads. If you fail to meet the franchisor's projections, you still must buy the advertising and further erode your net profit. Get rid of this provision if you can. At the very least, negotiate a very low first-year projection, or add a clause saying you will make up during the *second* year any shortfalls in ad expenditures during the first year.

Is this really so important? You bet. Suppose the franchisor projects your first-year gross income will be $100,000, and requires you to spend $5,000 on local ads. But you earn only $50,000. Under the clause, you would still have to spend the $5,000, although you could only reasonably support an expenditure of $2,500. There goes your vacation or a down payment on a new car or worse.

So negotiate a clause that relieves you of bearing the advertising burden during the first year should your actual gross income fall short of the projection.

Clause 9: Trademark-use restrictions. This clause is standard and usually nonnegotiable. It preserves the franchisor's rights, titles, and interests in all trademarks, trade names, copyrights, patents, signs, menus, insignia, architectural plans, and so forth. It limits your right to use them to the term of the agreement.

Clause 10: Training offered by franchise company. This clause identifies the location of the company's training center. It also specifies which members of your staff—your managers and you, supervisors, and so on—must receive training and for how long. It may describe the type and subject matter of your training in detail. In fact, make sure it does. Make sure the amount of training is commensurate with its cost, especially if you must pay for it in addition to other franchise fees. And ask for any discounts on hotel rooms, travel arrangements, and so on the franchisor can make available to you.

Determine whether supplemental training will be available, from whom, how often, and at what cost. Obtain a commitment to a continuous training program, not just an occasional newsletter, so you and your managers can be kept up-to-date on product and marketing changes. Include it in the contract.

Clause 11: On-site assistance and location preparation. This clause often states that the franchise company will assign you a staff representative, regional service rep, training rep, merchandising specialist, or similarly titled person to help you open your outlet or gear up your operation. It will also put a time limit on how long the rep will stay with you, and cite any additional costs to you.

One of the key concerns not usually covered is the assistance provided when you are building or refurbishing a store or outlet. Try to get on-the-spot assistance from the franchisor's real-estate and construction specialists, who can help you deal with contractors, architects, building inspectors, zoning officials, and so forth.

You can turn this clause to your advantage in several other ways as well. You can:

1. Specify what the duties and responsibilities of the franchisor's rep will be.
2. Make sure the person has helped at least five or more other franchisees in similar locations and with similarly sized stores open their doors.
3. Add more time to the rep's stay with you.
4. Negotiate a lower fee, make the rep's visit part of the franchise fee, or negotiate more time for the same fee.
5. Specify the type of assistance the company must provide when you get started: planning advertising and promotional campaigns; hiring and training employees; installing and testing equipment; and so forth.

In addition, make sure you specify who is responsible for building and equipping the outlet and who provides building plans and specifications for premises and layout and the like.

Clause 12: Use of operations manual. Each franchisor has a confidential operations manual that discusses in precise detail every practice, policy, and procedure you should follow to run a successful franchise. This is a gold mine of information, and you would do best to follow as much of it as makes sense or is required. But you do not own it. This clause may require you to promise not to divulge its contents or copy any part of the manual. And it requires you to return the manual when you sell your franchise or the agreement ends or is terminated.

Obtain a copy of the manual to study before you sign a contract and make the entire manual a formal part of the contract, so its contents are legally binding on both parties. Suggest any changes you can find that benefit you.

The operations manual is usually included as part of the franchise fee, but specify how it is paid for if it is not included and an extra fee is sought by the franchisor.

Clause 13: Operating practices. The manual and other contract clauses will require you to meet the company's standards of quality and uniformity of appearance in product, equipment, fixtures, and furniture; number, quality, quantity, type, size, shape, and so on of products; product availability; advertising and marketing controls; internal management procedures; internal bookkeeping and accounting controls; internal security and auditing procedures; employee conduct; and so on. As the result of several court decisions, a franchisor cannot require you to buy products or services only from it, but most can and do enforce quality standards and specifications. Flagrant violations of these will lead to the termination of your contract.

The important step to take about this is to make sure you understand exactly what is being required of you. Understand the costs, if any, of advertising materials, accounting and bookkeeping forms and reports, computerized reporting systems, and so on.

The contract may also dictate the days and business hours you must be open; set any sales quotas and penalties for not meeting them; explain any wholesale or discount purchasing plans available through the franchisor; show what purchases of inventory, goods, services, equipment, fixtures, and real estate are required from an appropriate source; and so forth.

You should require that the ways in which the franchisor profits from these requirements and specifications be included in the contract. Thus for the franchisor to change the terms and prices would mean a modification of the contract and would reopen other points for negotiation.

The key point is that these should be very detailed clauses. You need to clearly understand each of them and, most important, understand under what circumstances your failure to comply could allow the franchisor to cancel the agreement. Identify any combination of circumstances—late royalty payment, poor quality controls, a difference of opinion over standards—that could give the franchisor a legal crowbar with which to pry the franchise away from you. Include in the contract grace periods, preferably 60 to 90 days, in which you can correct the defects and meet the required standards and specifications and retain your franchise. Franchisors will want to limit the grace period to 30 days or less, so you may have to fight for this one.

Clause 14: Obligations to purchase. As was noted in Clause 13, you cannot be forced to buy directly from the franchisor. Normally, the franchisor makes it advantageous for you to buy from it by offering prices slightly above wholesale. The franchisor often pockets the difference as a profit for its trouble. Others, such as McDonald's, do not sell supplies or products at all, but operate very tough quality-control programs, even forcing supply vendors to meet the franchisors' standards before they are put on the "approved" list of suppliers.

Any obligation to purchase supplies, products, goods, and so on that must meet certain standards must be explained in the contract. Determine whether the prices you receive from the franchisor or a list of approved vendors are favorable to you. It is very tempting for suppliers to pay franchisors rebates or kickbacks. Get a clear understanding as well of how the company establishes and modifies its standards and specifications, and how it approves or revokes approval of recommended suppliers.

The enormous controversy over the quality-control issue has raged for more than three decades, and the key aspects of this issue are explored further in Chapter 10.

Clause 15: Equipment and premises maintenance. Most contracts require you to keep your premises, equipment, and furnishings in good repair. Some contracts also force you to replace older, depreciated equipment with new equipment that meets the franchisor's most recent or current specifications. This means that you could be faced with replacing equipment in good working condition every three to five years. If you have exhausted the depreciation tax deduction, you may want to buy new equipment. But if you have a cash-flow problem, you may not want to do so at the end of the depreciation period.

Other contracts can force you to renovate or refurbish your franchise as the franchisor dictates to keep up or improve the appearance of the franchise outlet. The renovation may include equipment replacement, redecorating the interior, repaving the parking lot, relandscaping the grounds, refurbishing the exterior, putting up a new building or storefront facade, and making other structural improvements and changes. These can be very expensive, so negotiate these clauses. Limit the expense for maintenance and rehabilitation you can be required to incur to a low percentage of your gross sales or a low, fixed dollar amount per year.

Clause 16: Right of inspection. A corollary to the operating practices, this clause allows the franchisor's district or regional rep to inspect everything about your operation. You are required to provide reasonable cooperation and allow the inspector to inspect. Make sure the inspection can be done only with reasonable notice—48 hours is not unreasonable—and again, include a grace period in which to bring any problems up to standard.

Clause 17: Right to audit. This clause allows the franchisor to examine and audit your books, records, and supporting information, such as cash register tapes. It may also include a requirement that you submit an audited profit and loss (P&L) statement and a balance sheet prepared by a CPA (certified public accountant) within a certain time period (60 to 90 days) after the end of the fiscal or calendar year. You may also have to submit an unaudited P&L statement within 30 days of the end of a quarter, and forward copies of sales tax reports to the company when you send the original to the state tax authorities.

Be sure you understand exactly what is required, when, and in what format. A franchisor may recommend a CPA firm, but you have the right to choose your own.

Clause 18: Similar business or noncompetition clause. Another very controversial clause, this one tries to prevent you from entering a similar line of business not only while you own the franchise license, but for a period of years after the agreement ends. It may allow you to get permission from the franchise company so you can go into a similar or competing business.

Many franchisees bitterly oppose these clauses and with good reason. The franchisor seeks to deprive you of the means of making a living after the contract expires or is terminated. On the other hand, franchisors need protection so every franchisee does not learn their successful formulas and simply open up a competing business in a different part of the same territory. You could avoid paying royalties and fees and simply let the franchise die on the vine while your new, competing, and almost identical business flourishes.

You should make sure a specific definition of similar lines of business is spelled out in the contract.

This clause also usually specifies a geographic limitation in which you cannot compete, possibly a 25-mile radius of the franchise location. This clause can be used in your favor if you turn it around to negotiate for more protected market territory in your franchise area. Of course, a franchisor does need some protection to prevent you from opening a competing store with a similar name across the street from your franchise, but you do not have to give the franchisor the right to prevent you from starting or participating in another business altogether.

No legal resolution exists to clarify this situation, but it is clear that you cannot operate a similar business, in which only the "window dressing" is changed, and get away with it. If you sign a noncompetition clause and violate it, you will probably find yourself threatened with a serious lawsuit and loss of your rights.

It would be easier to specify in the contract a distance requirement for a competing business. And try very hard to end the noncompetition part of the agreement when the agreement itself ends, or you may find yourself unable to make your own livelihood.

Also use this clause to negotiate the right to first choice for new franchises in adjoining or nearby territories. Point out that the franchisor would do better to keep you busy and growing than to alienate you.

Clause 19: Trade secrets. This too is a real bugaboo in the industry, and requires you to promise not to disclose or reveal any franchise trade secrets. In most cases, this is silly because few trade secrets exist. Anyone can grill a burger; there's no possible way to patent the process. But consider the Coca-Cola formula and the recipe for Kentucky Fried Chicken, which, among other industrial secrets, have indeed been kept secret. By and large, the franchisor has a good point here. Keeping the secret is to your advantage as much as the franchisor's.

Clause 20: Cancellation clause. Under many circumstances, the franchisor claims the right to terminate or cancel the contract. Most of these clauses say the franchisor can cancel the deal for "good cause" and specify what "good cause" means. (Beware of any that do not specify what "good cause" means.)

Most contracts say that the franchisor can cancel the contract if you:

- Fail to pay when due *any* money, fees, payments, and so on you owe the company.
- Fail to correct any defects or meet standards and specifications.
- Repeatedly violate the conditions of the contract.
- Falsify any report to the company.
- Cease to do business at the specified location.
- Are adjudicated bankrupt, or make a general assignment or a trust mortgage for creditors.
- Allow a receiver, guardian, conservator, and so on to take over your franchise and its operations; and/or
- Fail to live up to the terms and conditions of any lease, mortgage, promissory note, installment loan, security agreement, or other financial instrument the franchisor holds on your premises or franchise.

Your best defense is to make sure you have a reasonable length of time (90 to 120 days is a reasonable time period) to correct any circumstances that the franchisor may contend are good cause to cancel the contract. Many franchisors, however, give only ten days in their standard contracts, so this point will have to be negotiated. As a corollary to this, let your banker or sources of financing review these clauses and find out whether these terms are satisfactory to them.

Clause 21: Franchisee termination. Fortunately, you are not without your rights to end the agreement if the company fails to live up to its end of the bargain. A liberal clause would allow you to end the agreement with 30 to 60 days notice if you do not owe the franchisor any fees, ad payments, rents, installment payments, or other debts. If you terminate the agreement, you will be required to give up all interest in equipment, furnishings, fixtures, licenses, trademarks, and so forth.

However, many clauses found in the contracts are not so liberal and allow you to cancel only if and when the franchisor fails to live up to the letter of its promises as set forth in the contract, and only after a grace period in which the franchisor shall also have the right to remedy the problems. And you may be required to send all notices of failure to perform by certified or registered mail, or even legal summons. In many cases, a franchisor may refuse to let you cancel, and a nasty legal dispute may result.

Clause 22: Accurate representation. The contract should include everything about the franchise that the franchisor told you during verbal discussions and negotiating sessions and in the contents of printed brochures and materials. You should add an accurate representation clause to tie together any loose ends concerning the type of franchise; the fee structure; the franchisor's obligations to you; the training provided; your geographic and market territory; the franchisor's obligations for financing; co-op advertising; management support; regular advice and supervision; your obligations to buy supplies and materials from the franchisor; in short, everything promised to you either in the printed offering or verbally. Although you may be able to force a franchisor to honor its obligations as given in a printed offering, you will have a hard time forcing a franchisor to fulfill verbal assurances not put into writing.

Clause 23: Right to transfer or the right of first refusal. Determine what the contract says about your right to transfer or sell your franchise to someone else. Franchisors almost always reserve the right to approve the party to whom you wish to sell or transfer the franchise. Just as often, the franchisor also reserves the right to buy back the franchise within 90 days of the date the franchisee gives written notice of a desire to sell to the company. You can, however, make sure the franchisor does not unreasonably withhold that approval. And you should reduce the amount of time the franchisor has to make up its mind.

The franchisor often sets certain conditions the buyer must meet before it will give its approval. They are that:

- The buyer must have a good credit rating and be of good moral character.
- The franchisor must approve of the buyer's business qualifications.
- The buyer must promise to meet the franchisor's training requirements.
- The buyer must agree to the terms of the franchisor's current agreements with new franchisors.
- The current franchisee's debts and financial obligations to the franchisor must be paid off (these can usually be handled at the closing of the sale of the franchise as in a real-estate transaction).
- The selling franchisee may be required to pay the franchisor a legal fee.
- The seller must pay up any deficits in his advertising account with the franchisor.

Negotiate these terms, especially the franchisor's legal fees, and place the burden of future compliance on your potential buyer, not yourself. Make sure the contract specifies that you are not responsible if the approved buyer does not complete training or fails to fulfill obligations after the sale is completed. It is doubtful a franchisor could enforce such clauses in any case. But you could run up some nasty legal bills if it tried.

Clause 24: Right to inherit. Many franchisors refuse to let a spouse or other family member inherit a franchise if the proprietor dies. Under most contracts, the franchise reverts to the parent company. The easiest way to avoid this situation is to make your spouse or a capable family member a partner to the original agreement. Or get the franchisor's permission to incorporate and make your spouse or family member president or operating officer of your corporation. It is so easy to avoid this difficulty that you would be foolish, if not irresponsible, if you failed to arrange the structure to protect your family's interest in the event of your untimely death.

Clause 25: Sale of equipment. This clause governs the franchisor's "absolute" right to buy back all the equipment, furnishings, fixtures, and so on when the agreement expires or is terminated. But the franchisor only agrees to pay the depreciated value of the equipment. And the clause may seek to set the depreciation rate for all of the equipment. However, the tax laws set different depreciation rates for different types of equipment and furnishings. You should negotiate the buy-back prices based on the most favorable depreciation schedule.

These 25 clauses cover the major points of most franchise agreements. It is essential that you work with your attorney and accountant to review each clause and negotiate more favorable terms and language.

It is likely most franchisors will willingly enter into the give-and-take of active negotiations. If you run into an obstreperous franchisor, however, that will not negotiate even on relatively minor points, you may decide to find a different company to do business with. But don't expect any sensible franchisor to give away the store; that is, to compromise fundamental rights over trademarks or standards of quality control and operating procedures. These shape the heart of what the franchisor has developed, and both of you would be foolish to dismantle the things that protect the reputation, standing, goodwill, and image that create your opportunity to profit.

Don't expect the franchisor to volunteer to hand you on a gilt-edged certificate any nonessential clauses it has incorporated in its standard contract, either. Even with the most cooperative franchisors, you will have to bargain for what you want. So plan your negotiating positions carefully with your advisors and decide beforehand what you can give and take during your sessions with the franchisor.

Remember that the contract is the "law" by which your franchise will be governed. And like all laws, the most important parts of it will be found in the fine print. To avoid big trouble and establish a mutually beneficial relationship with the franchise company, study the contract carefully and negotiate wisely.

6

Financing Fundamentals: Know the *True* Cost of Starting a Franchise

The fee quoted by the franchise company is just the beginning of the costs of buying and opening a franchise business. You must expect the cash to flow out, like sap from a maple in springtime or worse, before cash begins to flow in. This outgo before income must be figured into the total cost of buying your franchise. If you underestimate it, you will lose sight and, possibly, hold of your primary goal—profit.

In this chapter, you will learn four important steps to making a profit, all based on the important knowledge of what your franchise really costs. You will learn:

- How to determine the total costs—obvious and hidden—of starting and operating a franchise
- How much money you will really need to buy and start a franchise
- Where the money will come from
- How to determine whether the profit from your franchise will meet your profit goals—not someone else's

The first three steps lead to the fourth, which is often overlooked as hopeful franchisees scurry to figure out the dozens of little costs that eat up their startup budgets. But to succeed, don't lose sight of the forest (adequate profit) for the trees (any profit at all, no matter how small and tenuous).

Who is to determine the adequacy of your profit? You, mainly. You should know ahead of time how much you absolutely need to make to cover your business and personal expenses, and how much more will let you take a profit from the business. The franchisor wants you to make a good profit too, of course, so that it continues to receive royalties and fees. But its idea of good may not be yours.

Although it will be difficult to determine exactly how much profit you can expect from any given venture—franchise or otherwise—you can get a reasonable idea. First, determine the total of your franchise fees and your startup costs, and how you plan to finance them. Second, use the franchisor's earnings claims or your own income predictions. Next, subtract your expenses and loan payments from your predicted income to get bottom-line cash flow and profit margins. The best sources of projected income and cash flow are:

1. A franchisor's earnings-claim statement within the FTC-required disclosure statement.
2. The actual experience of other franchisees in similar locations. This is another time when it's important to speak with other franchisees in your business, as long as their business is of similar type and size in a similar neighborhood. They may not tell you precisely how many dollars they bank for themselves, but you'll be able to get a good feeling for it. Observe their operations, and file hints about their lifestyles that may help you judge whether their experience is likely to be adequate for you.
3. The experience of independent businesspeople in the same line of business and in similar locations. Talk with these people too.

Be Skeptical of Earnings Claims

As you will see below, the FTC closely regulates earnings claims, and a franchise company must give complete details of four aspects of its claims. However, one caveat is in order: Franchisors do *not* have to present earnings claims at all. And fewer and fewer of them present written earnings claims because disappointed franchise buyers often file complaints against them for supposedly exaggerated earnings claims. Although many franchisors abused their statements of earnings claims before the rule took effect in 1979, the lack of any claims at all leaves the potential franchisee in the dark. When a franchisor does not include any earnings-and-profit projections in its basic disclosure statement, you have to rely on your own or your accountant's investigative ability.

One good way to create your own earnings-claim statement is to work backward from your total costs. Add a reasonable profit margin to your total costs and then determine how much product you must sell or what quantity of services you must provide to make that much money.

Here's a simplified example. Let's say it's for a sandwich shop.

Your total startup costs (amortized over a period of months or years) and monthly expenses (including supplies, labor, overhead, and so on) together equal $1,000 a month. You want to net a profit of $250, or 25 percent per month. To work backward, you divide the price of your major products into the total expenses and profit. How many sandwiches at $2.00 each would you have to sell to make $1,250 a month? The answer is 625 sandwiches, or more than 20 each and every day of the month. Then you have to consider whether you strongly believe, or can find the facts to support, a projection that your shop will sell at least 625 sandwiches per month.

Ask both other franchisees and independent business owners whether they believe, based on their experience, that the amount of money you expect to make from your franchise is reasonable. If they are very skeptical or downright gloomy, think again. Of course, ask several to make sure you don't act on the basis of speaking with a Gloomy Gus or a Pollyanna.

Above all, check and double-check any earnings claims made by the franchise company, especially those made to you verbally and not given in writing. And you must weigh even the earnings claims in a required disclosure statement very carefully. These claims always come with disclaimers, which are required by the FTC.

And don't forget to check that the type of operation on which the written earnings claims are based is similar to yours. For example, if the franchisor bases its claims on a 1,500-square-foot store in a 150-store regional shopping mall, it should earn a lot more than a store of 500 square feet in a neighborhood shopping strip with a dry cleaner, a self-service laundry, a convenience store, and you. If you're buying the second type, scale down your expectations.

The Strict FTC Rules on Earnings Claims

The FTC rule regulates four aspects of earnings claims:

- Potential earnings (example: "You can make $4 billion a year selling Vita-Meta-Vegamin.")
- Past earnings performance ("Our average franchisee made $2 billion a year during 1984 selling our Roly-Poly Burgers and Waist-Waster Belts!")
- The parts of the disclosure statement that describe any earnings claims

• Earnings claims made in any media—newspaper and magazine ads, TV and radio commercials, and so on

The FTC applies a broad definition of "earnings claims," including anything that suggests a *specific* dollar amount, level or range of potential or actual sales, income, and gross or net profits. And any specific statement need only be spoken, written, shown, or broadcast to either a prospect or the public at large for it to come under the rule. The FTC definition also includes any statement from which you can infer an earnings claim, such as "You can make enough money to buy the Queen Mary cruise ship in just six months," or "Earn 4,000 percent return on your investment in weeks." However, general claims, such as "Make fantastic money in your spare time," are not covered. If anyone acts on the basis of those, he needs more help than the FTC can give anyway.

The FTC also requires that claims follow strict standards that, when considered, seem like common business sense. The FTC requires that:

• There must be a reasonable basis to support the accuracy of the claim. Even the FTC has a hard time defining "reasonable" and uses a "prudent man" rule; if the facts would allow a "prudent" businessperson to make a reasonable investment decision, the claim is okay.

• The franchise company must already have in hand the facts to support its earnings claim *before* it is made. This information may include market research, statistical studies, actual profit and loss statements from existing franchisees, and so forth. And the franchisor must make this supporting evidence available to you with reasonable notice.

• The claims must be location-specific; that is, they must apply to the geographic market in which you plan to put your franchise. However, this does not prevent a franchisor from using claims based on earnings by franchisees outside your area if it can support the notion that the areas are very much the same. If a franchisor uses earnings in Saskatchewan, for instance, to make a claim about how much you will make selling snowshoes in Florida, it had better have evidence that market conditions in both are very similar. These conditions would include demographics, climate, type of location, local social conditions, psychographics, and so forth. And the franchisor must discuss factors from one location that significantly differ from or have an adverse impact on the claims made for your area.

All earnings claims must be packaged in an "earnings-claim document" and given to you either at the first personal meeting, as the FTC defines that meeting, or ten days before you sign a contract. This document must include the claim itself, the reasoning behind it, a notice that you can inspect the supporting evidence, and one or two cautionary disclaimers.

One disclaimer cautions that the figures are only estimates and do not include assurances you will do as well. It also places on you the risk of not doing as well if you choose to believe the figures. That's simple enough: Don't believe the figures.

The second disclaimer is similar, but refers to claims about franchisees' past performance. This one notes that some outlets have sold so much product or earned so much money, but warns you may not do as well. Caution? Sure. Don't believe the figures.

The last section of the earnings-claim document discusses claims made in the media, such as any type of advertising, public speeches, press releases, or other types of general dissemination engaged in by the franchisor. For media claims, the FTC does not require supporting evidence on the instant; it need only be available for inspection by the FTC. Notice of supporting evidence also need not be given in these instances, and the claims need not be geography-specific.

Not covered at all under the FTC rules is information given to financial journals or the trade press by the franchisees (after all, there may be misquotes) or information given to financial institutions when franchisees are seeking loans.

By and large, the FTC rule has reduced to an absolute minimum the abuse of earnings claims by legitimate franchise companies. If you are given clearly exaggerated earnings claims by a company that claims to offer a franchise, run, don't walk, to the nearest FTC district office. And demand from the franchisor that all supporting evidence be provided as required by law.

Remember also that even very accurate earnings claims do not necessarily mean net profits into your pocket. Study the assumptions very carefully to see what kinds of expenses are subtracted, whether the figures given are before or after income and other taxes, and if the claim is based on seasonal or temporarily exaggerated sales. Find out the dates involved in working up the claims. If the claims are made during a boom period, and you find yourself in a bust, you'll have to take the claims with a large grain of salt.

Only then should you go to the bottom line, and ask yourself whether the remaining figure, the net profit (if you reach it), will satisfy your desires. If not, it is unwise to fool yourself about it. Don't theorize that:

- "The business will grow," or
- "The neighborhood will improve," or
- "The economy will turn this business around in a few months," or
- "I can make this business grow because the other franchisees are dopes,"
- *Ad infinitum.*

Be very realistic. Take a minimalist approach. Use very conservative projections. If you exceed those projections, that will mean more money for you. Don't base your success on a high profit margin either, particularly at first. Startup costs and short-term loan and interest payments make it highly likely your first few years will be relatively lean ones.

Know All the Costs of Starting a Franchise

Almost any franchise requires its new franchisees to pay an up-front license or franchise fee. Many people interested in obtaining a franchise believe this initial fee covers most of the cost of going into business. This is not the case; the initial fee is just the beginning of the money you will have to spend before you open your doors.

Franchisors charge up-front fees so they can recoup their substantial up-front investments in founding the franchise; more rapidly expand and add more franchises; and count on a profit from selling you the right to use their system, image, know-how, and reputation. Franchisors must incur least 16 types of expenses just to get started, including costs for product development; marketing plans; market research or demographic studies; architects' drawings; interior and industrial designers' plans; site selection studies; lease and construction costs for model or startup units; carrying charges on inventory and loans; interest payments; payroll and payroll taxes; training program and materials development; legal and professional fees; management salaries; and sales and marketing salaries. Added to this is the expense of meeting federal and state requirements.

Clearly, franchisors are justified in charging some type of fee. The problems arise when you have to determine exactly what fees and charges you have to pay, to whom, how, and when. Clearly, it is in your best interest to hold back, even until after opening and cash flow begins, as many costs as possible. This may or may not be acceptable to the franchisor, not to mention trade suppliers with whom you'll contract.

A Dozen Types of Fees

The costs of obtaining a license and starting operations can be divided into two general categories: the franchisor's specific fees and charges, and the general costs of opening that any new business incurs. The costs that belong to each category vary from franchise to franchise. In fact, depending on the franchise, you may have to pay up to *12* types of fees to obtain the license and get support from the franchisor. These fees include:

• *The basic franchise fee.* For this fee, you may receive a wide range of personal training, licenses, operations manuals, training materials, site selection and location preparation assistance, and so on. You may receive some of these, or virtually none of them. These matters should be worked out through negotiation and added to the contract. Whatever ends up being included, however, you'll have to pay this to get into the franchisor's business.

• *Royalties.* You most often pay royalties on gross sales, revenues, or income, most often on a percentage basis. You may also pay a percentage royalty or fee that goes into an advertising fund or pool. These fees will be incurred as you operate, and will be payable the same way. They won't be part of your up-front costs, but they should be factored into your profit projections for the year.

• *Rents/lease payments.* If you rent or lease equipment, a building, land, and so on from the franchisor, you will have to pay rents. *Hidden cost:* Up-front security deposits usually required by landlords, franchisor-landlords, or leasing companies.

• *Prepaid capital expenses.* A broad category that usually includes all of the cost of fixed assets and equipment required to open your operation.

• *Business goodwill fee.* An additional cost, sometimes levied once a year or at the beginning of a new franchise agreement, for the privilege of benefiting from the franchisor's good name and reputation in the community.

• *"Special value" location fee.* An additional payment to pay the franchisor for finding your location for you, although the franchisor might also own the location, has been desperate to lease it to someone, and fully intends to charge you the going rate for rent.

• *Training fee.* More and more often, franchisors are "unbundling," that is, separating a training fee from the franchise fee. This is the charge you must pay to obtain required training either at the company's training center or in your location. *Hidden costs:* In almost all cases, you have to pay for your travel expenses to training sessions and your room and board for the duration. You may also have to agree to assume these costs for additional required seminars in the future, either at headquarters or regional training centers. These expenses can mount up quickly.

On the other hand, some franchisors will pay for your room and board, but not transportation; some obtain discounts for their franchisees from airlines, local hotels, and rent-a-car outlets; and some pay all of these expenses. Of course, one cannot expect a franchisor that charges a small initial fee ($1,000–$5,000) to provide room and board and transportation. The question of training expenses exemplifies the difficulty of determining who—franchisor or franchisee—pays for what.

• *Startup or grand opening fees.* These may include the costs of sending a regional or district representative or manager to help you with the grand opening and to help train your employees, if any. It may include the costs of store displays and promotional and advertising expenses. But some or all of these charges may be part of the franchise fee.

• *Ongoing management assistance.* You may have to pay an hourly rate or flat fee every time you ask the company to send a representative to help you solve a problem.

• *Build-to-suit fee.* This could be a very expensive charge if the franchisor must adapt its architectural plans or basic layout to conform to a location you choose. One franchisee had to pay an unanticipated $28,000 build-to-suit charge for a small outlet, more than doubling the planned startup budget. This makes it doubly important that you find not only the right location, but one that offers something very close to the franchisor's basic plan if you are to save these fees.

• *Accounting and bookkeeping fees.* Some franchisors will provide, as part of the initial fee, several months' worth of accounting and bookkeeping forms to help you streamline your own accounting procedures. Most franchisors provide a lot of this material because it helps them collect their royalties, service fees, or advertising contributions more efficiently too. Or you may have to develop your own accounting procedures. But almost no franchisor will simply throw you to the bookkeeping wolves without introducing you to an efficient way to handle the task.

However, many franchisors make up these costs to them by charging you for data you receive from them or for computer processing of bookkeeping data for you. Some may lease you electronic cash registers linked directly to their central computers and charge you for the dedicated telephone lines, long-distance or telephone charges, communications costs, service and maintenance costs, and so on under the label of "accounting fees." As computerized cash registers become less expensive, this type of accounting system in a franchise will become more prevalent.

• *Renewal fee.* This is a charge over and above the regular franchise fee for the privilege of renewing the agreement. *Hidden cost:* At renewal, you may also have to pay any increases in the basic franchise fee since you first bought the license.

Now and Forever After

In regard to any of these fees, there are a few key questions, besides the raw numbers, you'll need answers for, including:

1. Is the fee a one-time charge, a continuing fee based on sales, or a fixed fee paid quarterly, annually, monthly, or per use?

2. What are the terms for payment of the fees? Lump sum, cash up

front, trade discounts (2 percent discount for payments received within ten days), monthly payments for so many months? Also, at what interest rate will installment payments be computed? Are any late charges imposed on payments 30 days or more overdue?

3. Must the basic franchise fee be paid up front, or may it be paid in two or more installments? For example, suppose the franchise fee is $30,000; can you make a $10,000 down payment at the signing of the agreement, $10,000 more 6 months later, and $10,000 more 12 months later? Will there be any interest charges on such deferred payments?

Some franchisors require only a down payment and either finance the remaining balance themselves or help you arrange a bank loan. *Hidden cost:* The franchisor's interest rate is likely to be substantially higher than the bank's rate. After all, the franchisor had to borrow the money from the bank itself so it can lend the money to you. Thus your interest payments will be more costly on a monthly basis than if you obtain the credit from a bank yourself.

4. How "flexible"—that is, *negotiable*—are the fees and their terms? Wise negotiators state that it is often better to negotiate terms than price. In buying real estate, it is clear that buying a $100,000 house at 9 percent interest for 30 years is a better deal than buying a $75,000 house at 15 percent for 15 years. The difference in monthly payments is equal to $1,050 minus $805, or $245 per month in savings to the buyer. Keep this in mind when negotiating fees and terms, and calculate the cash flow and short- and long-term savings in each instance as well as the price itself.

Additional Payments to the Franchise Company

These dozen fees and charges are just the beginning of the costs you may have to pay the franchise company. Your largest cost involving the franchisor may well be startup inventory, equipment, and supplies. Many franchisors make a significant percentage of their profits by selling you equipment (special ovens and ice cream machines, for example) and supplies (paper goods with the franchise's name printed on them) at discounts. You must include these expenses in your startup budget in one category or the other. Determine also whether any supplies or equipment are included in the initial fee, although this is rare.

However, you can save money and lower your startup costs if the franchise company will help finance your initial purchases of equipment, inventory, and supplies. This lets you pay for them from actual sales. You may also be able to negotiate liberal credit terms and/or trade discounts with the franchisor. You may be able to use the company's influence to obtain trade credit and discounts from other suppliers, and/or to obtain credit from a bank at favorable, short-term interest rates as part of a franchise startup and construction loan package. In short, to avoid spending your cash up front, use as many innovative financing arrangements as you can handle without getting overloaded with long-term debt. It is almost always better to preserve your capital and pay your expenses out of cash flow.

On all fees and charges by the franchisor, be sure to obtain the exact details on the amount; financing terms, if any (equipment is often leased, rented, or sold on an installment basis); and at what point in the startup process you must pay these fees and charges.

Remember that for each franchise and each contract, certain legal terms will mean different things. Most often, these words, which should be clearly defined in writing, will be: *initial fee, initial cash investment, down payment, cash requirement, total cost, initial cost,* and so on. Make sure your attorney reviews these definitions closely and determines how they are applied in your contract. And when you must pay such amounts. And how.

Your Own Startup Costs

Beyond the fees and charges you pay the franchisor, there will be an additional array of up-front expenses you must meet just to go into business. If you do not pay the franchisor to lease, rent, build, or buy your premises, this will be your most important cost. There are as many ways to handle premises as there are ways to deal in real estate, from simple rental of existing storefront space to complicated ground lease, building ownership, and construction arrangements. Commercial leases are explained in more detail in Chapter 7.

The key thing to remember is to have an expert help you obtain a commercial lease or purchase commercial property. Commercial contracts are fraught with pitfalls for new and unwary business owners, and a professional's advice will probably save you more than his services will cost. Of course, you'll also need to have enough money for a lease's security deposit or the down payment on a mortgage.

In your startup budget, be sure to include at least three to six months' rent or mortgage payments to allow yourself time to get your franchise off the ground without draining your initial income.

Hidden cost: In any lease, whether with a franchisor or a private owner, be wary of escalator clauses that tie rent increases to changes in the Consumer Price Index, the Treasury bill interest rate, the Wholesale Price Index, the Producer Price Index, or similar government indexes. In times of low inflation, these can benefit you; when inflation soars, you will be severely handicapped. It is preferable to negotiate rent increases at a flat continuing rate to be applied from year to year or lease to lease, or to negotiate some "not to exceed" clauses. Also beware of assessments and costs the landlord can pass on to you, such as installing new air conditioning in his building.

Other essential expenses you will face include:

1. *Insurance*. You will need a variety of insurance policies, a topic to be discussed in detail in Chapter 9. Among the types of insurance you may need are: premises insurance; plate-glass insurance; office-contents insurance; inventory coverage; automobile and vehicle insurance on company vehicles; and other coverages required or recommended by the franchisor. You should also obtain an umbrella policy that covers many liabilities and eventualities not covered by other types of insurance; this is very inexpensive and is meant to help out in the event of crippling, million- or multimillion-dollar lawsuits. It is so inexpensive because, most of the time, your other insurances will cover all claims. The umbrella policies are meant to shelter you in the few instances when other policies have reached their limits. They cannot, however, be emphasized too strongly. Just knowing one is there is a good bit of needed business reassurance.

Insurance companies usually require at least a three-month, if not a semiannual, payment to be made when a binder is issued for the coverage. Thus, you can be forced to spend thousands of dollars *before* you open.

2. *Opening product inventory*. If an initial inventory of products and supplies is not included in the franchise fee, you will have to obtain enough to open your store and maintain proper inventory levels until your cash income is adequate to pay for more. The franchisor can help you determine the proper inventory for your store or outlet and may set minimal inventory levels you must keep in stock.

3. *Remodeling and leasehold improvements*. In most commercial leases, you will be responsible for the costs of improving the property, installing essential services such as plumbing and electrical outlets, decorating the premises, and providing signs.

This category also includes any zoning changes required for signs or premises uses. Neon signs often require variances. And many places require community approval—you have to get the neighbors to sign a document allowing you to open your doors—for businesses that make a lot of noise, serve liquor, create a defined public nuisance, and so on. In addition to time, you may well incur legal costs in these cases.

4. *Utility charges*. This category covers any deposits required for electrical, gas, oil, telephone, or water service and enough capital to cover the first month or two of projected expense for them. If you require any dedicated or special electric wires or telephone lines, you can expect to pay hefty deposits and first-month estimated usage as well.

5. *Payroll.* If you plan to hire any employees, this should include the costs of hiring and training as well as having them work in the store before the grand opening. Include a reasonable salary for yourself and any family members who will work with you. Don't forget to include withholding, workmen's compensation, and Social Security taxes as well as state and local income, disability, and other taxes due on the salaries in your calculations. Many small businesses try to skimp on these payments, but quickly find government tax collectors are endlessly patient and very persistent at collecting.

6. *Debt service.* This includes the cost of financing monthly principal and interest payments from all sources, including banks, investors, the franchisor, and so forth.

Hidden cost: Loan terms that fluctuate with some key index, usually the Treasury bill rate. You should always remember that this rate rises more often than it falls—it has for the past 40 years over the long term—and you need to consider what a higher interest rate would mean to you in monthly payments as you grow.

You should also negotiate the number of "points"—percentage points of interest above the given rate (the prime rate or the T-bill rate) that applies to your loan. For example, major AAA-rated corporations can borrow short-term funds at as low as one-half point above the prime rate, while small businesses often cannot borrow money at less than two, three, four, or even five or more points over the given rate. Banks usually set the rates that are most favorable to them. But you may be able to use the power of the franchisor's name and reputation to lower that rate and improve the terms for you.

7. *Bookkeeping and accounting fees.* There are almost bound to be others, besides any the franchisor may charge. In any case, it is always wise to use your own CPA or bookkeeper to protect your interests. The extra cost of this will be well worth it.

8. *Legal and professional fees.* The cost of hiring an attorney to review the franchise contract, represent you during the negotiations, file and obtain any required zoning variances, planning permissions, and so on, and handle any unforeseen legal conflicts that arise as you establish your franchise must be factored into your opening-costs projections. You may, of course, negotiate with a professional such as this to either reduce the fee by a percentage point or two for prompt payment, delay payment until after opening and cash flow begins, or accept installment payments.

9. *Training requirements.* In most states and cities, at least one, if not all, managers and employees in food-service industries must take an inexpensive course in food care and handling. This should be a small cost, but you will probably have to take the time to attend several day or evening classes and

obtain a training certificate. Myriad franchises could bring with them individual state or local training or education requirements, and you must bear the costs of meeting these, too.

10. *State and local licenses, permits, certificates.* These run the gamut from liquor-serving licenses to building permits for renovation. You must have them or face suspension or the shutdown of your business. If you plan to locate in any special zoning districts, perhaps a historic rehabilitation area, you may need special permission to change the exterior or interior of a structure, and you will have to comply with extra zoning and planning codes and procedures. This can often be a time-consuming, nerve-racking, and expensive experience; again, your attorney may need to be involved.

11. *Your own ad and promotional expenses.* It is not a good idea to rely only on the franchisor to provide enough advertising and public relations to give your operation a grand send-off. Rather, allocate some part of your startup budget to generating media exposure. Chapter 11 discusses many low-cost ways to get the best results for each marketing dollar.

12. *Coupon costs.* Related to ads and promos is the adverse effect of any discount coupons or giveaways you use during your grand opening celebration. If you calculate your early income based on full-price purchases, you could face a significant shortfall in income if, instead, you hand out a lot of discount coupons.

Now you can draft your startup budget. Add together all your payments to the franchisor and all your additional costs. It is essential too to figure these costs as accurately as possible, and then add a substantial contingency—some recommend 20 percent, others as much as 50 percent—as a buffer against the inevitable unexpected costs. Remember Murphy's Law—whatever can go wrong will, at the worst possible moment. As a new-business owner, consider yourself a likely victim of Murphy's Law; anticipate and plan for the worst. When better events happen, you will be pleasantly surprised and have some money left to put back into working capital.

Understanding Equity Capital and Working Capital

As you establish a startup budget, you need to do long-term planning to see where your future financial resources will come from. Obviously, you want to earn a lot of income, but that is just the beginning of an adequate supply of financial resources for the long haul. One of the two secrets of long-term success is adequate capitalization. (The other is good management.) Simply put, this means having enough cash in the bank, trade credit, a bank line of credit, cash flow, and borrowing capacity to steer you through any type of economic seas—clear sailing, seasonal doldrums, or howling tempests. Besides poor management, not having enough capital is the single greatest cause of small-business failure. In fact, the two go hand in hand; poor management often directly leads to wasted capital resources and business failure.

Recalling that "adequate" varies from franchise to franchise, nevertheless, you must have adequate amounts of two kinds of capital:

• *Equity capital.* This is money invested in fixed, or "hard," assets—buildings, equipment, land, machinery, fixtures.

• *Working capital.* This is money used to pay ongoing expenses, such as payroll, supplies, materials, rent, and the myriad other costs of doing business. Naturally, you want to use your cash flow for this, but there will be times when you can't.

You should have at least three and preferably six months' to a year's worth of working capital in the bank before you open your doors. Establishing equity capital, beyond what you initially have tied up in the nuts and bolts of your business, will not be as important at first as working capital. Why? You want to develop cash flow, and will lease most of your fixtures, if you can, to do so. As you grow and need tax deductions, however, you may want to change your emphasis to building equity capital and taking the tax benefits, depreciation, and investment tax credits (ITC)—if they still exist after 1986. The 10 percent ITC on equipment and machinery that existed in 1985, as this book was written, would be abolished under the Reagan tax reform program as it was proposed in late 1985. It is likely that any tax reform act passed in the next few years will at least nibble at the ITC issue.

Businesses in general, and small businesses in particular, stand to lose their incentive to keep their equipment up-to-date and in good condition if such tax reforms become law.

Look at wealthy people. They build wealth with equity capital—interests in businesses such as yours, real estate, and other hard assets. It is important, if you are to build lasting wealth, that you build equity capital as you become successful.

How to Finance Your Franchise

As you determine your need for startup funds, short- and long-term working and equity capital, you may begin to worry about where you are ever going to get the money. Fortunately, few franchisors expect you to pay cash for 100 percent of the costs and working-capital requirements. Many expect and encourage you to obtain outside financing for anywhere from 50 to as much as 80 percent of your startup costs and working capital. So you may need no more than 20 percent of the total startup costs in cash. In fact, it is economically unwise to try to pay cash to start your franchise business.

Why? By paying cash, you can put yourself in a deep hole as you try to recoup such a heavy cash outflow from your initial cash inflow. You can easily run out of cash you will need later as your franchise begins to grow. You also lose the power of leverage that a loan can give you through the advantages of investment tax credits, depreciation, and loan interest deductions. And there is a very dangerous psychological tendency to play faster and looser with your own cash than you would with someone else's—especially if you are accountable to that other party through loan payments.

So if you shouldn't use your own cash or cash equivalents (stocks and bonds) as startup money, what do you use? You use the same thing people of wealth have long used as the secret to making more money: OPM—other people's money. OPM comes in many forms, many of which you may never have thought of. OPM ranges from a bank loan to investments by your friends and neighbors to publicly sold stock and beyond.

The First Source—F&F Loans

Most small businesses get started with a loan from that well-known financial institution F&F Finance, also known as Family and Friends. Borrowing money from family members and friends to start a franchise is a proven method, but it has "proved" to have as many drawbacks as advantages. So go slowly and carefully before you borrow from F&F Finance. Be sure the people involved can spare the money. Be sure they are not going to indenture you in ways you cannot legally, financially, or very important, psychologically afford. Be sure that you regard these funds as loans, not as funny money never to be repaid.

Other Sources

Before you approach F&F for money, explore other, possibly overlooked, sources of ready money. A franchise company—and banks—will be interested in, if not adamant about, knowing whether you have exhausted your own sources of money before they are willing to finance your operation. Of course, you must make sure the franchise company is not unreasonable in its requirements, and you should not lay everything on the line. You will not want to lose your house or go bankrupt simply because a franchise venture fails, no matter what the expectations of others are. You never see a bank or franchisor go bankrupt to loan you money, do you? In fact, it is illegal for a bank to do so, and completely contrary to good business sense for a franchisor as well. Take a lesson from them, and refuse to loan yourself so much money that you risk disaster. Rather, use your assets and personal net worth to show the franchisor that it should negotiate favorable financing terms for you. In this case, a franchisor will act as a bank often does: It will be more than happy to loan you the money if you don't need the money in the first place.

Here are several additional sources of financing, none of which require you to take your cash cushion out of the bank or pillowcase you've stashed it in:

• *Low-interest loans against insurance*. If you have a whole-life insurance policy or other policy that has been building cash value as you've paid for it, you can borrow from the insurance company against that cash value—usually up to 70 or 80 percent—at interest rates below the going rate.

• *Personal assets*. Many people have personal assets that they are not using: heirlooms, paintings, jewelry, collectibles, equipment and machinery, and so on. You can use these to secure a loan from a bank. In most cases, if your credit rating is good, you will—at worst—need to secure only a portion of the loan. Thus you retain ownership of the assets without jeopardizing the equity in your essential property—that is, your home and car. Stocks, bonds, mutual fund shares, money market accounts, and other paper financial instruments all can be used this way.

• *Special retirement plans*. You *cannot* use IRAs (individual retirement accounts) as collateral for loans. However, self-employed businesspeople and professionals can form a special type of pension plan that they may invest in a wide variety of business ventures, including franchises. This program is the 301-K retirement plan, and more than 100,000 of these plans have been formed. They allow self-employed people and professionals to put up to 25 percent of their gross income into the plan each year, deduct the amount from their incomes, and use the funds to make investments. If you are eligible for this plan, there are no restrictions on your using the money in your plan to invest in another venture in which you have an ownership interest.

Nor are there reasons why other self-employed people and professionals shouldn't invest in your business. Contact physicians, dentists, CPAs, attorneys, and other successful professionals in your area. They may have funds to invest and would be glad of a chance to invest locally with the backing of a well-known franchise shoring up their investment as well.

• *Equity loans*. These are loans against the value of real property, usually a residence. But they can be obtained against income property (apartments, rental houses, office buildings) or even undeveloped, vacant property you own. An equity loan from a bank can be for up to 70 percent of the amount of equity you have.

Beware of underrating your equity. Many people believe that equity is simply the amount of money they have paid for a property so far. This is not the case. Equity also includes the value of appreciation of the property, and this could enhance your equity position greatly.

For example, suppose you bought a house in 1965 for $15,000 and you have only $4,000 left in principal to pay for it. But suppose that, on today's market, your house is worth $50,000. The amount of equity you have would be the $11,000 in mortgage principal you have retired *and* the $35,000 in appreciated value, or $46,000. If your credit record is good and you show you can pay the loan back, the bank may lend you $30,000 as a second mortgage. Mortgage bankers and private lenders may lend you even more, up to 80 percent of the value of the house.

Of course, if the neighborhood has declined drastically, it is possible you have paid in cash more for your property than it is currently worth, but this is not common.

Using "Personal Capital"

An equally good way to raise money is to borrow against your "personal capital"—your knowledge, skills, experience, successful track record, even your rights in the current and future value of royalties from copyrighted works, patents, trademarks, trade names, mineral holdings, and so on. You can use these things to present your case to a bank for an unsecured loan. Often, however, you can best borrow against your "personal capital" by forming partnerships; you put up the expertise, future expectations, and so forth, and the partner or partners put up the cash.

It is popularly believed that, in forming a partnership, you give up control. But you're going into business partly to gain control, right? The truth is, you can still run your own show by setting up limited partnerships, in which you are the general manager—and in complete management control—and the partners are inactive, or "silent."

In these cases, the partners are looking for tax shelters or a future return in cash flow, but they do not want the hassles of managing a day-to-day retail business. As general partner, you may put up no money at all, or the 10 percent of the total that is common. But you receive up to 50 percent of the gross profits, while each partner buys a share for a specified percentage interest or sum of money. The amount each share costs will depend on how much money you need to raise and how many partners you want to take in, but shares usually cost $5,000 or $10,000 per unit, although you can sell them for two cents each if you want to.

Partnerships are very tricky and complex, and you should use the services of a lawyer and CPA to set one up. But as real-estate partnerships have shown for decades, this is an effective way to raise money, provide tax shelters, and generate positive short-term financing for a solid business venture; if successful, it also provides a healthy long-term capital gain for the investors.

Your CPA and attorney may be excellent sources of leads to potential partners, clients, or others who are looking for solid ways to invest their money. The types of people often looking for partnerships include: doctors, attorneys, CPAs, stockbrokers, real-estate salespeople, successful executives in major corporations in your area, and successful small-business owners of all kinds who want to expand their opportunities to profit.

The most attractive partnerships to the silent partners are those that maximize the amount of money that can be sheltered from taxes during the first year or two of the partnership. If your franchise requires a lot of equipment and machinery purchases—as restaurants do, for example—you can pass the tax advantages of purchasing or leasing the equipment on to your partners. Partners are fond of buying land and building facilities on them, one reason you see so many fast-food franchises in freestanding structures. But again, this is a complex area, and you should only form a partnership with sound professional advice.

Of course, the drawbacks to a partnership include: loss of complete control (although as general partner you retain day-to-day management powers) and loss of profits, in that you have to share the profits with the partners. Still, it is better to have 50 percent of a successful business than 100 percent of an underfinanced failure.

• *Secured loans from other people.* If you do not want partners, you can try to arrange loans from private lenders in two basic ways. No, this does not mean a visit to the local loan shark. This means that there are numerous private individuals who make personal loans to good credit risks; they do charge interest rates somewhat higher than the local bank's, but the loan will be perfectly legal and aboveboard. Your CPA or financial adviser can recommend reputable individuals in your area. Likewise, he can probably steer you away from the not-so-reputable ones.

Here are the ways private investors may work with you:

First, you can ask for an unsecured loan backed by your good credit rating. For it, you will pay a higher rate of interest (four or five points) than the local bank will give you on a personal loan.

Second, you can ask for a loan secured with real assets or property, a house or a savings passbook, as collateral. You will probably not have to collateralize the entire amount. If you have a good reputation and a good plan, expect to collateralize about half of the loan.

Private lenders, however, tend to be tougher than a bank in recouping their investment. They often move to foreclose on loans backed by real property very quickly if you miss a payment or default. These lenders very well understand the value of your franchise, and may not mind taking control of it if you falter. So be aware that private lenders, who do not share in the risk of the franchise, should be used as a last resort.

• *Subordinated officers' notes.* This is a way in which you or your other sources lend the franchise money in exchange for promissory notes from your franchise business. Then you go to a bank with these notes and an agreement from the holders of the notes that they will subordinate them to any bank loans. In short, you and anyone who lends you money promise that in case your franchise fails, the bank will get its money before the holders of the promissory notes. This reduces the bank's risk and will help make most banks more eager to loan you money.

These are a few of the lesser known ways to raise money to buy and run a franchise business. It is likely that you will use at least one of these uncommon methods as well as one or more of the three better-known ways to raise money.

Conventional Borrowing Methods

The three better-known ways—banks, Small Business Administration, and the franchisor itself—are not necessarily the best ways for you to go, depending on your circumstances and your personal preferences. You may prefer to use F&F loans rather than a bank. You may find partners more palatable than borrowing from the franchisor. You may find dealing with the SBA bureaucracy leads to too much red tape and too many strings attached to suit your point of view; you may prefer even tough private lenders to that. These three ways have, however, been proved through the years and are used successfully by many businesses.

Just because there is a wealth of other money sources, don't form the impression that the conventional methods—unsecured bank loans, Small Business Administration assistance, and franchise company financing—are hard to come by. In most cases, these three will be readily available. In fact, you may want to use a mix of conventional and unconventional ways to finance your franchise so you can preserve as much of your own available cash as possible.

The Franchisor's Financing

If your credit is good and you own your home or other property, it is likely the franchisor will help you finance the franchise in one of several ways, especially if the franchise fee is a substantial sum (over $10,000 or so). First, it may let you pay the franchise fee with a down payment and installments paid over a period of time. The length of time, the interest rate, and other terms are completely negotiable, and they vary from franchisee to franchisee. Often the rate will be tied to the rate for one-year Treasury bills and the payback period will be relatively short, usually a year or so. Often the installments are quarterly payments.

Second, a franchise company may work with you to obtain a bank loan; often franchise companies have strong relationships with banks with which they work on a regular basis. You may or may not want to consider this step; to maintain your independence would require borrowing from your own sources and using the franchisor's preferred bank as a last resort. Third, and fairly rarely, a franchisor will guarantee a bank loan, but you may have to put up your inventory, equipment, and fixtures as security.

If the franchisor really wants you to run one of its stores and you have a good personal and business track record, you will be able to obtain financing at reasonable, if not favorable, terms.

Some larger franchisors even have their own SBICs, Small Business Investment Companies, formed under federal small-business legislation. SBICs make relatively low-interest loans and mortgages guaranteed by the Small Business Administration. They differ from other SBA loans in that they are made by private companies, not commercial banks.

SBA Loans

SBA loans are not necessarily a good source of financing for franchises because of the length of time and paper-shuffling hassles one has to endure to get the money. Even then, the SBA is not giving you the loan; it primarily guarantees loans from banks, or at best participates in a loan and shares the amount with a bank or banks, depending on the amount you want. And the SBA does not often get involved in amounts of money under several hundred thousand dollars, nor does it usually loan money to those who can get the money from other sources. The SBA, perhaps more so than a bank or franchisor, will force you to use all other sources of financing before it will participate. And the project must usually involve some specific worthwhile purpose, such as manufacturing a scarce but worthy product, or employing large numbers of unemployed or poverty-level people, and so on.

If you want to work with the SBA, get your local congressman on your side. He has a specialist on staff who can help push your loan through the SBA a little more quickly than it might go otherwise.

The advantage of an SBA loan is that it can be a source of money when no other source is available, and it can make starting out easier for you than other methods. But to get one you will have to go through a trial by red tape.

For addresses of SBA district or field offices, contact your congressman, look in the phone book of the nearest city or metropolitan area, or contact the U.S. Commerce Department.

The Banking Method

Forbes magazine has christened the typical small-business banker "The One-Minute Lender," a facetious term for bankers who rapidly turn down loan applications from small businesses. It does appear at first glance that banks are getting more skittish about loaning money to small businesses, but this does not necessarily include franchises. In fact, if you are opening a well-known franchise, you may find local banks competing to provide services, including cash management, payroll servicing, bill paying, accounting, estate planning, lines of credit, and much more. In the deregulated banking environment, banks are finding they must compete with each other for desirable business.

In any case, banks follow the same general procedure in granting business loans that they follow in giving consumer loans, with a few key differences. They will want to know:

- The amount you want to borrow and what percentage of your total estimated financial requirements this represents.
- The purpose of the loan—inventory purchase, financing initial accounts receivable, purchasing equipment, other.
- The ways you intend to repay the loan—from sales and cash flow or higher profits made possible by use of the money.
- Your "backup" payment method in case higher sales and profits do not materialize. This could include personal assets, a guarantee, security or collateral of the real assets of the franchise, collection of accounts receivable, real estate, or other sources of income belonging to other family members—a spouse's income from a job or profession or his or her own personal assets.

Negative factors a bank will consider will be a heavy personal debt load and a lack of knowledge of how to run the business. These factors make it important that you provide the lender thorough, but concise, financial, income, and expense statements and business plans. Having the franchisor go to bat for you will also help.

The franchisor should help you prepare any plans and paperwork for the bank, and go with you to visit the lending officer when you discuss the loan. Even if you have a solid, longtime relationship with a banker, a franchise representative should go with you. The banker will want complete reassurance that the bank is loaning money to a reputable concern with good long-term prospects.

If business conditions are mildly favorable, and you do all of your homework, you should be able to obtain a reasonably sized bank loan—up to one half of your financing—at a reasonable interest rate. For example, if the prime rate is 11 percent, a loan of 13 percent should be considered reasonable.

If you get turned down by one bank, don't despair. Ask the banker exactly why you were turned down, and analyze what other information you could have presented, how you could have acted differently, any additional support you could have marshaled in your favor, and so forth.

Often loans are turned down simply because the bank has been asked to put up too great a percentage of the total amount of financing. Start again. Work on ways to raise more money from other sources, and then go back to your bank. Or go to another bank. Bankers differ in attitude and approach. One week, the bank may have tons of money to lend, and the next it may literally be dry. Lenders have quotas of money to lend that vary all over the map. Bank A may have loans for business and Bank B may be emphasizing condominiums. Don't give up; keep looking. Try unconventional types of banks—U.S. offices of foreign banks, private banks that do not offer checking accounts, foreign banks in overseas locations, any financial institution whose lending powers may not be affected by the local or even U.S. situation.

Try the full-service branches of foreign banks. Some with branches in many states include: Banco Popular and other South American banks with branches in Florida, Texas, the Southwest, and California; Canadian banks with branches in states in the northern tier. especially Michigan and Minnesota; even European banks with full-service branches and commercial branches in many cities. On the West Coast and major eastern cities, Japanese, Chinese, Korean, and Southeast Asian banks may be helpful.

Try competitors of local banks. Play them against each other to your advantage. Negotiate favorable terms and ask another bank to better them. Negotiate a plan to keep your business accounts at the bank that gives you the loan, and volunteer to keep a certain balance, called a "compensating balance," in that branch, if you must. Agree to use the bank's payroll and check-cashing services for your employees. There are many ways to convince a bank to do business with you. Work with your CPA and your banker to discover them and to use them to your advantage.

Ask for What You Want

The single biggest mistake small-business operators make is that they do not ask for what they want. Even if they do ask and are rebuffed at first, they stop trying instead of working even smarter to make it work the second time they try. Few of them, indeed, go out fully prepared the first time, with a business plan they can use once or a dozen times if need be.

How to Prepare a Business Plan

The most professional way to show any lender, from your great-uncle Maxie to the Bank of America to a Saudi Arabian oil prince, what you want is with a well-thought-out business plan.

When approaching franchisors and lenders, you need to create a good impression before they will consider giving you what you want. More important even than your appearance or personal background will be the impression they get of your business savvy. Of course, credentials and fancy titles from previous positions and experience all help mold that impression, but an essential piece of the puzzle for which franchisors and lenders look is a comprehensive business plan.

By a solid business plan is not meant a bank statement or a franchisor's application. A business plan discusses in concise and precise detail these areas:

- Your franchise's projected activities
- The projected performance of your management team (even if that's only you and your spouse—or just you)
- What features distinguish your business from the competition
- A serious survey of your proposed market
- Financial projections for your business
- Actual and proposed sources of financing

Much of this information will come from the franchise company's own offering prospectus and literature, but you must develop your own additional answers to fit local conditions.

This plan need not be a Pulitzer Prize–winning tome. The length will vary according to the size and scope of the franchise. In fact, tailor the length of your business plan to the complexity and expense of your franchise. A $15,000 franchise will simply have fewer complications and details than a $250,000 one.

In general, a business plan should be between 15 and 50 pages long. But that length does not include the franchise application itself or related personal documents, such as tax returns and personal financial statements.

A business plan serves another important function as well. It is the best way to give yourself an overall picture of exactly what you want to do. Ideas and plans in your head often remain fuzzy and general; a business plan helps you be very specific and clear in your thinking. And it will help you more accurately target your true markets. Suppose you want to open a maid service franchise, and you initially think your market will be wealthy individuals who can afford maid services. The market research part of your business plan makes it clear to you, however, that you could make more money offering a once-a-week service to young married professional couples.

Later you can use the plan as a foundation on which to monitor your business's progress during the first year it is open. By comparing your actual results and progress with your plan's projections, you can quickly see where you are on target or off the mark and make adjustments in time.

As you prepare a business plan, use it not as a static document carved in stone, but as a flexible, dynamic picture of which direction you want your franchise to take. Use it to study the projected results and consequences of various strategies. Use it to determine how many employees you will need to reach various financial goals, how much physical equipment, how many sales, how much startup capital, and so forth. In short, a business plan, used primarily as a tool to sell yourself to franchisors and lenders, should also serve as a monitoring device, like those at nuclear power plants that prevent meltdowns. By writing down all your goals and plans to reach them, you are creating a warning signal—if you simply remember to look at it once in a while. Without this monitoring device, your franchise could self-destruct before you even have a fair chance to succeed.

Plan for a Business Plan

Here is a concise outline of what a thorough business plan should include:

I. SUMMARY—1–2 pages

Highlight important features and the prime business opportunity. Do not sell yourself short here; make the business sound attractive, worthwhile, and convincing. (This is not puffery; after all, if it lacked these things, why would you *want* to go into it?)

II. THE FRANCHISE ITSELF

A. Company Background—Basically describe your products and services, potential customers, and market area. Give a short discussion of how you got interested in the franchise.
B. Business Background—Discuss what you know of the franchise

you want and the industry in which it participates. Describe any major trends in the industry.

III. PRODUCTS AND SERVICES

A. Product/Service Description—Describe these in detail. Use franchisor material to help fill this in.

B. Product Potential—Discuss any ways you can extend the available products and services in your market area.

IV. MARKET ANALYSIS

A. Potential Customers—Define who you expect your most important customers will be (the 20 percent that will buy 80 percent of your goods or services); where you will find them; why, how, and when they will buy. Explain the difficulties you face in appealing to your customers.

B. Market Trends—Define how big the *total* potential market is for your franchise and discuss trends that affect that market—both for better and for worse.

C. Competition—List the strengths and weaknesses of your competition and their products and services. Use a table to compare your products and services with those of the competition. Assess and discuss why the competition's customers now buy from them, and assess how you plan to appeal to these current buyers.

V. MARKETING PLAN

A. Sales Goals—Outline your estimated quarterly sales for the first two years you are in business.

B. Sales and Service Plan—Describe your sales, service, pricing, distribution, advertising, and promotion strategies.

C. Strategies—Discuss which customers will be targeted first and those to be targeted in later stages, how you will find these customers, and how you will cope with seasonal sales.

D. Prices and Costs—Discuss various pricing strategies compared to those of the current competition. Justify prices higher or lower than the competition's and consider how you intend to become and stay profitable.

E. Sales and Service Tactics—Discuss how you plan to sell and distribute your products. Discuss any guarantees, warranties, or service plans.

F. Advertising and Promotion—Describe how you will bring your product to the public's attention. Outline initial advertising costs and programs.

VI. PRODUCT RESEARCH AND DEVELOPMENT

It is unlikely most franchisees will do their own research and development, but discuss here what the franchise company plans to offer and how your own efforts will blend in with the company's.

VII. OPERATING PROCEDURES

A. Location—Discuss where you will locate, why, and the advantages and disadvantages.
B. Equipment and Shops—Describe the facilities you need to get started, where they will come from, and how much they will cost.
C. Production Procedures—Discuss how you will make the products you will sell, even if they are hamburgers (consider the differences among McDonald's, Burger King, and Wendy's!). Describe your "make-or-buy" policy and your sources of supply.
D. Employees—Discuss where they will come from, what kinds you need (full-time or part-time, students or experienced engineers, and so on), the training they will need, and the cost of such training.

VIII. EXECUTIVE TEAM

A. Key Management Roles—Describe who will actually manage the operation on a day-to-day basis and what functions each will perform. List the responsibilities and duties of each manager.
B. Management Pay Structure—Discuss which managers will get paid how much for which functions.
C. Management Training—Describe in detail any training the managers will require.
D. Professional Support—Describe your attorneys, accountants, consultants, advertising agency, bank, and service organizations.

IX. STARTUP SCHEDULE

A. Project Schedule—List on a project schedule the interrelated steps you must take to get started and how and when you plan to take them.
B. Deadlines/Milestones—Pay special attention to key deadlines and milestones.

X. CRUCIAL STARTUP PROBLEMS

In this section, discuss in detail the possible problems that could adversely affect your start-up, including:

- Negative economic and market trends
- Responses from existing competition
- Rise of new competition
- Failure to meet project schedules
- Trouble obtaining financing for start-up or growth
- *Ad infinitum,* remembering Murphy's Law

XI. FINANCIAL PROJECTIONS

A. Profit and Loss Projection—Include income statements for two or three years.
B. Cash-Flow Forecast—Discuss how the dollars should come in and flow out for two or three years.
C. Pro Forma Statements—Do balance sheets of assets and liabilities to show bankers and franchisors.
D. Financial Controls—Describe your accounting procedures and controls over cash.

XII. FINANCING

A. Needed Financing—Describe your financial requirements and the sources from which you plan to obtain the money. (Make sure this is put in capsule form at the end of the summary.)
B. Capitalization—List the shareholders and the number of shares each holds.
C. Use of Funds—Describe how the financing will be used.

This seems like a lot of work to obtain a franchise, and it is. But franchisors and successful franchisees will attest that this plan represents the kind of serious, sophisticated thinking you will need to succeed today. For smaller franchises, many of these answers will be short or self-explanatory, but mention them anyway. Whether you open a large or small business, you'll need to learn as quickly as possible to think and plan in a manner that suits your business. Using this outline will help.

Through the Haze: Financial Glossary

Franchisors and lenders use various financial terms with which you may not be familiar. They are basic to understanding what franchisors and lenders mean when they talk turkey. Yet how one franchisor uses the terms may differ from how another defines them. The brief glossary below explains how various franchisors may define these common terms.

• *Cash requirement.* This phrase may mean the total amount of cash, exclusive or inclusive of the fee, the franchise company requires you to put up. It may or may not come from outside sources, but it is likely it means the amount of cash you must raise *without* the franchise company's help. It may or may not include cash available for working capital and operating expenses.

• *Down payment.* This may mean an up-front payment on the franchise fee, the more conventional meaning of a down payment on a mortgage, or it may be synonymous with initial investment.

• *Earnings claim.* Any claim made by a franchisor concerning the level of income, profit (gross or net), earnings, or profit margins of a franchise.

• *Equity investment.* This too can have many meanings, but it usually means startup capital from your own sources for real-estate leases, fixtures, machinery, equipment, and so on. It may or may not mean the same thing as initial investment, although initial investment most often includes the franchise fee, and equity investment often does not.

• *Initial investment.* This may mean the franchise fee alone; or the fee with a required inventory purchase; or the fee, inventory, and equipment and fixtures; or something entirely different.

• *Initial license fee.* This can include the franchise fee and a variety of additional services, such as training, opening assistance, and so forth, or it may not.

Do *Not* Borrow Too Much

After all this, you may want to restrain your urge to borrow. Leading franchisors say they get very concerned when a franchisee borrows a very high percentage (more than 80 percent) of his working and equity capital. You should worry, too, because loan payments and high interest rates (still 15 to 18 percent in late 1985 for small-business loans despite three years of very low inflation) can sap your profits.

There is no set formula for determining how much you should borrow to get started. But it makes good sense to borrow less and emphasize partners or YOM (your own money) more if the franchise is in a relatively slow-growth industry. If the franchise is in a boom phase, you may be able to borrow more and sustain payments at high interest rates.

But if you see that you will have to spend equity capital, dip into your family's cash reserves, or raid your children's college fund to start your franchise, stop and think again. You will start with your resources stretched very thin. And it will only take one or two fairly bad months to knock your franchise down for the ten-count. Few franchises today are get-rich-quick schemes. You should plan your finances for prosperous long-term growth. And plan to manage your franchise for long-term financial success and personal satisfaction.

In Part I, you learned how to buy a franchise. In Part II, you will learn how to manage one for the best possible results.

Part II

Secrets of Managing Your Own Franchise

7

Firm Footing: The First Steps in Setting Up Your Franchise

You've bought your franchise. You've persevered and found an excellent business that fulfills your desires and matches your talents. You're working with a financially sound, reputable franchisor that is eager to help you hit the ground running. "Well," you think, as you breathe a sigh of relief, "the worst is over." In a way, that's true. Now the fun of making money by running your own business begins. But temper your joy with understanding of your changing roles.

To succeed, you must make the transition from being the enthusiastic buyer to working as the enthusiastic owner. You will assume the roles of purchasing manager, personnel manager, marketing director, sales manager, production foreman, bookkeeper and accountant, public relations expert—anything and everything up to and including chief executive officer. Unfortunately, you don't have time to learn these roles one by one; you've got to do it simultaneously. But remember, that's what you wanted—and that's half the fun. There are, besides, rules to help you through it, until each role slips on like a second skin.

Four Startup Rules

Remember first of all that your main goal is profit; without it, you won't be in business for long. Beyond that, obey these four simple rules and you will be well on the road to success:

Rule No. 1: Follow the franchise company's operations manual. Franchisors repeatedly say, "It's all in the manual," and for their specific type of operation, the advice you need to correctly implement their business system will indeed be found in their operations and management manuals. So follow them, and follow them religiously as you get started.

Rule No. 2: Keep overhead—your operating costs—as low as possible. You will have already paid large sums of money—first, to the franchisor; second, to contractors and landlords; and third, to what may seem like every merchant in five counties. Now that you are ready to open your store, you must concentrate on cash flow. Delay petty expenditures, purchase goods and services carefully, limit hiring to filling only the absolutely necessary positions, and borrow as little as possible. It is unlikely customers are going to flock to your store immediately, although suggestions on how to improve your grand opening can be found in Chapter 8. And Chapter 11 will show you how to boost sales with inexpensive advertising and promotional methods.

Rule No. 3: Think small in terms of markets and big in terms of profits. At first, concentrate on what is likely to be the most profitable segment of your market. You should know this already from your own and the franchisor's market research. Stick with these results, and don't try to be all things to all people. You'll save time and can more precisely aim your advertising at your preferred customers.

Rule No. 4: Most important, do not be overconfident. Fledgling franchisees tend to see their new world through rose-colored glasses. While no one would endorse being overly pessimistic, a contagious condition that could scare away customers, there is a middle ground. Robert J. Ringer, author of *Looking Out for Number One,"* advises using the "presumption of negative results." While planning for positive results, assume that you will get negative results, despite your efforts, and plan to react to them. For example, if sales are slow at first, don't convince yourself that "Things will pick up in a few weeks." Assume they won't, and work your smartest to overcome that assumption.

Breaking these rules has been shown time and again to cause new franchises to fail early and often. Let's see how you can put these basic rules into practice, from start to finish.

How to Arrange a Commercial Lease

It is unlikely you will own or buy the office or building in which your franchise will be located. Usually, you will be required to lease a space. (The best-known exceptions to this are the freestanding fast-food outlets, which are most often in buildings created specifically for the franchise, usually in advance by the franchisor.)

Although you may well be used to renting or leasing a home or apartment, commmerical leases are quite different from residential leases. For one thing, they often place far more of the burden of expense and perform-ance on you. But working in your favor, if you are smart enough to use it, is the fact that the terms of commerical leases are open to negotiation.

Below are the major points a commerical lease will deal with and hints for arranging them in your own best interest.

The first point to consider, though not in the lease itself, is this: Have your attorney help you negotiate the lease. This is the best hint of all. But you also need to be able to understand the lease, and you must recheck the points the attorney brings up to be sure you agree; remember, you *can* overrule your attorney or any other professional you hire if you feel it's in your best interest to do so.

Second, consider what name will be signed to the lease—the name of the business you formed to operate the franchise? Or your own and/or partner's names? The most serious implication here is this: If you sign your name to a lease as an individual or sole proprietor, you become personally liable for the lease. Even if your franchise goes out of business before the lease expires, you may have to pay the rent *until* the lease expires. To protect yourself and your assets, you may wish to incorporate and put the name of the corporation on the lease. You or another officer of the corporation should sign the lease, but only as an officer, not as an individual. The property owner, however, will often want your personal backing of the lease or a guarantee from the franchise company, something it may or may not be willing to give.

Third, make sure the property, buildings, furnishings, and so forth are completely and accurately described in the lease. Otherwise, you could lease the wrong office, or discover too late that the fixtures you assumed were permanent belonged to the landlord. Moreover, you could be accused when vacating of removing something from the building, unless all these details are spelled out in writing in the lease.

Fourth, consider the term of the lease, or how long it gives you the space. It is best to negotiate the lease for the term of the franchise agree-ment—usually five or ten years with an option to renew for a similar period. If this is not possible, make sure it is long enough to allow you to retain the location after you have built a successful business. Nothing is more disruptive than to be forced to change locations just as you begin to prosper.

Include in the term a provision or option for renewal. An option gives you the right to extend the lease for a given period. In almost all option clauses there will be a provision to increase the rent. And option clauses often make the extension contingent on the landlord's approval. The most important thing an option clause does for you is to let you know years in advance how much rent you will be paying in the future. This helps you plan for long-term growth.

Watch out for escalator clauses in the lease tied to various price indexes. It is better for your planning and peace of mind to have fixed percentage increases rather than percentages that vary according to questionable and unknowable economic conditions in the future.

The term of the lease also spells out the day the lease begins, the day you must start paying rent, and the date the building and space will be available for your preparations, among other information.

Fifth, the lease should give the precise details of how much rent you must pay. In home and apartment rentals, this is simple—you pay a flat sum each month. But most commercial leases are "triple net" leases. Under such a lease, the rent includes a host of additional fees and charges described in the fine print. These may include:

- Real-estate taxes and a proportional share of any future real-estate tax increases
- Annual cost-of-living increases
- Utility escalation charges if the landlord pays for any utilities—water, sewer, gas, electric, fuel oil, and so on
- Insurance escalation fees
- Business or occupational license fees
- Common-area maintenance charges, increases, or assessments for maintenance to or upgrades of lobbies, hallways, elevators, parking lots, and so on
- A percentage rental fee, which means you pay the landlord a percentage of your gross sales in addition to the flat monthly rent

As you can tell, these fees and charges add significantly to your cost of doing business. You should know exactly which of these the landlord plans to make part of your rent and, as important, when you must pay them.

Sixth, the lease will discuss who is responsible for which repairs. With few exceptions, you will be responsible for all repairs inside the space you rent. The landlord may be responsible for the roof, exterior plumbing and wiring, and similar items, but most often the landlord need only make a reasonable effort to ensure that these systems work. And usually, the landlord is not liable if they don't.

Seventh, determine who pays for which insurance. You will very likely be required to protect the landlord's property by paying for various kinds of insurance against various kinds of risk. If you plan on opening a retail store, you will undoubtedly have to provide plate-glass insurance. You will have to carry public-liability insurance to indemnify the landlord for any claim, suit, or judgment in case one of your customers is injured on your premises. And you will be required to have an appropriate fire-insurance policy protecting the landlord's property as well as your own. Usually, your insurance will have to give the landlord preference for payments.

Eighth, accompanying the insurance section should be one that describes tenant's and landlord's obligations in case a disaster strikes and the leased space is unusable. Normally, you have to give notice to the landlord in case of fire or other disaster, and the landlord is required to make necessary repairs "as soon as practicable." This loophole allows a landlord to delay repairs because of labor strikes, material shortages, and similar events. Another common clause also allows the landlord to delay repairs until *after* an insurance settlement. Since insurance settlements may take months or even years, try to negotiate a clause that requires the landlord to repair any damage as soon as it happens, regardless of other allied eventualities, such as insurance settlements and so on.

The same section should discuss a rent abatement in case of disaster. No commercial lease lets you escape paying some rent unless the damage is almost total. Even then, the landlord is usually given the power to cancel the lease with 30 days' notice. If the damage is minor or the landlord begins repair work quickly, you will have to pay the rent unless you negotiate a clause that states otherwise.

Ninth, the lease will probably prevent you from subleasing the space without the landlord's permission. Although the language itself is a loophole, as we saw earlier, and the power of the clause varies from state to state, it is wise to include a clause stating that, if you want to sublease, the landlord's permission will not be "unreasonably withheld."

Tenth, there is likely to be a paragraph that will prevent you from making any changes or additions to the structure of the building without the landlord's approval. And the lease will make clear that any improvements you make to the building become the property of the landlord. If you don't want your furniture and shelving to become the landlord's property, you must specify exactly what is and what is not considered a leasehold improvement, keeping your belongings out of that classification as much as possible. Take this right down to the rugs and tiles if you can.

Eleventh, one of the toughest sections will outline the landlord's power in case you default on rent payments, or fail to carry out the terms of the lease. Every commercial lease is loaded with weapons for the landlord, including:

- Power to take possession of the premises with only a few days' notice. How many days varies from state to state.

- Power to take possession of your equipment and inventory and sell it to obtain the amount owed on the rent.
- Power to rerent the same premises and collect the new rent while he sues you for *all* the rent owed through the end of the lease. For example, suppose you have a total rent of $100 a month for five years. If you default on the first payment of the second year, the landlord can throw you out, rent the store for a higher rent, and still sue you for the remaining $4,800 rent owed under the terms of the lease.
- Power to relet the store as your agent—in effect, to sublet the space in your name—and collect the rent for his own benefit. He can rent the space for more money and keep the difference as well.

Finally, there will be clauses about sundry other matters, including concerns about government condemnations, subordination, landlord's access to the store, your right to freedom from harassment from your neighboring tenants, and so on.

With a commercial lease, a good, aggressive attorney *must* review and negotiate the lease with you. And beware the landlord who adamantly and absolutely refuses to negotiate any of the lease's provisions. This is a far different attitude from the "wish list" attitude; landlords who practice wish listing load up the lease with benefits for them—but they also know they must negotiate some of them away. Carefully study the lease and make up your own "wish list" of protective clauses for yourself. You had better work hard up front so that you will feel safe and comfortable in your franchise's new home for years to come.

In addition to your own attorney, you may seek aid from the franchisor. It will have commercial leasing experts who should be able to give you free advice. However, they may not know the specifics of a standard commercial lease in your state—still another good reason to have a good attorney of your own.

What if the franchisor is your landlord? The lease and its provisions and conditions are still negotiable. Consider well the same points, and hire your own attorney to negotiate for you.

Which Business Structure Is Best for You?

About the same time you seek a specific location to lease, you need to decide what type of business structure will benefit you most. By this is not not meant a building or physical structure, but a legal structure: a sole proprietorship, a partnership (limited or general), a corporation, a Subchapter S corporation, or other form. You must have a legal business structure because every local government requires you to at least register a business name in order to legally conduct business in that place. The two main reasons for choosing one structure over another are: (1) tax benefits and (2) limiting your personal liability.

Of course, some franchisors dictate a legal form for your business. A franchisor may not allow a corporation to buy a license because the franchisor prefers to hold you personally liable for the fees, payments, and operations. Most small businesses, however, incorporate in order to limit that very liability. If you run a food, medical, or fitness-related product or service franchise, incorporation may be necessary; being sued by customers who find roaches in the salad is not uncommon.

In short, negotiate with the franchisor the best possible protection you can for yourself, while satisfying its need to hold someone accountable for the firm's good name—and possibly royalty payments later on.

The details about and advantages and disadvantages of each type of business could—and do—fill many volumes. After some preliminary research, based on the descriptions below, ask for advice from both your legal and tax advisers; often they will have opposing views it will be up to you to decide between.

Sole Proprietorships

Sole proprietorships are just that, one-person businesses in which the owner is responsible for all debts and liabilities, but also receives all the profits. You may have to register a trade name at city hall, pay an occupational license fee, get a sales tax certificate from the state or local taxing authority, and in many professions—medicine, real estate, barbering, plumbing, and so on—obtain a state license.

The best part of a proprietorship is that, unlike a corporation, you pay no tax on your net earnings. You pay taxes only on the combined net of your profits and losses from the business and all other sources of income. You pay only as an individual at personal income tax rates. And you can take advantage of all legal opportunities for lowering your net income.

The worst part is your responsibility for everything. To satisfy business debts, levies, and lawsuits, everything you own—home, automobiles, equipment, and so on—could be seized. Other disadvantages include difficulty in raising outside capital (banks will be your best, if not only, source of loans); total involvement of your personal life and finances in the business; and the end of your proprietary interest when you die. There are also restrictions about deducting for health and other insurances for yourself that are fully deductible to corporations for their employees and principals.

Partnerships

Partnerships have the same liability disadvantages as proprietorships, but the liability is spread among two or more people. Partnerships do offer significant tax benefits. Partnerships pay no tax per se; they spread the profits or losses proportionally among the partners, who then pay taxes at individual rates. They do not have to pay special corporate taxes, such as excess profits, personal holding company, or accumulated earnings taxes. Husbands and wives can be partners and benefit from substantial tax benefits, such as the much higher retirement deductions available under Keogh and 301 retirement plans. An IRA is limited to $2,000 for each working spouse, while each spouse in a partnership can deduct up to $30,000 or more with a Keogh plan, depending on income levels.

A disadvantage of partnerships is that total liability for claims, damages, and lawsuits is spread among the partners, unless a partnership agreement specifically spells out who is responsible for what. (Limited partnerships, however, generally limit the liabilities of the limited partners, and usually place the burden on the general partner.) Even worse, all partners may be responsible for the business actions taken by one partner in the name of the partnership, even if the others did not know or approve of the actions.

The worst problem with partnerships is that partners often disagree, if not get into colossal fights; one partner may develop personal, emotional, mental, or legal problems—and on through the panoply of ways two or more people can destroy business and personal relationships. The only protection for you as a partner is a very detailed partnership agreement, but even this must be enforced in a court of law. Frankly, unless you plan to run a franchise with your spouse and you are equally enthusiastic, a straight partnership might not be the best way to run a franchise. A limited partnership in which you are an investor or the general manager works better. The general manager has total day-to-day control; this prevents most of the situations in which disputes and disagreements arise.

Corporations

In franchising, the main reason to incorporate is to limit your personal liability. A corporation, as a legal "person," is responsible for its own debts. Your personal assets are protected from the corporation's liabilities. Corporations can own and lease property, sign contracts, make investments, buy stocks and bonds, act in business any way a real person can, and assume the final responsibility—in most cases—for their actions. Executives may be responsible for fraud and other crimes, but the degree of criminal responsibility varies widely.

There are several types of corporations, including:

- Closely held or closed corporations, in which private individuals or a family hold all of the stock.
- Publicly held or public corporations, in which the initial owners sell shares in the corporation to other people. Public corporations, of course, are subject to the myriad reporting and behavior rules of the federal Securities and Exchange Commission and state securities departments.
- Subchapter S corporations, ingeniously helpful structures that limit personal liability of the shareholders while passing through corporate income to the shareholders as personal income.

Benefits of corporations include these points:

- The owners risk only what they invest in a corporation, not everything they own, as they do with a proprietorship.
- A corporation can stay in business permanently without the inheritance difficulties faced when a proprietor or partner dies.
- A corporation may establish a better relationship with financial institutions and increase its borrowing power.
- Corporate tax rates may, depending on the individual's circumstances, be lower than they would be for a proprietor, partner, or shareholder.
- The salaries and benefits of corporate executives—who might otherwise be the sole proprietor—are deductible business expenses, and can substantially reduce the corporation's tax liability.
- Corporate managers can take advantage of a wide range of benefits and expenses they might not be able to deduct as sole proprietors. These include pension plans, stock-purchase plans, profit-sharing plans, medical and health insurance payments, life insurance premiums, and other fringe benefits.
- Shareholders do not have to pay taxes on corporate income if no dividends are paid.
- It is easier to sell a corporation, and the selling price is likely to be higher than for a sole proprietorship.
- If the business fails, shareholders (of whom you would be one) can deduct stock losses from income taxes.
- The owner of a closely held corporation can shield a significant portion of his income—perhaps as much as half—in a pension plan.

Corporations have disadvantages, too. Since they are relatively expensive to set up ($200 to $3,000 or more, depending on the state in which you incorporate), someone buying a very inexpensive franchise might not want to increase startup costs so significantly. Further, corporate income is taxed twice, once to the corporation as its own income, and again to the share-holder as personal income. Dividends are not deductible expenses to the corporation. And if you are an officer, your salary will be taxed.

As important, if the corporation loses money, the owner or shareholders cannot deduct the losses from their personal incomes. (This is not the same as deducting stock losses if the business fails, which is allowed.)

And there are limits to how much protection from liabilities and debts a corporation can offer. Often banks will not loan money to small corporations without the personal guarantees of the major stockholders.

Also significant for franchisees is the fact that corporations must pay unemployment insurance taxes for their executives and managers. Partner-ships and proprietorships are not subject to these payments on owners (though they are subject to them for other employees). Small franchisees may find the added cost of unemployment compensation a drawback unless they plan to keep their salaries very low in the beginning.

The Special Attraction of Subchapter S. Subchapter S corporations are marvels of protection for the small-business owner. If your franchise qualifies for Subchapter S status with the IRS, it will not pay corporate income taxes, eliminating the double-taxation headache. Instead of an income tax return, it files an "information return." The income is taxed exactly like the income of proprietors and partners, but the Subchapter S corporation form of business offers all of the other protections of the corporate structure against liability for debt.

There is no doubt that any franchise owner whose operation involves even a minor risk of injury to customers should consider the Subchapter S structure. Only very wealthy individuals needing a more secure tax shelter may prefer a regular corporate structure. As you work with your accountant and attorney, determine which method will best lower your tax obligations. In general, the lower your tax bracket, the better off you are with Subchapter S.

The Best Structure. If you are an individual or family setting up a franchise that does not carry an extensive inventory of warehoused goods, your best structure could be a Subchapter S. By "inventory," I do not mean your normal inventory of products for sale; in this instance, I mean a warehouse or manufacturing operation. If you have bought a retail or service franchise, consider these possible steps:

1. Incorporating and electing Subchapter S. (If you don't specifically elect this form, you will automatically be considered under the other form.)

2. Operating on a "cash basis." This is an accounting term that means you determine your profit by subtracting actual expenses from actual income.
3. Deducting your startup expenses immediately. These usually create a tax loss because of short-term negative cash flow. However, in reality, you may enjoy a highly positive personal income.
4. Deducting, as the only or a major shareholder, your proportion of tax losses, reducing your investment and sheltering your actual income.
5. Reevaluating your situation as the cash flow improves and turns positive. You may later choose to revoke your Subchapter S status and become a regular corporation, or you can stay with what you have. As your cash flow improves, analyze the benefits of Subchapter S in your higher tax bracket, and follow the most advantageous course.

Naturally, both corporations and Subchapter S corporations are far too detailed to be completely discussed as part of a book such as this. Ask your tax and legal advisors about them, in depth, before you decide.

Time Your Move

In some cases, you may need to time your incorporation. Incorporation means going public with your intentions, and your new business will quickly become known to hordes of federal, state, and local inspectors, who may want to make sure your business is operating in accordance with dozens of rules and regulations you do not even know exist, much less are prepared to deal with. You must also assume credit bureaus, trade suppliers, bankers, competitors, and others will find out about your new business and react accordingly. Credit bureaus may start a file on your business, making reports available to trade suppliers.

This can be a problem or a benefit. It can benefit you because it may also become known that you are a franchisee of a well-known and reliable enterprise. On the other hand, reports on new companies often encourage suppliers to put them on a cash-payment-only basis.

So consider the timing of your move to incorporate or register your partnership. Work with the franchisor if it objects to an incorporated business's buying its license. Perhaps the best time to incorporate is just prior to obtaining a lease. You do not have to be incorporated to buy the franchise; with the franchisor's permission, you may transfer the license to your new corporation. But you do want the corporate protection when you sign the lease, to prevent the landlord from attaching your personal assets in case your business fails.

Getting the Greatest Benefit from Training

The period after you sign the franchise contract and before you open your doors for business will be very hectic. If you plan and use the time right, the most helpful time you spend will be at the franchise company's training sessions.

With occasional exceptions, few people who buy franchises are experts or have extensive experience in the franchise they choose to buy. That's natural because many people who buy franchises are changing careers. But in order to succeed, a new franchisee must learn an awful lot about a new kind of business very quickly and very well.

The best way to do this is to make the most out of the franchisor's training program. Here is a simple ten-step plan with which you can master the intricacies of running a franchised business. Remember, any reluctance to be trained can only harm your chances of success.

1. *Be prepared.* Before you attend any training sessions given by the franchisor, do some legwork on your own. Identify your strengths and weaknesses as they relate to your new franchise. For instance, if you are buying a franchise for a Duraclean-type service, you get a general idea of how the cleaning machines work. Got that? Maybe you're weak in accounting. Read a few basic books about it. Write down your personal strengths and weaknesses for the business, and draw up a list of questions for the franchisor's trainers to answer.

2. *Assume a positive attitude.* Prime yourself to attend the franchisor's training sessions to study, work, and learn, not take a vacation before you open your franchise.

3. *Demand the best training.* If you are obtaining a franchise with a small territory, or with no exclusive territory, it is not likely the franchisor will offer extensive training. If little or no trainig is required, ask for it anyway and insist that the franchisor do as much as the company can to get you started on the right foot. This will give you a leg up on your competition.

4. *Set aside personal resources.* Make allowances of enough time, money, and energy to complete the training course. Do not leave the training sessions early because you are too tired or don't have enough money. Include in your franchise purchase budget enough money to get *all* of the training you need.

5. *Train key employees.* Make sure your key employees receive the same training you do, preferably at the same time, so all of you start working on the same wavelength from the beginning. If the franchisor does not train key

employees as a matter of course, make that an important point during the contract negotiations. Even consider paying for it yourself.

6. *Train at an actual location.* If the franchisor offers training at a "college" at its headquarters, take one step more and obtain training at an actual store or franchise location. Work for a week or two in a functioning store: Make french fries, clean carpets, sell shoes, sweep floors—whatever it takes to make that franchise operation work. This will give you a far more realistic picture of what you have to do than classroom training. If you can afford it, do this for free.

7. *Get the franchisor to train your regular employees.* Some franchisors send a field training representative to train your new employees before the grand opening, but many do not, leaving you to do this. But training them yourself is time-consuming and expensive because you may not fully understand the operation yourself. So try to get the franchisor's training reps to do as much employee training as possible at your location. You can also make this part of your contract negotiations.

8. *Guarantee continuous training.* Most franchisors offer some type of on-going training, but often this is confined to newsletters or annual or semiannual seminars and concerns only new products. Make sure your franchisor will also offer advanced training on new or improved management techniques and new accounting and computer systems as well as new products and marketing ideas. Find out who does this continuous training, how often and where it occurs, how much it costs, and whether or not it is required.

9. *Find out how good the training is.* Although most franchisors have spent thousands of dollars on preparing modern and effective training programs, not all are equally good. Find out from existing franchisees just how valuable your franchisor's program is. If it does not meet your standards, get help from other franchisees.

10. *Put it in writing and follow through.* Make sure the details of the training, both those that the franchisor requires and those you have negotiated for, are included in the final written contract. Then follow through and give the training your very best efforts.

By putting a strong emphasis on training, you will impress the franchisor with your energy, determination, and willingness to learn. And you will probably be able to get your business started at a more professional and more profitable level than if you paid scant attention to your training duties.

8

On Your Own— But Not Alone— at Last

After you arrive home from the training session, you will face the nitty-gritty details of starting. The most frustrating and time-consuming task you face is building or renovating your premises—whether it is a freestanding structure, a storefront, or an office—and installing equipment. The franchisor should have a detailed list of procedures for you to follow. But expect frustration—from moderate to soul-crushing—in dealing with any local builders and subcontractors. Handling contractors is fraught with peril—no-shows, poor-quality workmanship, incompleted jobs, theft, trouble with angry building inspectors, *ad infinitum*. Unfortunately, few people take advantage of the protections offered. Don't let yourself be talked out of taking the following simple precautions:

• Always interview the contractors yourself.

• Always take bids from several contractors, even if the bids are informal, spoken ones. For the one you accept, get the bid in writing, and get it in detail, down to the very last nail, so to speak.

• Always ask for references and follow through on them; check them out with the local chamber of commerce, Better Business Bureau, your banker, other area franchisees, credit bureaus, attorneys, realtors, and so on.

• Always require performance bonds, so that if the contractor does not finish the work, you can extract the money and hire someone else to finish the work. If a contractor cannot get a bond, deal with someone else. This will also save you from the capriciousness of contractors, who have been known to file liens against their clients over disagreements as to work completion; in many states, the amount of the lien need have nothing to do with the amount of work or cash in dispute.

• Always obtain signed contracts, and always include incentive and penalty clauses and ongoing quality inspections. If the contractor does the job right the first time and meets specific deadlines, you may choose to add a bonus. But if the contractor does poor-quality work and misses deadlines, you can legally penalize him—and protect yourself—by deducting the specified amounts from his final payment.

• Always set fixed fees for each job. Never agree to pay a contractor by the hour or on a cost-plus hourly rate or percentage basis. The hours tend to accumulate very quickly, and costs tend to escalate.

• Always hold back at least 20 to 25 percent of the payment until *after* the job is completed. This is your only real protection to make sure the job actually gets done. Put it in the contract.

• Closely supervise the work yourself. Maybe it isn't fair, and maybe it shouldn't be that way. After all, you've contracted a contractor so you won't have to do the contracting. However contracting is far from an ideal world. To get the best possible job for the best possible price in the best possible length of time, you'll have to be the worst possible pain in the neck. Visit the site early and often. Be a nitpicker. The contractor won't like it, but you're not trying to win a popularity contest. Question and inspect everything, from the invoices to the carpet underlay. If there's something you don't like, close down the job until it is performed to your satisfaction. You have every right to do this, and you owe it to yourself.

• Finally, do as much of the work as you can, buy as many of the materials as you know how, and use all of the skills you, your family, and your friends possess. It will save you time, money, and hassle.

(If this sounds like words from the mouth of an older but wiser person, you're right. *Ignore these steps at your own peril.*)

Hiring Employees

As your physical facilities take shape, you will need to hire employees so they can be trained and ready to go before you open. The length of time needed for this may well be dictated by the franchisor. And it may give you some how-to advice as well or even on-the-spot help. No matter how it's handled, keep these all-round hiring tips in mind, both for your opening and your continuing hiring tasks:

• *Don't hire too many people.* This is a corollary to Rule No. 1—"Keep overhead low." It is easier to start with your key managers and supervisors and teach them the entire operation, so they can train others. And it is easier and more pleasant to hire than to fire. Always beware of getting overstaffed.

• *Follow—very closely—all of the equal employment opportunity and human rights regulations federal and state governments require that you follow.* Make sure you know what these antidiscrimination rules are before you even begin to interview. Some statutes do not apply to companies with only one or two employees, or to sole proprietorships or partnerships in which only family members work. Call the district office of the Equal Employment Opportunity Commission (EEOC) and/or state government offices, perhaps a human rights division, state EEOC, labor department, attorney general, or similar agency to find out the specifics that apply to your situation.

• *Hire for the job.* Do not hire people who are overqualified for the position. Some new employers make the mistake of looking for the best available person—the best educated, the most highly skilled—instead of matching the requirements of the job with the intelligence, skills, and experience of the applicants. Overqualified employees in unskilled jobs may quickly become unhappy, quit, or stir up dissatisfaction among the other employees. It is better to hire someone to whom the job *as it exists* will be a challenging and rewarding task.

Preopening Shakedown

To get your doors open, you will most likely follow a project schedule the franchise company either gives to you or outlines for you. All of your preliminary work and training will lead to a grand opening of your store or the launch of your service business. Actually, it is better to have your doors open for a few weeks before you hold a "grand opening" celebration. Operating at a low-profile, low-volume level can help bring to light any operating problems so you can take care of them before the general public becomes aware of them. You can use the preopening period to make sure you have enough inventory in stock, to get all employees adequately trained and used to procedures, and to reveal any problems with construction and equipment installation.

Beyond careful preparation, another key to a successful grand opening is to keep inventory as low as feasible. You may face initial inventory stocking requirements from the franchisor, but do not exceed these requirements. If you can choose your inventory levels, keep them low, but make sure you can replenish that inventory quickly, with same-day or overnight deliveries. Why? To make sure you pay for inventory and supplies as you go, instead of adding that expense to your startup costs and working-capital requirements.

A Grand Opening

With your shelves stocked and your operation already running smoothly, you can stage your grand opening. A successful grand opening depends primarily on these three things:

1. *Enthusiasm, both yours and your employees'.* Purposefully build up your employees' anticipation of finally getting the chance to show the results of their training and hard work. Many companies pay less during the training period than they do after the doors open, so employees have a built-in incentive to look forward to opening. Do this if you can, but go beyond it. Be your own best cheerleader and wear a smile on your face, even through the expected adversities of opening. What your employees don't know about any problems that have cropped up won't hurt you.

2. *Appropriate public relations and advertising.* Obviously, you must have your public relations and ad programs timed correctly. Carefully target your advertising expenditures and the placement of the ads themselves.

While you narrowly target the advertising you pay for, broadly spread your public relations efforts, which cost nothing or at least a lot less. The day or two before you open, have a press conference or briefing and serve good refreshments; the press is, indeed, a jaundiced lot, and how you treat them will have an impact on how they treat you. Here's a true-life example: A few years ago, a major electronics manufacturer served warm orange juice and stale cookies to a press conference of editors and writers in the electronics industry. The representatives from at least one popular and valuable magazine so resented being treated like poor relations that the company got no help—and no coverage—from that publication. This does not mean the press wants to be bought. Rather, the press wants to be treated liked valued guests, which, in effect, they are.

If you own a fast-food restaurant, invite the press in to sample your menu. Most publications wouldn't view accepting as a conflict of interest. If you own a cleaning service, however, or other highly personal or very costly product or service franchise, don't expect to give the press a free sample of that. Publishers probably would consider a free housecleaning a conflict of interest, and it would be too expensive for you to provide for the benefits gained, in any case. Rather, in such cases, simply have a grand opening party. Serve a few good-quality refreshments, be on hand to answer questions, have press packs available if possible, and demonstrate any unique products or equipment you are selling or using.

You can even stage a media event, hiring clowns or people in chicken suits, or any similar but appropriate means of attracting the press and public to your door. Also make use of any "grand opening package" your franchisor might provide. Grand opening signs, bunting, flags, and the like have been used thousands of times, but they still work.

Be sure all your efforts are sincere; you can't expect to snow the public, or the press either. They will go one round with you, but if you fail to follow up with good products and service, no matter how well you've treated them on the first round, they will resent having the wool pulled over their eyes, and it will be the worse for you—justly so. By all means put your best foot forward, but beware of following up like a stumblebum.

Finally, don't overlook the more businesslike promotional opportunities, such as appearing before local community clubs—the Kiwanis, Civitan, Rotary, and so on—to discuss your new business venture. Personally visit with the business editor of the local daily and weekly newspapers and any local business publications, and visit chamber of commerce representatives or invite them to visit you.

If you like, you can even take numerous smaller steps to back up your main efforts. Have teenagers distribute flyers in local shopping-center parking lots or place them in screen doors in nearby neighborhoods. Invite the local softball teams to have a free soft drink if they come in wearing their team shirts. Have your staff volunteer to answer phones for the local public television station's fund-raising week, especially if it's close to your opening. Be creative. Getting the word out—the good word—is essential to a successful grand opening.

3. *Special incentives.* Customers expect something out of the ordinary at a grand opening. It need not be lower prices, but perhaps something that can attract equal attention, such as a raffle, a lottery (where allowed), a contest, a drawing for prizes, and so on. Use your imagination and ask for the recommendations of the franchisor or other successful franchisees.

The Myth of Goodness

Finally, beware of a myth about a grand opening. Many people believe the timeworn adage that building a better mousetrap means people will flock to your door. If you feel you have a better mousetrap (and you should, for you have chosen the business, after all), you may fall into the trap of neglecting to promote your business. You offer a quality product or service, you think, and at a reasonable price, so customers should and will come to you. Completely false.

Dozens of companies build better computers than those IBM makes, many experts say, but who sells the most computers? IBM, of course. So forget the myth of goodness. You must promote your franchise before, during, and after a grand opening. You must sell yourself and your business wherever you go on business and even during your leisure hours. It is not the better mousetrap that succeeds, but the better promoter with an equally good or even just an adequate mousetrap.

Short-Term Strategies

After your grand opening, you will probably feel a warm glow of success. Customers piled in and a lot of cash piled up. But suddenly, a few days or weeks later if you are not careful, you may look around and begin to wonder what happened to all of those smiling, happy customers. Of course, you should plan for some falloff in trade after a grand opening, but don't let it go too far. In fact, plan ways to counteract this drop-off with a good short-term strategy to keep customers coming in. Here are some proven techniques:

• *Distinguish your operation from your competition's, even from others within the same fast-food franchise.* First, emphasize the name and reputation of the franchise itself, if it is well known and respected. Then make use of the reasons people frequent small businesses instead of large ones, by emphasizing these advantages of your business:

1. *Service.* People go to many franchises for personal service with a smile. Emphasize creating customer satisfaction more than any other skills your employees possess.
2. *Quality.* Quality does not mean perfection; it means meeting the standards as the market demands and the franchise company requires.
3. *Cleanliness.* No one has ever objected to shopping in a spotlessly clean environment. People go into franchises expecting products and services of a certain quality level, usually that established in their minds by the franchisor's advertising campaign. You would do well to meet or exceed those expectations.
4. *Convenience.* Do everything you can to make it easy for customers to buy your products and services. People should find it more convenient to locate what they are looking for in your store than in all the others; they should find using your service so pleasant that they are glad to call again, and to pay for it.
5. *Pleasure.* People go to franchise outlets because they find the experience more pleasing than discount stores, department stores, large cafeterias or huge restaurants, and so on.

• *Build customer traffic,* but be wary of offering too many discounts or specials that eat up your profit margins.

• *Keep a close eye on product lines.* Offer as few products as the franchisor requires or concentrate on the products that are already selling. It is easier to expand a product line, creating an image of improvement and growth, than it is to drop items. Promote those products and services that are already selling best. In short, give your customers what they want first before you try to wean them onto something else.

• *Reduce unit costs—that is, the cost per item—to the minimum.* To find out what your unit cost is, determine your total costs for a given period and divide that by the total unit sales. For example, suppose your total costs for one week are $2,500, including everything—products, supplies, apportioned rent and utilities, salaries, and so on. If you had sold 1,000 hamburgers, then your unit cost would be $2,500 divided by 1,000, or $2.50 per unit, or burger. If you had charged $2.50 for each burger, you would be breaking even, not a good position to be in. If you have just opened, you will find it hard to raise prices, so you'll have to find a way to reduce costs. Ask yourself whether you are buying too many supplies, hiring too much staff, buying too much advertising, offering too many discounts, and so on. Take appropriate action to cut costs in any area in which you have overspent or oversupplied yourself.

• *Make everyone a salesperson.* Successful companies understand that what they are really selling, regardless of what product or service they charge for, is customer service and satisfaction. This creates goodwill, which translates into sales, company revenues, and profits. So be sure every employee, from the cash register operator to the cleaning staff, is selling service. The most important words on any employee's lips are, "How can I help you?" Their most important attitude is really meaning it. Their most important act is following through. Encourage all employees at all times to find ways to satisfy the customer's needs.

• *Recognize employee efforts.* The best way to keep employees happy is to recognize—always in a positive manner—their efforts and achievements. Even if they fail or make a mistake, while pointing out the error and correcting it, praise the worthy parts of their activity.

Early Warning Signals

After you have been in business a month or so, analyze your position. Answer the questions below to determine whether you are slowly—or perhaps rapidly—sliding into trouble.

1. Are minor operational problems—customer complaints, production bottlenecks, and so on—ignored or, worse, dealt with in a harsh manner? If so, carefully and objectively find the source of the problem and correct it.
2. Is there a recurring cash-flow shortage? If so, take steps to reduce costs, stretch out payments, and boost sales.
3. Have you forgotten to plan your intermediate and long-term strategies? Do you suddenly feel as if you are drifting, without a goal and without a plan? If so, spend time modifying your short-term strategies and determining what you need to do for long-term success.
4. Are inventory and unused product piling up in your storeroom, or is the amount of wastage increasing? If so, reduce your orders and

hold special promotions to get rid of excess inventory. Remember that inventory carrying costs average 2.5 percent ($2.50 for every $100 worth of goods) per *month*.

5. Are you experiencing frequent delays in receiving shipments? If so, pressure the supplier to meet schedules. If possible, institute sanctions, such as withholding payment or switching some of your order to another supplier.

6. Are your accounts receivable and days sales outstanding—the amount of time between the day a sale is made and the day it is paid for—increasing? If so, increase your collection efforts, and hire a credit bureau or professional collection agency to collect very overdue debts if need be.

7. Are employees audibly and visibly disgruntled? If so, calmly find out why and retrain supervisors or correct your management practices if you are at fault.

8. Has equipment started breaking down frequently? Find out why and improve maintenance schedules. Retrain employees on its use.

9. Are you or your managers confused, feeling overwhelmed, or doing extraneous tasks instead of concentrating on the important functions—satisfying customers, managing employees, and making money? If so, analyze what is important at this time and make time to do those things. Delegate less important tasks, checking only to make sure they get done.

10. Has communication among departments or work areas broken down? Even if this is no more serious than the french fry cook not talking to the hamburger cook, it could lead to bottlenecks and customer complaints as well as lower morale. Without taking sides, get to the bottom of the dispute and encourage those involved to resolve their differences.

If you recognize any of these or similar problems already cropping up in your new franchise, take corrective action immediately. Business problems—even in a franchise—do not, like old soldiers, fade away. Like boils, they tend to fester until they burst, damaging your business and reducing your profits.

However, armed with the training, experience, and backing of the franchisor, if you also follow common-sense business practices, you will avoid these pitfalls and your first few months as a franchisee will be prosperous ones.

9

Going Strong: Secrets of Day-to-Day Successful Operation

Running a successful franchise is much like running any other business, with one major exception—the input of the franchisor. It may seem to be alternately helping you with advertising, promotional ideas, and management assistance, or breathing down your neck if you miss royalty payments or reporting deadlines. Franchisors consistently insist that if you strictly follow their operations manuals and their systems, you can succeed. But it's not that easy. If it were, franchisors would manage their franchises with robots, not flesh-and-blood businesspeople.

Running a business requires diverse skills; the most important of these are not making perfect hamburgers or balancing the books like an auditor. For such tasks, you can easily hire others. No, the three most important skills in running a business are keeping an eye on things, serving customers, and managing people. None of these can be done by a robot, especially the last and most important of the three, managing people.

The Critical Skills: Managing Employees

Contrary to the myth that people managers are born, not made, managing people is a business skill that can be learned by anyone willing to follow a few basic principles.

First and foremost, especially in a franchise that runs with two or three shifts a day (most fast-food places and restaurants), is hiring a good second-in-command. You can't work 16 or 18 hours a day every day, so you have to have someone who is competent, reliable, trustworthy (especially with the cash receipts), loyal, and good with people and who complements your strengths and weaknesses. If you are not comfortable with hiring and firing, hire a manager who is experienced in it. About the only thing you really cannot allow your second-in-command to completely control is the accounting, unless, of course, that person is your spouse. You must feel completely confident that you can leave your franchise for a week, or even a month, and the operation will not significantly suffer.

And as hard as it may be, you need a manager who is not afraid to disagree with you and will point out problems as he sees them. Too many owners surround themselves with "yes men" who bring only good news while burying the bad news on the back pages, so to speak. It is only human to want to give and hear only good news. Unfortunately, it is also the way to fail. Smart and successful owners and managers not only hear, but seek out and discuss, the bad news. Then, they can correct problems before they get out of hand.

The Pete Rose School of Managing. Second, unless you are purely an investor, you should manage your franchise the way Pete Rose managed the Cincinnati Reds baseball team during the 1985 season: as a player-coach. Pete Rose was the model player-coach, breaking supposedly unbreakable records, yet hustling his team, one of the worst in baseball during 1984, into contention for a division title. Pete Rose, nicknamed Charlie Hustle for his nonstop, flat-out, enthusiastic play, could easily have let his pursuit of Ty Cobb's record for the most hits distract him from his duties as a manager. However, despite the hundreds of daily distractions of his pursuit of the record, Pete Rose managed very effectively.

He did this by knowing that each player had to be treated as an individual, and each individual required different methods of treatment. He was quoted as saying, "You have three different guys. One you pat on the head, one you kick in the butt, and one you have a long talk with. The difference is knowing which one gets the pat, which one gets the kick, and which one gets talked to." That is a pretty good summary of what good people management is all about.

As a "player-coach" owner, you need to be the first at work in the morning and the last to leave, not only to impress the other employees, but to handle the cash receipts. Remember, cash is unbearably tempting to many people. Avoid trouble by removing the temptation.

Although you may have a thousand pressing worries, be outwardly enthusiastic and positive. Bear in mind that example is the best teacher. So show everyone that you know the operation and are willing to do what is necessary to keep it running smoothly.

Third, get to know your employees. Small businesses often assume the aura and configuration of a family. Like the mama or papa, you must know each member's personality, his strengths in regard to the business, his weaknesses, his personal aims in working for you, and even a bit about his family situation. Don't pry. But don't ignore the possibility, indeed the likelihood, that personal lives have an impact on professional performance. There may be nothing more to do about it than be aware that this is so. Go further and you may be meddling, unless you are invited to give advice. But don't be understanding to the point of business failure. If you have an employee who won't leave personal problems at home, who won't seek help, and who is destroying your business, remember that charity begins at home and take appropriate action in your own best interest.

Fourth, learn to delegate responsibility, but make sure each employee remains accountable to you. Make sure every employee knows exactly what his duties are and how his personal goals and those of your business coincide. Make sure he knows that he will be accountable to you for his actions and that his actions determine his own future.

Fifth, emphasize the quality of the work environment. You need not go so far as providing carpeting in the dishwashing room. But do make your business a clean, attractive place not only in the customer reception areas, but in those areas where employees "regroup"—the washrooms, break rooms, supply areas, and so on.

If the business itself requires hard, physical, dirty labor, nonetheless, keep your place clean as a sign that you respect your employees and your customers and expect them to respect themselves and you. Provide clean, adequate facilities for cleaning up and resting, even to the point of employee showers (automotive franchises often supply these) and chaises on which employees can spend a moment when they're feeling weak.

More important than the physical environment, however, is the psychological one. If you act like a tyrant, your employees may become resentful, and this will be reflected in poor-quality work, high turnover, employee theft, bad-mouthing to customers and other businesses, and so much more.

Naturally, you can't act like a Caspar Milquetoast either, or your employees will take advantage of you. Rather, seek a happy medium in which your employees enjoy their work and want to do their work well, but are fully aware that you are the boss.

Despite your best efforts, since we are not robots, disagreements will arise between employees and between you and your employees. That's okay, and a perfectly healthy sign. However, you can't let the problems slide. Handle them in one of these ways:

- Encourage employees to bring disagreements among them to you. Make it clear that you do not want any dissatisfaction to fester, and back up your statements with action.
- Bring all involved together and listen to their complaints. Ask ques-

tions about the situation, and make them listen not only to you but to each other's point of view.

- If they make unsupported claims, have them get more information to support their contentions.
- Show them ways to work out solutions among themselves, but with your guidance.
- Provide an atmosphere in which a solution or settlement develops from a feeling that everyone involved participated, that everyone had a fair chance to be heard and to persuade the others.

Sixth, in any business, it is a very good idea to make salaries, wages, and bonuses confidential. Avoid giving employees a chance to compare their pay checks by having them distributed by your bank, if need be. Make it well known that you will look askance at any discussion of wages and salaries. This helps circumvent resentment and the "You make more than I do, but I work harder than you do" syndrome.

Finally, be very vigilant for any signs of poor employee morale and high turnover. Poor morale leads to employees' quitting at the worst possible moment. Repeatedly hiring and training new people is very expensive; it wastes your valuable time, and it wastes money because new employees get paid, but usually have very poor productivity. And disgruntled employees may steal, cause customer dissatisfaction, sabotage equipment, upset the other employees, and so on in a vicious cycle.

Personnel surveys and franchisor studies show that the main reason people quit their jobs is poor management. Other reasons commonly cited all lead back to poor management: poor working conditions; working in the wrong job for one's skills; and badly arranged workloads.

So despite the pain that may be involved, have a talk with any employee who quits. Ask careful questions about why he is leaving. An employee who is quitting will be very reluctant to tell you the truth, but ask what are called "open-ended" questions, which call for more than a yes or no answer. Questions such as "Why are you dissatisfied?" or "What happened to make you unhappy?" may help the employee talk more freely than might, "Did my reprimand last week upset you?"

There is no mystery about the methods that a good manager follows. Simply exercise careful judgment and a reasonable sense of authority to keep your employees content and working productively.

The Critical Skills: Customer Service

After managing employees, the way you manage customer relations determines how well your franchise operates. In most franchises, this too boils down to following simple, time-proven methods and training your employees in following them as well.

Customer service is essential to a franchise, as it is to any small business, for two simple reasons. First, satisfied customers are the best source of advertising. Not only is this free advertising, but the advertiser actually pays for the privilege of spreading the good word about your franchise. Second, repeat business saves money and increases profits. How? By allowing you to spend less on advertising and promotion to reach new customers and by helping you buy products more efficiently and in larger, more cost-effective units.

Here is a list of several proven methods of developing customer satisfaction:

1. *Treat every customer courteously and with respect.* Never, ever treat a customer rudely or abruptly. "I don't have time to talk to you now" or a harsh "What do you want?" will lose a customer fast.

2. *Establish and maintain an image appropriate to your type of franchise.* In short, customers buy from franchises because they know they can expect a level of quality and professionalism they do not expect from a mom-and-pop shop. So work with your franchisor to fulfill its standards. Your link with the franchisor is a badge of professionalism that it is your duty—and the source of your profit—to uphold.

3. *Establish a policy for handling complaints as quickly and painlessly—for you and the customer—as possible.* Although the customer may not always be in the right, every customer does have the right to be listened to attentively and to have action taken on his complaint. In that, at least, the customer is always right.

4. *Give customer complaints precedence over other routine matters.* If you show customers that their problems take priority over a telephone call or another chore, they will respond favorably. You may be able to compromise more effectively on whatever they seek; they will certainly be more likely to come back again than if they are treated cavalierly, no matter how their problem is resolved.

5. *Learn how to say no to a customer the right way.* When the customer is wrong, and you cannot satisfy his request or complaint, do three things:

- Listen carefully to the customer's problem, restate it in your own words, and make sure your understanding is correct.
- Explain in detail why you cannot fulfill his request or satisfy his complaint.
- Try to find another solution or, if possible, compromise with the customer. A half a loaf is better than none, for both of you. Be reasonable, and the customer is more likely to respond in kind.

The Critical Skills: Keeping Your Eye on the Business

If you manage people well and keep your customers happy, you are well on your way to continuing success. But you might still falter if you do not keep a tight grip on your finances, from sending the required reports to the franchisor and government taxing departments, to counting your cash and keeping it flowing—inward.

Make it your goal to know as precisely as possible where every dollar in your business comes from and where every dollar goes, not just once a month, but every day. Good record keeping will help you; do the preliminary accounting yourself, even if you have a bookkeeper or accountant to keep things legally shipshape at intervals. Keeping frequent track will enable you to better make sound business decisions, not ones based on ignorance.

Don't, however, keep this information on snippets of paper or in your head. The IRS and state tax agencies may require good records, as will your bank or investors, or even the franchisor. You can use your record keeping to give your accounting professionals a head start, saving you money in the long run, by keeping organized written records for them—and you—to work from. Not fancy, mind you, just neat and complete.

There are any number of business record-keeping primers for you to base a simple system on. Or get your franchisor or accountant to help you set up a useful system. Here, however, are the basics of a simple, useful system:

A journal and a ledger are the basics of all record keeping. These are created from receipts, check stubs, petty cash vouchers, cash register tapes, and electronically stored data.

You'll need two journals: cash receipts and cash disbursements. The former records *all* cash received by your business, and the latter records *all* payments you make to others. Payments in cash or by check are included in the normal accounting definition of "cash." But identify payments made by cash and payments made by check within the disbursements journal. You'll want to have a record of the check numbers, in any case, so you can easily follow up any that are lost or in dispute.

The ledger is a record in which you separate your income and expenses into various accounts: rent, telephone, utilities, payroll, withholding taxes, postage, cleaning services, and so forth. You use the ledger to organize and summarize all of the transactions recorded in the two journals. At the end of each month, you balance the ledger to make sure the income (credits) equals the expenses (debits).

From the ledger, you create a chart of accounts that lists every category of income (or revenue) and expense (or payments). This list should be as detailed as need be to sensibly organize your records. You may find that a fast-food franchise may have an account for each menu item. With this detail, you will know exactly how many double cheeseburgers with bacon you sold, on what days, and at what price—essential information for planning your future purchases of beef, bacon, cheese, and buns to avoid waste and also avoid running short.

With summaries from the chart of accounts, you divide the financial information into three categories that form a basic financial statement: assets, capital, and liabilities. Your assets include cash on hand from all sources, accounts receivable, inventory plus the value of depreciated equipment and plant. Your capital includes certain types of capital assets, such as real estate, physical plant, shareholders' equity, and surplus. These can be added together on your balance sheet and will provide a look at the positive finances of your business.

Your liabilities include your outstanding bills or accounts payable plus unpaid taxes or tax obligations. A look at this will let you know the negative finances of your business. Needless to say, your aim is to get the positive to far outstrip the negative.

Figure 9-1 outlines a basic balance sheet or statement.

The balance sheet shows you the overall financial condition of your franchise. If your liabilities are way out of line, and you have little capital left compared to your assets and liabilities, you need to take corrective action. If your long-term debt outweighs your fixed assets or perceived ability to pay for it, you need to reevaluate your position and take steps to reduce the debt.

P&Ls and Budgets

Two other essential types of financial statements are profit and loss (P&L) statements and a budget. A P&L simply calculates for a given period—a quarter, a month, a year—your net income, and summarizes the sources of income and expenses. It shows you in a nutshell whether you are making any real profit. Figure 9-2 shows a simple P&L statement.

You may want to prepare a P&L statement every quarter or even every month. Then by comparing it to planned or previous results, you can see if you have any problems and where they lie. P&Ls are also commonly presented to banks when loans are sought; it will be handy to have a recent one on hand when you want interim financing.

Another simple instrument you can use to keep track of your franchise's progress is a budget. Possibly you use one now to schedule family expenditures and savings; a business budget need be no more complicated. And you'll use it for the same general purpose—planning.

Set up your franchise budget at the beginning of each year. The first year, you will have to seek help from the franchisor, your accountant, and your research to estimate how much you are likely to gross; after that, you

Figure 9-1. A basic balance sheet.

BALANCE SHEET

Current Assets

Cash on hand and in bank	$ 10,000
Inventory	50,000
Accounts receivable	5,000
Total current assets	$ 65,000

Fixed Assets

Real estate—land		$ 75,000
Real estate—buildings		
Original cost	$ 150,000	
– Depreciation	50,000	
		$ 100,000
Furniture and fixtures		
Original cost	$ 50,000	
– Depreciation	25,000	
		$ 25,000

TOTAL ASSETS	$ 265,000

Current Liabilities

Accounts payable	$ 50,000
Notes payable (one year)	25,000
Total current liabilities	$ 75,000
Long-Term Debt	$ 100,000
Capital	$ 90,000
TOTAL LIABILITIES AND CAPITAL	$ 265,000

will have previous years' actual figures to base the estimates on. Follow the same procedure in estimating a sales forecast and the anticipated cost of those sales.

Use your budget to plan for future growth by clearly identifying when, how, and how much your cash flow will be so you can anticipate when you can take expansion and improvement expenses from cash flow and when you may need to borrow money instead—and how and when you can pay it back.

Figure 9-2. A basic P&L statement.

PROFIT AND LOSS STATEMENT

Year Ended December 31, 1985

Sales	$250,000
Cost of sales	100,000
Gross income	$150,000
Operating expenses:	$ 55,000
Selling expenses ($25,000)	
General expenses ($30,000)	
Operating income	$ 95,000
Other expenses	
Loan interest	$ 7,500
Net before-tax income	$ 87,500
Income taxes (50%)	$ 43,750
Net income	$ 43,750

Besides helping plan equipment purchases, the budget will help you decide when to hire new employees, conduct sales promotion campaigns, and take other steps to make smooth the crests and troughs in the business cycle.

Remember to compare your budgeted figures with your actual results over time, and make adjustments as needed. A budget should not be seen as written in stone. Keep it flexible so it and you can adapt to changes in the marketplace. Figure 9-3 outlines a basic budget you may supplement with your own income and expense categories. The more details you want to know about your operations, the more categories you will want to have.

From these simple financial records, you can assemble all of the information you need to manage your business, plan for expansion, borrow money, or obtain financing. Of course, they will need to be accurate. Consistency and frequent maintenance of the records are the keys.

Make time at the end of each month to plug your actual results into the budget and to bring your P&L statement up to date. Use your cash register tapes, credit-card forms, check stubs, and petty cash receipts to keep your cash income and disbursements journals up to date every day or every few days. You simply cannot afford to let any of the financial record keeping get too far behind. Without good records, you are trying to steer your business like a ship without a rudder. Like such a ship, you may well end up lost and going around in circles.

Figure 9-3. A sample format for a franchise budget.

MONTHLY BUDGET

	June Budget	Actual
Projected Income:		
Cash sales		
Accounts receivable collected		
Interest income		
Miscellaneous receipts		
Total income		
Projected Expenses:		
Selling expenses		
Inventory		
Payroll		
Advertising and promotion		
Equipment purchases		
Loan payments		
Tax payments		
Administrative expenses		
Total expenses		
Projected cash balance (Start of month)		
Cash increase or decrease		
Projected cash balance (End of month)		
Working cash balance needed		
Short-term loan, if needed		
Cash available (Purchases or investments)		

Using Financial Ratios

From the information in these records and statements, you can do simple calculations—nothing more than adding, subtracting, multiplying, and dividing—and know instantly whether your business ship has lost its bearings or is sailing full speed ahead toward greater profits. These calculations are called, in accounting jargon, *ratios,* and they let you take a quick and accurate snapshot of the condition of your business.

The most important ratio is called the *current ratio,* and it determines how solvent—how financially healthy—your franchise is at the moment. Determine this simple ratio by dividing current assets by current liabilities. For example, if you have $250,000 in current assets and $200,000 in current liabilities, your current ratio is 1.25. For most retail or small businesses, a ratio above 1.0 is considered adequate, and the higher above 1.0 the ratio is, the better off you are. (This varies from industry to industry; your accountant can help you with accurate ratios for your industry.)

What can you do if the ratio is around or below 1.0? Try to convert some short-term liabilities—bank notes and loans—into long-term loans. As often as possible, be sure you use long-term liabilities, such as bank loans, to pay for long-term assets, plant, and equipment in the first place. Short-term loans for such lasting equipment are wasteful of cash flow.

Another significant ratio is the inventory turnover ratio. Determine this by dividing the cost of goods sold by the value of inventory. This ratio too should be as much over 1.25 as possible. If it shows a pattern of slumping, evaluate your stock. Stop ordering slow-moving products, and even have a clearance sale to rid yourself of their weight. Remember, carrying inventory that won't be sold is expensive.

To determine whether your assets and hard work are earning a satisfactory percentage of return, determine your profitability ratio. Calculate this by dividing your pretax income by net sales. For example, if you had pretax income of $100,000 and net sales (after the cost of sales is subtracted) of $500,000, your ratio would be 0.20, or 20 percent, a healthy net profit. If your pretax income were $25,000 divided by net sales of $500,000, the ratio would be an anemic 0.05, or 5 percent; you'd quickly see the need to boost sales and/or reduce expenses.

None of these techniques involves more than simple math skills—all you need to effectively manage your franchise's finances and net ever larger profits. Use them carefully, but consistently.

Franchise Insurance: Defeating Murphy's Law

As you establish your franchise and develop a healthy financial condition, you'll need to protect them from both natural and man-made disasters. As much as you may try to prevent them, accidents do happen and people do try to steal. Protecting your financial and personal investment from risk requires that you know what kinds of insurance and security you need to use and how you need to use them.

Unfortunately, evaluating and obtaining the myriad insurance policies you need to protect your investment is not as exciting as setting up shop. Co-insurance, deductibles, parties of the first, second, and third parts, and other insurance jargon are boring stuff compared to the thrill of ringing up sales. But beware: If you do not carefully insure your business property, you will be very sorry if something unfortunate happens. At some point, often sooner than later, you will stand convicted of violating Murphy's Law. But with study, foresight, planning, and a reasonable amount of money, you and all of your investment can be properly protected.

First, get acquainted with the myriad types of insurance you may need. The types you require may vary from franchise to franchise or location to location, but many of those listed below will be required by government, the franchisor, or good common sense.

• *Fire insurance*. In addition to fire, this insurance also generally protects against loss caused by all kinds of natural disasters, including flood, windstorms, hail, lightning, and so forth. Location and type of franchise will generally determine the amount and cost of this kind of insurance.

• *Casualty insurance*. This is part of any loss protection policy, a fancy way of saying a policy that offers protection against robbery, theft, burglary, larceny, broken glass, and similar incidents. It may also include the required workmen's compensation and employee disability coverage as well as policies for health or medical insurance, although these are more often considered employee benefits covered under separate policies. If you use an automobile for business, you must have state-required auto casualty policies for all drivers.

• *All-risks coverage*. This is a particular casualty policy that covers more types of *physical* risks, losses, and problems.

• *Business interruption insurance*. No one plans for his franchise to be destroyed by a fire in the building next door or to be put out of business for a month because of a flood. This sort of policy protects against temporary interruptions and pays for loss of profits as well as covering all or part of your fixed expenses (rent, loan, or lease payments, for example).

• *Your own disability*. Never magically believe that you will remain in perfect health just because you have a business to run. You can become seriously ill or injured in an accident and be out of work for some time. You may have a manager or family member who can take over temporarily, but who will pay your own personal bills even if someone can pinch-hit for you? What if your "take" goes completely to cover the pinch-hitter's compensation for doing the job? Disability insurance is your best bet, beyond stacking up, as quickly as possible, at least a six months' cushion for yourself in a savings account. Be warned, however: This kind of insurance is very expensive for the self-employed and unconscionably hard to obtain. You will probably have to undergo an unreasonably difficult and thorough physical, agree to an amount one-half or less of that you project you would need in such an emergency—and pray to whatever gods there are to let some insurance company slip up and issue the policy.

• *Business liability.* Your franchisor may require you to have a sizable liability policy to cover potentially catastrophic losses arising from third-party claims. You could easily be held liable for enormous damages, and a liability policy is the best way to protect yourself. The franchisor may even force you to make *it* an insured party while you pay for the policy.

• *Umbrella policy.* This is not strictly a business policy, but it is a useful, extraordinary degree of protection for you personally. Most accountants would strongly recommend that you get a $1 million or more umbrella policy that covers you against all kinds of liability. These policies are very low-cost, as low as $70 a year for the seven-figure coverage for a personal policy. Figures for strictly business umbrella policies rise sharply, however. Check with your accountant and attorney to see if the personal policy will be adequate for you.

• *Business life insurance.* This includes life insurance on you, "key man" life for your top managers, partnership life, and loan and credit life. The latter two pay off outstanding loans and protect your business's credit rating.

• *Fidelity insurance.* This is additional protection against employee or internal theft or loss. You may trust your employees implicitly, but it's better to be safe than sorry.

Where to Obtain Insurance

Finding good sources of all this insurance will take time and careful effort. First, inquire what policies the franchisor can help you obtain; it may have access to group policies for its franchisees. Group rates will be much lower in most cases than those you could obtain on your own. Just be sure the group policies meet all of your requirements.

Second, use the franchisor's loss-prevention experts to help you devise every reasonable way to prevent losses and protect the safety and security of your property, employees, and customers.

Third, strongly consider doing your insurance business—that not covered under available group rates through the franchisor—with a local independent insurance agent. Single-underwriter agents will argue that their way is best, offering you a direct line to the clout of a huge nationwide firm. But there is much weight on the side of the independents where franchising is concerned. Several points that are strongly in the independents' favor are:

1. They are self-employed like you and understand your problems both instinctively and by experience.

2. They are far more likely to find the policy "diamonds" among the many hunks of policy "coal." They can search the offerings of dozens of companies to find the best deal for you.

3. They are far more likely to help you when you are in trouble. You are their valued customer; it is in their best interest to go to bat for you in times of trouble—after a fire or other disaster, for instance.

Often, too, they can bind insurance coverage for you by phone, something single-underwriter agents generally cannot do (or will not do). This is valuable when you discover a need too late to mail a check, or if you have forgotten to send a check for insurance already in place, and ask for this service. The independents can do this because they will learn whether you are a reliable customer, and can advance the money to their underwriters out of their own business accounts.

Independents also frequently trip over better deals for clients while researching other matters. The independent will call it to your attention and ask if you'd rather switch, often even if it means a slight reduction, in the short run, in his income. A single-underwriter agent doesn't have this possibility, so neither do you.

And the fortunes of the independent are much more closely tied to building a good local set of business relationships, as are yours. The single-underwriter agent, on the other hand, may have little interest in your locality, being able easily to pick up his business and move it across the state or across the country.

The worst choices for a business owner, however, are "shopping mall" agents, who are not really agents at all in the strict sense of the word. They are merely commissioned order takers for national companies. They may be fired, or they may leave for personal reasons; they are not themselves a part of the business community. As such, their interest in aiding you extends only as far as each single commission in their pocket, not to a long-term relationship.

Principles of Insurance Coverage

Follow these seven guidelines when selecting insurance to protect your new franchise:

1. Be wary of policies with co-insurance clauses. These often mean you get no more than 80 percent of the *current* value, not the *replacement* value of the property, inventory, and other items you lose.

2. Obtain replacement value insurance where feasible, but be prepared to pay much more for it.

3. After securing the minimum insurances required by law and by your franchisor, protect the greatest risk of the greatest loss first. If you are in a

marginal neighborhood, your greatest risk might be vandalism. If this is not covered by other policies, cover it first. If you discover your business sits on a floodplain, cover it for potential flooding. And so on.

4. Use high cash deductibles to reduce your premiums. Instead of using low $100 or $250 deductibles, determine whether you have enough cash resources to adequately cover losses of up to $5,000 or $10,000, and set your policy deductibles as high as you can. High deductibles will cut the cost of a policy, often by more than half.

With high deductibles, you essentially follow a practice common among major corporations called *self-insurance*. The term means what it says—you insure yourself against minor losses. You trade the risk of minor losses for the immediate, substantial savings in cash. For example, one franchisee saved more than $750 a year by using a $10,000 deductible for his major medical insurance plan. With a "normal" $250 deductible, the policy would have cost $900 per year; with the $10,000 deductible, the cost fell to less than $150 per year. He was willing to keep on hand, earmarked for that potential, the $10,000 amount of the deductible.

5. Reevaluate your insurance protection at least once a year, twice a year if your business is growing especially fast. Add to it as needed to keep pace with your business's growth and inflation.

6. If you find after these exercises that you cannot afford reasonable insurance protection for your franchise, you may not be able to afford the franchise! Give this principle serious consideration because of guideline 7 . . .

7. Take firmly to heart Murphy's Law: It is the only law in the world with no exceptions. Emblazon on your soul: Whatever can go wrong will go wrong—at the worst possible moment. Then protect your franchise, your investment, and yourself with adequate, but not extravagant, insurance.

An Ounce of Prevention

Although you can buy insurance to pay for losses caused by burglaries, robberies, and the like, no single outside threat is the one most likely to cause financial losses. Most losses, especially in franchise or retail businesses, are caused by employees.

But rather than concentrating on employee security problems, most franchise owners install elaborate burglary alarm systems and hire security guards to patrol doors and exteriors. Of course, you need basic security systems to prevent burglary, fire, and theft. The best modern devices are based on ultrasound and anti-intrusion alarms, not wire taped to windows or big alarm boxes attached to the outside of a building: Both of these can be easily circumvented by knowledgeable thieves.

The easiest way to prevent employee theft is to remove temptation. The vast majority of employee thefts are thefts born of opportunity. And the opportunity was available because the business owner did not look for and close the gaps in his accounting or security procedures.

The most tempting and most frequent theft from a retail franchise is taking cash from the register. The major franchises prevent casual cash register theft with sophisticated, computerized cash registers that each day compare the items sold and money received with end-of-day inventory levels. If you are on your own and cannot afford an elaborate inventory-matching cash register, you will have to protect yourself the hard way. It's known in business as "counting the buns," that is, keeping a very close eye on your inventory, and matching the amount sold with the receipts in the cash drawer—particularly if you are not on hand to run it yourself.

While bun counting is a pain in the neck to anyone who must do it, it is not difficult. You simply keep a record of every transaction, including credits, corrections, employee purchases, even "free" goods such as meals to employees. For example, you know that at the beginning of the day you have 100 hot dog buns. Hot dogs sell for $2.00 each. At the end of the day, you have 35 hot dog buns. You should have written slips or cash register tapes that show you sold or used 65 hot dog buns. Your tally shows: 55 hot dog receipts, 5 slips for employee hot dogs, and 2 buns broken and thrown away. What happened to the other three? Ask the people selling hot dogs and ringing up the cash register. It may be a mistake, or it may be theft. Require that each broken or thrown away bun—or any other item—be accompanied by a slip of paper saying so. Of course, these are easily faked, so if a serious problem develops, you'll have to require that all "deep six" items be saved for your personal inspection.

Beginning to feel like Ebenezer Scrooge? Three hot dog buns doesn't sound like much. But multiply that by 365 days a year at a cost of even 10 cents a bun and you have wasted more than $109.50. And add to that the hot dogs, hamburger buns, sodas, pickles, chips, and pizzas, and your business could easily bleed slowly to death. At the very least, your profit is going into the pocket of someone else, someone who hasn't taken the risks you have. Is that fair to you? Hardly.

While bun counting is a necessary evil, you can minimize the necessity for it by adopting a strict stance about employee theft from the outset. First, make it clear when each employee is hired that honesty is expected. Make it a condition of employment. In other words, evidence of chiseling will be cause for immediate dismissal. One smart franchise owner of a rib shop marked some bills. Sure enough, late one afternoon, a waitress asked him to change a ten-dollar bill for her—the one with his mustache on it. She was invited to leave, and she knew he could prove why.

Second, consider having experienced undercover investigators check out your operation at random intervals and report any employee thefts to you.

Third, immediately have arrested, fire, and then prosecute any employee caught stealing. The rib shop owner let it go with simple firing; he no longer lets any hands but his into the cash register. His is a small shop, and that may not work for larger ones. And, too, he may have been following the common notion that to have an employee arrested and prosecuted will embarrass the business and harm its reputation. It will, indeed—among thieves. And letting it go merely transfers the problem from one business to the next as the fired employee simply finds another job and starts the pattern again.

Fourth, be aware that employees may be in league with outsiders, particularly delivery people and burglars. Make it known that you know this could happen, without accusing anyone, and will prosecute anyone caught. Make this a written policy all new employees read at hiring and make sure all current employees read and sign once a year that they understand and accept your security policies.

Fifth, give employees substantial discounts on purchases of your products and services. It is known that the larger the discounts, the less employee theft there is. But do not *give* products away. Giving things away, except in recognition of a job well done, teaches employees you place no value on your products, and they may feel free to take them.

Sixth, be wary of any large shortages or series of small ones from cash registers operated by the same person. Be on the spot whenever the cash register is read and the cash balanced. Balance the registers on a random basis.

Seventh, do not encourage employees to steal by poor management practices. Managers should never be allowed to give employees extra discounts or price breaks on damaged or returned goods at their own discretion. This would inadvertently teach employees to damage goods and buy them at a significant discount.

Eighth, establish a policy that allows you to make random checks of employee packages, briefcases, and handbags.

Ninth, do not allow employees to bring bags, coats, carrying cases, or the like into working areas.

Tenth, counteract large-scale or big-ticket thefts at loading and unloading areas. Prevent confusion, and do not allow more than one delivery truck to be on your premises at any one time. Carefully count the items, comparing those delivered to those on the bill of lading. Note any damage or discrepancy between the type of goods on the order and those being delivered. Do not allow deliveries to be made late in the day or when you or your trustworthy manager are not on the premises. Make sure all containers are sealed in the same manner and find out the reasons for any resealed or open boxes.

Finally, take steps to prevent the potentially most dangerous type of theft—embezzlement and fraud. If you ship or deliver goods from a warehouse to customers, or use computers for your accounting procedures—accounts receivable and payable and payroll—take extra precautions to protect yourself. Carefully controlled paperwork and audit trails will help prevent embezzlement. Make sure all orders, invoices, bills of lading, pay checks, and so on are prepared in numerical order. Make sure every one—even if torn, damaged, or voided—is accounted for.

Keep a close watch on items that are returned, orders that are canceled or voided, invoices for damaged goods, and the like because these can be easily manipulated outside the mainstream of your business's flow of paperwork.

Above all, check, double-check, and check again all facets of your business, from accounting to inventory. Do it randomly: Have trustworthy outside accountants come in at odd times; hire a private investigator; take inventory without warning to anyone, not even the managers; change auditing controls at odd times; rotate employees from cash register to cash register, and note where the income and records change dramatically.

It is a nice theory that people are honest, but the facts don't bear this out. You needn't treat every employee like a red-handed crook from the word go, but don't take for granted that your employees aren't. Establish policies that promote honesty, then follow them up. Counting buns is the only sure way, literally and figuratively, to be certain your profits go into your pocket.

10

The Win-Win Syndrome: Keeping Good Relations with the Franchisor

When the franchisor and the franchisee both do well, it is fairly easy to maintain a pleasant working relationship. Franchisees don't mind paying royalties because their incomes are skyrocketing, and franchisors can afford to provide high-quality advertising campaigns and support. But franchise relationships are much like marriages. These "honeymoons," which tend to last as long as the economy and market grow steadily, often evolve into troubled marriages, if not acrimonious divorce battles.

Besides arising from economic issues, disputes between franchisors and franchisees may arise from other causes, causes that are symptomatic of the tension that must exist between franchisor and franchisee. This underlying tension, briefly discussed earlier, arises because the franchisor tends to jealously guard its system and reputation and the franchisee tends to want to operate independently.

In fact, the founder of Dunhill Personnel System, Robert Kushell, has noted that the tension in franchise relationships should be considered franchising's "nuclear bomb." Like nuclear energy, franchise relationships have the power to unleash fantastic energy and growth potential, but they also have the power to destroy the franchise.

Franchisors, especially those with the entrepreneur/founder still holding the reins, believe they are giving franchisees a wonderful opportunity to cash in on the franchisor's years of hard work. The franchisor has paid a high cost in dollars, time, and emotional involvement to establish a successful franchise and must be constantly concerned about legal risks: product liability, antitrust, disclosure regulations, illegal earnings claims, and hard-sell hype by overly enthusiastic salespeople and franchise brokers. The franchisor must juggle the legal requirements for franchise registration in dozens of states while keeping an eye on the FTC. It must join with other franchisors to protect its interests before Congress and state legislatures.

On the other hand, franchisees may consider burdensome and annoying the strict conditions and specifications in the franchise contract. They may resent paying royalties when they do not receive continuous advertising and promotional campaigns and hand-holding by regional managers or field representatives.

When a franchise's growth slows, or hard times hit, these basic tensions, often covered with a bed of financial roses in good times, spring up like weeds in a schoolyard. Franchise companies depend on very positive cash flows from royalties and sales of new franchises to finance their rapid growth. When an economic slump hits, the royalty streams slow down and fewer people have the money to buy new franchises. These pressures squeeze the franchise company, which, in turn, is tempted to put the squeeze on franchisees. It may tighten collection procedures, sponsor frequent or excessive discounting and coupon programs, increase sales quotas, increase inventory stocking requirements, and so forth.

But even in hard times, the relationship between the two is governed by the contracts they've signed. Franchisees in general have been unsuccessful in breaking these contracts in court battles unless the franchisor had committed fraud. Almost the only way to change the contractual relationship is to negotiate with the franchisor. This makes it absolutely essential to negotiate every clause and paragraph in the contract. During the euphoria of buying the franchise, you may have looked at the contract and persuaded yourself that you could ignore particularly tough requirements. "What could go wrong?" or, "That's not going to happen," you thought.

Causes of Conflict

Following are fourteen possible causes of conflict. Read how to avoid them and how to work out a negotiated settlement if they do arise.

1. *Accounting procedures and requirements.* This is where many franchisees, unwittingly or not, bring unpleasantness upon themselves. Some fail to file accounting and management reports when required. Sometimes, too,

franchisees file false reports and are caught when the companies audit their books.

Expect franchisors to be tough about reporting deadlines and accurate accounting. If you keep accurate books, but are simply snowed under by work, ask for extensions. Or you can ask for help from the company's regional rep, or can hire more accounting help. But above all, file accurate reports.

If you truly believe there is simply too much paperwork, much of it inessential, build a case and show the company in terms of wasted time and dollars how much you spend. You can strengthen your case and chance for success by first developing more efficient ways of obtaining the same information, and showing this to the company too.

2. *Discount and coupon practices.* As noted earlier, extensive coupons, discounts, and special deals can ruin your profit margins while boosting the franchisor's image and royalty income at your expense. You should have negotiated a contract clause allowing you to choose whether to offer discounts and coupons; if you weren't able to get this concession in the contract, renegotiate it later if the problem becomes severe. You can handle it in a letter agreement for legal protection.

You may also be able to make a case exempting for you from coupons when you have low profit margins or losses.

3. *Diversion of advertising funds.* Many franchises set up advertising funds in which any specific advertising fees or royalties are pooled. Many, however, do not have such a pool, and put ad fees into their general operating budgets. It is tempting for franchise companies to use these ad dollars to boost their profit margins, or subsidize activities that promote pet projects of the franchise founder.

To prevent these abuses, encourage the franchise company to set up an ad fund and administer it with an advertising committee dominated by *franchisees*. Successful committees have included two company members— usually vice presidents of sales and marketing—and three independent franchisees.

4. *Running company-owned stores in competition with franchisee-owned stores.* Company-owned stores tend to be more profitable because they pay no royalties, have the best available management, and can avoid various reporting requirements; this information is gathered for them by corporate employees.

You should have made sure when you bought your franchise that no company-owned stores were close enough to cut into your profits. If some pop up, encourage the franchise company to sell its company-owned outlets to others. During the early and mid-1980s, some franchisors were doing this on their own to eliminate this cause of conflict. Develop figures to present your case; if your profits rise, so do royalties, after all. The franchisor may stand to reap the same rewards in the long run.

5. *Price-fixing and antitrust activities.* When company-owned stores consistently charge lower prices than franchisees, the company could be price-fixing, which is illegal under the Sherman Anti-Trust Act.

Here's an example: Suppose a company-owned outlet charged $10 for a product for which you had to charge $15 to make a profit, and did so again and again. You could not compete and could build a case for both price-fixing and unfair trade practices.

Further, franchisors cannot force you to charge a particular price. They can make suggestions, but they cannot penalize you if you choose to charge a different price. Keep a close eye on pricing and build a case against anticompetitive pricing by anyone, franchisor or a group of franchisees.

6. *Taking rebates and kickbacks.* Another practice that may be illegal is for the franchisor to receive rebates or kickbacks from suppliers or vendors of goods to franchisees. The company should pass through, in terms of greater purchasing discounts, any rebates or special arrangements with approved suppliers.

You can prevent this by keeping careful watch on all your invoices, and by making independent calls to suppliers for frequent price quotes. Speak with other franchisees too to see whether they suspect any kickbacks are going on. It's not something anyone, supplier or franchisor, is likely to broadcast, but you should get an inkling over time.

For remedy, change suppliers. It would not be easy, and probably not even legal, to accuse the franchisor of kickback schemes unless you had absolute proof and a means to prosecute.

7. *Territory divisions.* If a franchisee has not preserved the right of first refusal to expand into surrounding and nearby territories, his business is at high risk from a new owner's eroding the customer base.

If you have neglected this in the contract, again attempt to renegotiate it and solidify it in a letter agreement. If you are doing well, show the franchisor the logic of letting you expand, rather than taking a chance on a new owner or bearing the full cost of a company-owned outlet's start-up. If your franchise is in big demand, however, you may not have a lot of leeway on this one.

8. *Pricing and leasing equipment.* Another common problem occurs when a franchisor sells or leases to the franchisee used or refurbished equipment at new-equipment prices.

If you find this is the case, demand remedy from the franchisor. If it is not willing to make things right, gather your proof and take the firm to court.

9. *Arbitration clauses.* A major point on which franchisees have lost

several court battles is the arbitration clause in most franchise contracts. This clause requires all conflicts and disagreements to be settled by an arbitrator, such as those made available by the American Arbitration Association. Even worse, the clause usually states that you must abide by the arbitrator's decision and forfeit your right to sue in court. In two 1983 court decisions involving Quickprint of America, Inc., the clause was upheld even though the franchisees had made allegations of antitrust practices, misrepresentations, and fraud.

Because it will be very difficult to get a court to allow you to circumvent an arbitration clause, learn how to use the arbitration proceeding to the best of your ability.

First, attempt to resolve your problems in a face-to-face meeting with the franchisor. If that fails, call in the arbitrator specified in your contract or an arbitrator from the American Arbitration Association.

Gather supporting documents for your case. If you believe the amount of money involved warrants it, or if the principle you are trying to establish is significant, you may want to hire an attorney skilled in arbitration to help present your case. In the end, be prepared to abide by the results.

Arbitration can be a useful tool and most often saves thousands of dollars in costs and lawsuits. Experience shows that arbitrators tend to strike fairly equitable compromises and make reasonable decisions that benefit both sides; court suits tend to drag on for years and result in all-or-nothing decisions.

In most cases, arbitration is quicker, less expensive, and more beneficial to the franchisee as well as the franchisor.

10. *Lack of support.* After a contract is signed, the most common cause of conflict comes under the catchall term *lack of support.* This can include failure to provide promised or necessary expertise. A major pizza franchisor was sued by a Canadian franchisee for allegedly failing to provide the know-how to build a restaurant, causing the construction cost to rise to more than double the original estimate. This was one of the few lack-of-support complaints involving a tangible piece of evidence—the structure itself. Most such complaints are much less tangible and don't easily admit of a court solution as this one did.

Most lack-of-support complaints arise when field representatives fail to help during grand openings, do not respond to a franchisee's requests for help, and do not make clear, or help a franchisee fulfill, new requirements by the franchisor.

The problem with lack-of-support claims is that they are relative. One franchisee may be a Nervous Ned and need his hand held every time an employee complains. Others may not want to ever see the field rep and want no help or interference at all. These differences in personality explain why you must negotiate the specific types of help you feel you will need.

If you neglected to do this when you negotiated the contract, resolve the problem through a meeting with the franchisor. Before the meeting, check with other franchisees as to the level of support they are getting. Weigh the possibility that you are one of the Nervous Ned types before making your presentation; the franchisor will have done so. When you have met on some common ground—and that usually means you agree to less than the ultimate hand-holding and the franchisor agrees not to ignore you—write up a letter agreement.

11. *Lack of financial support.* An increasingly common conflict arises when a franchisor does not or cannot help a franchisee obtain new financing. Some franchisors force their franchisees to pay cash for their purchases, and do not even provide normal 10- or 30-day trade credit terms. Others do not help their existing franchisees obtain lines of credit or short-term inventory financing. Yet when franchisees run into slowdowns, they need short-term financing at reasonable interest rates to see them through.

Associations of franchisees can decide to act on their own behalf, with or without the support of the franchisor, and obtain the credit their members need from independent financial assistance organizations.

See the ComputerLand case study below for another situation in which a franchisee association successfully pressured the franchisor into doing this for its franchisees.

12. *Payment schedules.* Of course, the most common conflict arises over payment schedules for royalties, advertising fees, rental payments, and equipment leases the franchisees must comply with, and sales quotas they must meet. Be aware that a franchisor may create additional fees or require additional purchases when it has excessive inventories or needs a quick infusion of cash for any reason.

You have probably negotiated a grace period for payments. But you probably have not negotiated increasing sales quotas. Meet the quotas if doing so will make money for you. If not, resist. Build your case. Cite decreasing population, increased competition, higher unit costs—in short, all the factors that are causing your problems.

13. *Failure of the franchisor.* Although it may not be uppermost in your mind when you are buying a franchise, you must be aware that a franchisor may fail. If a franchise company fails, you could be left out in the cold with no image, no business goodwill, no reputation, no supplier, no support, and a pile of debts.

Be forewarned that if the franchisor goes out of business—and more than 60 did so during 1984—you are likely to be left holding the bag. You may sue in court, but even if you win, you face the more serious problem of collecting your settlement from a nonexistent or bankrupt business, a very difficult task.

If you begin to get hints that the franchisor is in serious financial trouble, negotiate the right to buy the permanent use of the franchise's name within your territory if the franchisor should go out of business. Whether the name will be worth anything may be open to question, of course.

Also carefully study your leases—real-estate and equipment—to determine what happens if the leasing company goes out of business. You could end up with no store, although usually a lease is binding on the succeeding company or buyer. In fact, you may be able to negotiate better terms with the new owner if he really wants or needs you to stay in the building.

14. *The quality-control issue.* Of intense concern to anyone in business, this issue has been adjudicated in the franchisee's favor in many courts. Nonetheless, quality control remains one of the least understood and most perilous issues a potential franchisee has to face.

What is quality control? In short, quality control in a franchise is that part of the contract which governs how and in what manner a franchised product line is sold and what standards the products, store, and management must meet. In a fast-food restaurant, quality control would include not only the content of the food products—the quality and grade of hamburger meat, for example—but also the cleanliness of the store and the employees' uniforms, to name just two aspects.

For at least 20 years, many franchisees have contended that a company's quality-control clauses are often used to force a franchisee to buy supplies, equipment, appliances, signs, "secret" ingredients, and so forth from the parent company. On the other hand, the franchisors contend that enforcing product quality and uniformity is the best available protection for the business image of each franchisee, the franchise system itself, and the public.

The International Franchise Association (IFA) pamphlet entitled "Investigate Before Investing" notes, "If bargaining away of such controls were common, a franchisor could erode by bits and pieces the standardization and quality controls necessary to protect each franchisee and the public who rely on the franchisor's tradenames and the entire system. There would remain no good-will and no national or chain image worth your investment." And it advises potential franchisees to look elsewhere if a company is willing to bargain away its quality-control protections.

Which side is correct? This issue does not lend itself to simple black-and-white answers. Consider a little of the history of this problem. Before 1970, franchisors could—and many did—force franchisees to buy supplies, equipment, and so on from them. Those sales were a very large part of franchisors' incomes; they remain an important, but not large, part for many franchisors to this day.

In 1970, a federal court ruling stated that franchisors could no longer *force* a franchisee to make those purchases. And in the late 1970s, in an even more important ruling, another federal court ruled that it was illegal for a franchisor to *influence or persuade* franchisees to buy supplies, equipment, real estate, and so on from the parent company. The federal jury reasoned that a large franchisor could, by its sheer size, force a one-shop operator to buy from it although the operator might buy supplies at a lower price from another vendor.

Since that decision, franchisors have had to tread a very fine line between their quality-control programs and their sales of supplies, equipment, real estate, and so on to franchisees. Many major franchisors, including the daddy of them all, McDonald's, do not sell supplies. But they strictly regulate the supplies and equipment the franchisee can buy with quality-control standards.

Of course, many franchisors are paragons of quality control. Their success shows the advantages that tight quality control can bring to a potential franchisee.

First, the public is drawn to a franchise outlet to buy products because people come to respect its image and understand the quality of product they can expect to receive when they shop at a particular franchise.

Second, that image and reputation and the knowledge that you can get consistent-quality supplies are probably some of the main reasons you are interested in buying a particular franchise. It is usually only *after* a franchisee has been in business for a while and finds alternate and less expensive sources of supply that he complains about being tied to the franchisor.

Third, the franchise's image and reputation for quality products and consistently clean, modern stores may be a new franchisee's strongest asset when he first opens his outlet. This gives a long leg up on the local competition. These factors play a large part in any franchise's successful marketing strategy.

Fourth, a franchisor's supplies sales can provide a buffer against sharp price rises and product shortages, reduce shipping charges, and make budgeting and management easier for the individual franchisee. This type of approach can be very effective in a time of rapid inflation to help protect franchisees from crushing price increases.

On the other hand, in a free market, individual shop owners may feel that they have paid for the franchise name with their cash payments and royalty fees. That is enough, they believe, and they have the right to negotiate the lowest price for their supplies with anyone they want to. And they contend that the franchisor must trust that the actions its franchisees take will directly benefit the franchisee and indirectly benefit the franchisor.

One thing is clear: There is a lot of leeway in contract language that can be used to provide more or less protection for either side. The goal of each party should be to achieve a fair balance, allowing the franchisee to obtain the best supplies at the lowest price and the franchisor to protect the image and reputation of the franchise's name.

Avoid a franchise with weak quality control or none at all. This demonstrates a significant lack of concern for the future of the franchise and implies a short-range outlook by the franchisor. Neither will be good for the franchisee who is interested in building a thriving business that will last for years.

Also avoid, however, any franchise that dictates quality-control standards with a heavy hand. These strictures could be used to take a new, thriving franchise away from a franchisee so the parent company could reap the benefits of his toil and trouble.

Undoubtedly, you must pay very close attention to the quality-control issue when you investigate a franchise. Talk to a wide range of current franchisees and be sure to ask them how they feel about the franchisor's quality-control standards and enforcement of those standards. These people are on the front lines and deal with the franchisor's quality-control inspectors all the time. They will also be the ones who would know best where to find the most reasonably priced supplies that meet a company's standards.

If the franchisor's quality-control behavior changes significantly after you are in business, find out why. If it gets suddenly lax, the franchisor may be in trouble and you'll need to protect yourself from its demise. If it becomes onerous, the franchisor may be trying to force out the franchisees in favor of company-owned outlets. Or it may simply be trying to upgrade the franchise's image for all concerned. Find out. Then negotiate what you need and want from the change based on facts and on a rational presentation of your case to the franchisor. Consider joining with other franchisees to pool your bargaining power and get the greatest good for the greatest number—yourself included.

Two Case Studies: The Adversarial Way and the Cooperative Way

During 1985, two examples of the tension in franchisor-franchisee relationships—one positive and one not so positive—grabbed headlines. Without saying which side is correct, let's look at how one major franchisor handled more than a year's worth of dissension among its franchisees and how another major franchisor has acted for many years to prevent any serious conflicts. By studying these examples, you'll know what to look for in a positive relationship with a franchisor.

The ComputerLand Dilemma

By summer 1985, Computerland, the world's largest computer-store franchise (more than 630 stores), was suffering from the sharp slowdown in the personal computer industry. Complaints from franchisees about poor support, inadequate financial assistance, excessive royalty rates, improper use of advertising dollars, and more buffeted William Millard, the billionaire entrepreneur who founded ComputerLand in the late 1970s.

(The franchisor was also involved in a very tough court challenge for control of 20 percent of ComputerLand's privately held stock, but that problem was ancillary to the franchisee relationship and will not be discussed here. It did, however, threaten to push ComputerLand into bankruptcy, although that possibility had been averted by the end of 1985.)

One of the most serious points of contention was a franchisee demand that the company lower its 8 percent royalty rate.

As ComputerLand's conflicts with its franchisees came to a head, many threatened to break away and sell public stock, a move strictly forbidden by the ComputerLand contract. Many threatened lawsuits, and one, Analytical Systems, Inc. (ASI), filed a lawsuit alleging that the franchisor forced it to open additional outlets in the Southeast against its wishes or face the prospect that ComputerLand would sell other franchises in ASI's territory. It also alleged that ComputerLand breached its contractual obligations to provide products at lower costs than ASI could find on its own. ASI has closed 12 stores and has removed ComputerLand signs from 5 others that remained open, and is fighting ComputerLand's own attempt to force ASI to close a warehouse computer sales outlet that ASI opened independently. ASI also claimed it tried to negotiate an end to the agreement, but said ComputerLand unilaterally revoked the agreement in August.

ASI's suit points out numerous causes of conflict, including the key one about territory definitions. ASI alleges that after it opened eight new franchises and converted three existing computer stores, it was forced to sign new agreements covering the new and existing franchises; these contracts, it alleges, include an unenforceable noncompeting clause. ASI asserts that the clause does not reasonably limit in time or territorial scope the anticompetition requirement.

Regardless of which side is right or wrong in this particular suit—which should take years to resolve—the allegations illustrate the problems that arise if the franchisor-franchisee tension gets far out of balance.

In addition to the 12 Atlanta stores, numerous other franchises closed down, and ComputerLand apparently refused to buy them out or provide enough support for them to continue. The closing of 5 stores in Miami, owned by a single local businessperson, brought the total closings by mid-September 1985 to 26; one franchise outlet in Houston filed for Chapter 11 bankruptcy protection to allow it to reorganize; and others threatened to make independent agreements with major vendors. Many others are up for sale at bargain prices.

To protect themselves, the franchisees had formed the Chicago-based International Association of Computer Dealers (IACD), which had more than 250 members in 1985 and was growing rapidly. The IACD had threatened to sue the company for a lower fee and wanted a moratorium on new franchise sales.

Another complaint centered on ComputerLand's use of ad dollars to launch a multimillion-dollar campaign, including full-page advertisements in *The Wall Street Journal,* to promote Millard's and his staff's solutions to world hunger. This campaign used such attention-grabbing headlines as "Why ComputerLand Decided Not to Send Money to Ethiopia" and alienated franchisees who needed more money spent on ads to sell computers. It may not be a lost point that, in addition to being noncomputer advertising, the ads may have been contrary to the viewpoints of franchisees whose money was being spent.

ComputerLand's Responses

In response to these problems and to rebuild its tarnished image, ComputerLand launched a series of reforms and turned its annual franchisee meeting into a rah-rah session to boost its franchisees' confidence. But it did make some significant offers and concessions to its franchisees, which you might keep in mind as objects of a similar quest if you feel the need. The offers included:

Reasserted commitment. Top management clearly and repeatedly reasserted its commitment to the franchise method, and reiterated that it would not open competing company-owned stores.

Reduced royalty rate. To ease the royalty burden, the franchisor launched an incentive program that would reduce from 8 percent to 4 percent the royalty rate for any franchisee whose sales surpassed its previous year's sales by 15 percent or more. If the franchisee exceeded fiscal year 1985 sales by that margin during fiscal year 1986, the royalty rate would be a flat 5 percent. The previous rate was 8 percent royalty and 1 percent ad fee on gross monthly sales.

Sales incentives. ComputerLand also launched an incentive program to award cash prizes of up to $100,000 to the ten regional franchises that record the largest annual sales increase. Smaller prizes will be awarded to other franchises showing significant increases.

New advertising campaign. The company promised that it would launch a new $6–$8 million campaign featuring television, radio, and print ads with an "institutional" flavor aimed at boosting the franchise's image and reputation.

Increased marketing support. Executives encouraged their franchisees to reorient their marketing thrust away from home- and small-business buyers to specialty markets and corporate sales. They stressed that franchisees cannot compete on price in this shakeout field, but must offer quality and service to obtain a better price for their products.

New training program. ComputerLand launched a new training program that teaches how to sell high-margin products and integrated personal computer systems to corporate and institutional accounts.

New distribution arrangement. ComputerLand initiated a new program through which three major software distributors can ship their products directly to the franchisees. In the past, most software purchases went through ComputerLand's warehouse. ComputerLand is also trying to reduce its costs of evaluating, reviewing, shipping, and supporting dozens of software programs that are not major sellers. The company planned only to support major software titles from large firms, such as IBM.

ComputerLand executives estimated in mid-1985 that these programs would add up to 3 percent to an average franchisee's net profits during fiscal 1986.

The franchisees' response to ComputerLand's efforts was generally enthusiasic, and it appeared the two sides were well on their way toward patching up their relationship.

However, a better idea than putting out raging fires of discontent is to prevent small causes of friction from turning into such major storms of acrimony. An excellent example of a franchise company that is known for its successful relationships is Midas Muffler.

Midas Muffler's Franchise Magic

Midas Muffler has more than 1,500 franchisees, each of whom has paid at least $142,000 in fees and startup costs. But Midas has avoided any significant difficulties with its franchisees for more than 20 years not only by providing support, but also by listening attentively to its franchise owners. Midas also puts prospects through what it calls a "grueling" two-day session that explains the offering prospectus and the disclosure statement. This makes absolutely sure each franchisee understands what is required of him and leaves no room for complaint later.

The support Midas provides is also extensive, including:

- A field force of division and district representatives who meet constantly with franchisees.
- Real-estate, marketing, advertising, and sales promotion executives who work in direct contact with franchisees.
- An open-door policy in which franchisees can get in direct touch with the president of Midas.
- A policy of going to the dealers and asking their advice *before* any new programs are put into effect. Midas holds that the franchisees must believe in and support new programs to make them work.
- Encouraging its franchisees to expand. Midas provides high-quality market research to back up such a move.
- Giving current franchisees first crack at expanding and opening new outlets in their areas.

The Successful Midas Franchisee Association

Most important, Midas franchisees have a very strong association, and that association works very closely and cooperatively with Midas management. An adage states that there is strength in numbers: The National Midas Dealers Association, Inc. counts 1,100 of 1,500 franchisees in its membership, a very powerful lobbying force, indeed.

Midas could, of course, take an antagonistic viewpoint toward the association, but Midas executives realize that such an attitude would be self-defeating. After all, an association is not a collective bargaining organization or a labor union. Association representatives have stated that Midas management and association reps meet on a monthly basis to discuss strategy for local ad campaigns, future marketing strategies, and more.

When a problem does arise—when Midas plans to do something that some franchisees fear will harm them—the association asks other franchisees to investigate the situation. If they find the franchisees are correct, they make recommendations to Midas itself for changes; if they feel the franchisees are wrong, the franchisees are more likely to listen to their fellow dealers and cooperate.

Midas prescribes large doses of preventive medicine to keep its franchisees healthy and wealthy. And it eliminates the conditions that most often lead to conflict: lack of communication; top-down enforcement of policies;

excessive financial burdens; feelings of lack of support and abandonment; and inadequate chance to expand and grow.

Franchise Associations and Councils

If the other owners of the franchise you want to buy do not have a franchisee association, consider working with them to form one. Responsible franchise companies will welcome the opportunity to work with a central group that can summarize and clarify the interests of all franchisees.

Here are important points to remember when setting up such an association:

- Make sure it is independent and franchisees pay their own way. Set reasonable monthly dues ($20 is common) no franchisee will have trouble paying.
- Make it clear to the franchisor that you wish to establish a "win-win" relationship in which your mutual goal is to discuss things that are best for your business. In short, adopt a conciliatory and cooperative attitude, not one of confrontation. Take an adversary point of view only as a last resort.
- Work with the franchisor to develop future marketing plans, improve the screening of prospective franchisees, plan advertising and promotional campaigns, and so forth.
- Keep the association tightly organized. Form committees to consider various problems. Provide opportunities for every franchisee to contribute.
- Encourage franchisees to hash out concerns before presenting proposals to the franchise company.
- Develop programs to provide support for franchisees. Above all, always work to promote a better franchise program for everyone.

New Support for the Interests of Franchisees

Even if you are not a member of a franchise association, you need not feel like a lone warrior on the front lines of a business battle with your franchisor and your customers. You are part of the greater nationwide group of 400,000 franchisees with similar interests and similar problems.

What does a Dunkin' Donut dealer have in common with a Midas Muffler man or a Frame Factory franchisee? Plenty, including franchisor relationships, taxes, labor relations, federal and state regulations, health and safety laws, to name just a very few.

And there is a national organization that represents all of their interests. This organization is the National Alliance of Franchisees (NAF), and it works with Congress and the federal regulatory agencies, state and local governments seeking to restrict the rights of franchisees, and the franchise companies themselves and their own associations.

In addition to individual franchisees, The NAF represents dozens of franchisee associations—including the National Midas Muffler Dealers Association; the Dairy Queen Operators Association; and the National Coalition of Associations of 7-Eleven Franchisees, with 10,000 members.

NAF Activities

The NAF lobbies for franchisees before federal and state governments on these common—and very serious—problems:

- Wage and hour regulations, including minimum wages and tip reporting
- Product liability
- Workmen's compensation and disability insurance
- OSHA and EPA regulations
- Small Business Administration loans and regulations
- Bank attitudes toward small-business lending
- Moves at the state, local, or federal level to restrict the rights of franchisees or weaken legal protection

As an example of these activities as a lobbyist, the NAF took a strong stand against a proposed Michigan law that would have weakened the Michigan Franchise Investment Law. The International Franchise Association (IFA) supported these changes, but in late 1984, a compromise resulted that eased reporting requirements, but kept enough restrictions to protect new and existing franchisees.

The changes eliminated the requirement that a franchisor must register the franchise with the state government and submit the franchise to a merit review by the state's Corporation and Securities Bureau. The NAF supported changes that the IFA also advocated that eliminated a lot of cumbersome paperwork and bureaucratic hassles in the sale of franchises in the state, a plus both for the franchisor and the franchisee as well as for a franchisee who wants to sell his existing outlet.

To boost its membership, the NAF has established State Franchise Councils to represent small franchisees or those not represented by franchise associations. The franchisees whose national associations already belong to NAF will be represented through those associations.

Setting Up Franchise Old-Boy Networks

Perhaps the most important overlooked effort the NAF makes is the creation of an old-boy network for franchisees. The NAF brings together members of the older, established franchisee associations, such as Pizza Hut and Midas Muffler, with small, young associations or franchisees who want to form associations of their own dealers. By sharing experiences and the legal know-how of the NAF, new associations can avoid some of the time- and money-wasting problems usually encountered in setting up new organizations.

Other Efforts

Although the lobbying efforts get the most publicity and the old-boy network that helps individual members gets the least, the NAF has helped create a another subtle, positive effect that is also unheralded. The NAF seeks to work with franchisors and their associations that speak for the interests of the franchise companies. The NAF works to improve franchisor-franchisee relations. The NAF members overwhelmingly believe that a nonconfrontational approach toward solving problems is not only beneficial to both parties, but highly desirable. In short, the NAF would rather talk than fight, and cooperate instead of bicker. This attitude is consistent with the fact that, at heart, both the franchisor and the franchisee seek the same goals—a profitable and growing business.

The NAF has also developed an educational program. It sponsors seminars on franchise management and provides published information on taxes, accounting, labor relations, banking, insurance, and other areas of business interest.

If you are considering buying a franchise, you can take advantage of the NAF's information programs and seminars. And it will certainly be good to know that although the franchisor will be a continuing source of help in running your business, you will have another helping hand to represent your personal interests. Your Congressman may consider your opinion as a small businessman if you write him about a problem, but he will be far more impressed if your opinion is backed by the same opinion expressed by thousands of other franchisees whose personal lobbyist is knocking on his door.

Most franchisees truly desire positive, cooperative relationships with franchisors. Emphasize that you believe a franchise is one situation in which both sides can maintain a "win-win" relationship for many years. But don't sacrifice your investment or endure unfair or illegal treatment. Use all the tools at your disposal, from personal effort to group action, to turn the potentially dangerous tensions into positive programs to benefit the franchisor's profits and, most important, your own.

11

A Shot in the Arm: Building Your Franchise with Modern Marketing Techniques

Franchises usually serve relatively restricted geographical areas, so local advertising—on radio, in newspapers and pennysavers, and on local or cable television—is generally very effective, especially when its effect is compounded by the franchisor's regional and national advertising efforts.

In this chapter, you will learn how to go beyond the joint advertising efforts you make with the franchisor. You'll learn to use modern marketing techniques even if you have a limited advertising budget.

You'll learn how to make public relations count. While public relations and promotion may get your name well known to a general audience, they do not necessarily zero in on the most important people—your potential customers. By their nature, public relations and promotion, while essential parts of your overall campaign, act like shotguns. They spray their "pellets" of exposure across a wide area. But by using PR and promotion techniques along with moderate amounts of the much more costly advertising, you can precisely target your customers, like the bull's-eye in the sight of a rifle.

The Secret of Effective Advertising

How do you identify the customers you do want to reach, so you can target your promotional efforts specifically to them? The secret is market research.

Multinational corporations spend billions of dollars on this each year. But you can use some practically free, but very effective, methods on your own.

You learned a great deal about your customers when you were selecting your franchise and choosing a location for your business. Understanding population demographics, identifying where different types of people live, and other techniques were described in Chapters 3 and 4. And the franchise company will probably have given you lots more general information about your customers.

So you've identified a broad base of potential customers. Use the techniques below to identify customers more specifically and to learn what makes them buy your products in your store. You may find, as many new businesses do, that the people you *thought* were going to be your customers are not. Or you may find you were right on target. Either way, you can then plan your advertising, public relations, and promotion to reach exactly those you want as customers for your business.

The Essential Difference of Psychographics

The research you did when you bought your franchise will have told you quite a bit about your customers' demographics—their income levels, ages, average number of children, education, type of house, cost of housing, the amount of money they spend, what they spend it on, how much money they spend on your product or service, and how often.

But have you *reconfirmed* or *updated* your assumptions since you opened? Probably not, and unless you have a cooperative ad plan, the franchisor may not have done it either. You'll want to update it. But when you do, go beyond demographics, or what your customers *can* spend, to psychographics, which will tell you *why* they spend, and help you offer products and services most appealing to them.

For example, two 45-year-old people each earn $35,000 a year and live in census Tract 201 on Houston Lakes Boulevard. These demographic facts strongly indicate they should both shop in your store. You are in the same tract, and your customers earn between $25,000 and $40,000 per year, according to your franchisor's and your own research. Yet one shops in your store and the other doesn't. Why? One is a truck driver. He has three kids, lives in a middle-income single-family home, and drives a Ford truck. He wears work boots, flannel shirts, and jeans, and enjoys drinking beer, watching football, and spending most of his spare money betting on horses.

The other is a female assistant professor of English literature at a small college in your town. She is not married, lives in a small condominium, and drives a Japanese-made compact car. She enjoys reading both serious novels and Gothic romances, but doesn't tell her friends about the romances. She also enjoys eating in small natural-food restaurants, and traveling to Europe during summer vacations. She supports the local opera and ballet companies.

Although both of these people earn the same amount of money, and live in the same part of town, they do not spend their money in the same ways. The difference is psychographics.

Low-Cost Survey Methods

You can find out who your customers are now, analyze their psychographics, and determine how best to reach them with an inexpensive survey. This is not a complicated survey like the Gallup poll or the "taste tests" conducted for national TV. It is, at most, a one-page questionnaire with 10 or 12 basic questions that establish who your customers are, what products or services of yours they buy, how often they buy, how much they spend, and what they like and don't like about your business.

There are several relatively inexpensive and painless ways to conduct a survey. They are:

• *In-store.* Ask your customers to fill in the questionnaire while they are shopping. Supermarkets do this frequently with some success. You may offer a small, one-time discount on current purchases or a small, inexpensive free gift to customers who participate.

The in-store survey is practically free and involves only a little of your own or your staff's time each day. This survey identifies *current* customers, and tells you why they shop in your outlet, what they buy, how much they buy, what they like and don't like about your store, and what they think of the quality of your store, its cleanliness, the service they receive, the courtesy and actions of your staff, and so on. It does not, however, tell you why people who are not your customers are not, nor what it would take to snag them.

• *Near-store.* If you are in a mall, shopping center, or downtown area, you can sample *potential* customers as well as actual customers by stopping people on the sidewalk or in the mall concourse and asking them similar questions. You may offer them a free sample or a coupon for helping you. The free sample may give them a reward immediately, and entice more of them to cooperate. The coupon, on the other hand, will bring them into your store, where you have another chance to make them a regular customer.

The kinds of questions you'll ask in a near-store survey differ somewhat from those of an in-store survey. You must ask more questions about where the respondents now shop for products similar to yours and why; then you can understand why you do not now receive their business. This survey too is practically free, using up a bit of staff time or your own time. (Family volunteers are a good way to deal with the time element, and teenagers, in particular, are both nonthreatening to shoppers and generally not shy about asking questions.)

By interviewing between 100 and 200 people over several days, you can obtain some reasonably accurate results. Once you have the completed questionnaires, simply total answers and responses to each question and study the results. You do not need a degree in statistical analysis or consumer psychology to understand what customers are telling you. If you ask a question about cleanliness and 57 of 100 people who *do not* shop in your store say they believe your store is fairly clean, but not very clean, you may conclude several things: (1) you need to clean more carefully; (2) you should analyze follow-up questions to see whether they prefer to shop in very clean stores; or (3) you should analyze other parts of the questionnaire to see if this is the main reason they do not shop in your store, or if other factors—high prices, poor service, lack of desired products, and so on—are the real reason.

If you do an in-store survey, and 75 of 100 existing customers say they believe your store is fairly clean, 15 say it is very clean, and only 10 say it is moderately dirty, you can safely conclude your store is adequately clean, and you should maintain your current cleanliness standards. Cleanliness is not a factor with people who do not shop there.

• *By mail*. You can send out a selected number of letters (a few hundred is more than enough) to residences in your neighborhood or to known customers if you have a mailing list. Keep the mailing list idea in mind; it is an essential aid to improving sales for many types of franchises. With it, you can send out notices of seasonal specials to customers you are fairly certain will be interested in buying.

In the letter accompanying your survey, offer a coupon to be redeemed when the recipient brings in the survey, or offer him a free gift for returning it. Also always include a return envelope addressed to your store, and pay for the postage—a good reason to keep the questionnaire to one page, so you can save postage costs. Use a postage meter or a bulk-mail postage-paid permit rather than stamps. Survey companies used to put uncanceled stamps on return envelopes, but found that as many as half of the people stole the stamps and used them on their own letters. Avoid this expensive mistake.

• *By telephone*. In small towns or selected neighborhoods for which you can obtain the telephone numbers, you can conduct a survey by telephone. For about $500, you can canvass about 300 households using local college students to make calls during the evening. Keep these surveys short and to the point, 7 to 15 questions at the most. Be sure your callers are relentlessly polite even when their efforts are rejected, or your store will get a reputation for rudeness along with the information you gather.

Creating a Questionnaire

The same sort of questionnaire would be appropriate for all four types of retail-store surveys. Each kind should contain the same types of questions, including:

- Yes or no questions
- Multiple-choice questions
- Weighted number or word scales that determine how strongly a person feels about an issue or statement ("How much do you enjoy XYZ's Super-Duper Butter Nut Sundae? —Very much. It's okay. Not so much. Never had it, never will.")
- Opinion questions
- Open-ended discussion questions in which a person is invited to express his true feelings about something

To double-check the information, some surveys repeat the same question, rephrased.

A sample questionnaire on which you may build one of your own design is shown in Figure 11-1.

As you can see, this simple questionnaire will quickly tell you what kinds of products your customers most often buy, why they like to shop in your store, what they think of your customer service practices, what advertising medium has been effective in reaching paying customers, and where your customers come from.

Armed with this information, you can design a targeted advertising campaign. For example, suppose half of your customers said they traveled at least half an hour to reach your store. Most of them also identified your Yellow Pages ad as the way they found out about you. You would then know you have a highly motivated group of customers willing to go out of their way to reach your location. That may indicate several things: First, you could be in the wrong location, and would do better to move closer to your customers. That area may contain more less motivated customers who could support your business. Second, you may have little competition for your goods. Look at this answer in relationship to answers given about price; you may find you can maintain somewhat higher prices. Third, you may be selling products or services your customers cannot find easily elsewhere, and you should try to maintain this competitive difference.

Remember, if you are successful, someone is going to emulate you—and fast—so you need to constantly bring in new products to keep your customers coming back.

Figure 11-1. Sample market research questionnaire for athletic apparel and shoe franchise.

1. How often do you shop in this store?
   _____Daily   _____Several times a week   _____Once a week
   _____Occasionally   _____Hardly ever   _____First time

2. What kinds of products have you purchased from this store?

   _____ Jogging shoes
   _____ Tennis shoes
   _____ Women's tennis wear
   _____ Women's aerobics clothing
   _____ Women's swimsuits and bathing apparel
   _____ Men's tennis wear
   _____ Men's swimsuits
   _____ Children's sportswear
   _____ Special T-shirts
   _____ Accessories

3. What is your opinion of the overall quality of the goods you have purchased in this store?
   _____Very high quality   _____Overall average quality
   _____Some very good, some very poor   _____Poor quality

4. How do our employees treat you when you come into the store?
   _____Always courteously   _____Most often courteously
   _____Somewhat courteously   _____Sometimes rudely

5. When you visit our store, what most appeals to you as a customer? Please give each of these a number: 1 is the most important and 5 is the least important.

   _____ Quality of goods
   _____ Customer service
   _____ Prices
   _____ Appearance of store
   _____ Wide choice and availability

6. How far did you travel to shop in our store?

   _____ From the adjoining neighborhood (name of subdivision)
   _____ From within a few minutes away
   _____ A 15-minute drive
   _____ A half-hour drive
   _____ More than a half-hour drive

7. Did you specifically come to this location (center, mall) to shop at this store?   _____Yes   _____No

8. If not, what other specific types of shopping do you intend to do today? Please answer all.

_____ Grocery shopping
_____ Women's clothes shopping
_____ Medical or dental office visit
_____ Men's or children's clothes shopping
_____ General browsing with nothing in particular in mind
_____ Other products or services

9. Do you regularly shop at any other athletic apparel shop?
_____Yes   _____No

10. If so, why did you choose to visit our store today?

_____ Sale
_____ Special discounts
_____ Happened to be passing by
_____ Prefer your quality goods
_____ Goods not available at other store
_____ Redeeming coupons

11. How have you heard about our store? (Answer all that apply.)

_____ Saw the signs
_____ Read Yellow Pages ad
_____ Read advertisement in daily newspaper
_____ Received coupons in the mail
_____ Read advertisements in local shopper
_____ Heard your radio commercial
_____ Saw your franchise advertised on local/national television

(To use this question list for telephone and mail surveys, you need only change the time element—*today* becomes *recently,* and so forth.)

No-Cost Survey Results

There are several ways to gather useful psychographic information to target your customers without spending an extra dime. First, you may be able to obtain quality market research simply by the judicious use of your own instincts supported by strong facts and clear evidence. Surveying by "walking around" is one way mentioned earlier. Census Bureau information on your neighborhood is another, although this will be light on the psychographics.

Second, although you probably use advertising mats provided by the franchisor, a local advertising agency may be willing to share, for free or at low cost, psychographic information it has collected. If you are now or plan to become its client, this should certainly be the case; in fact, you can require sharing of this information as a condition of your becoming a client.

Third, you can obtain a gold mine of information simply by reading your local newspapers, weeklies, pennysavers, magazines, business newspapers, and any publications put out by the local chambers of commerce, local or regional industrial development agencies, or municipal governments promoting business development in your area. They contain a wealth of information about the future growth prospects for your area; often, stories will predict more or less precisely what that growth will be if you read between the lines. For instance, a new high-tech research and development company coming to town will give you different psychographics among its 200-plus employees than would a manufacturer of farm equipment. The main caveat in this method is that such publications tend to present a very rosy view of the future. Take the editorializing with a grain of salt, and read them for their factual statistics.

Fourth, keep an eagle eye and a dog's ear alert for what is happening in your own backyard. You may hear the good news (a new real-estate development, a new shopping mall, a new highway) or the bad news (school closings, rumors of factory closings, population shifts) before anything is publicly announced. You can make quick changes in your ad campaigns and stay one step ahead of the competition by knowing more than they do. For example, suppose a new factory plans to open near your store within six months. You can design and have ready a promotional campaign to gain its employees' business, and then make future plans for growth and more profit because of its proximity. Make sure you determine first whether it will be a research factory or a factory farm; the psychographics will be vastly different. Bonus giveaways of season opera tickets probably won't fit the psychographics of the chicken pluckers.

On the other hand, suppose a new four-lane highway is diverted from your neighborhood to the other side of town. If you hear about it in advance, you can weigh its impact on your business. You may even want to get a jump on relocating near the new highway.

In short, market research, whether it is as simple as talking to your local banker at a civic-club meeting or as complex as doing a 5,000-piece mailing to established customers, helps you know in what direction your customers, and therefore your business, are going. Even on a small scale, in this age of rapid shifts in population and customer buying habits, market research is a "must-do" task for any franchise owner.

Inexpensive Advertising for Franchisees

Now that you know who your real customers are, how can you focus your advertising dollars to gain the maximum impact? First, concentrate and coordinate all of your efforts around your best customers and your best-selling products. In selling, you ignore, at your peril, the well-known Pareto rule: 80 percent of the business comes from 20 percent of the customers. This has been proved repeatedly, so your ads must cater to the 20 percent of all customers with the most money to spend and the most interest in spending it in your franchise.

Never, unless you have very big bucks available, pull out all the stops and advertise through all the local media. Such advertising for the grand opening alone may quickly swallow a year's reasonable advertising budget. Don't, on the other hand, shrink from advertising outside your own store windows just because of some initial discomfort in learning how to place ads and negotiate with the media, or because of uncertainty about what the results will be.

The Key Factors

You can easily avoid either extreme, using some proven, inexpensive advertising methods. First, however, consider the size of your ad budget. If you spent $1 million opening your McDonald's, you would probably have enough financing to use the parent company's cooperative advertising program and make a big hit in your territory. Yet most McDonald's rely on the franchisor's national advertising efforts to bring in the customers. They reserve local ad dollars for special promotions.

Most new franchises are much smaller, requiring under $50,000 in total startup costs, and their advertising budgets are consequently much, much smaller.

How big should your advertising budget be? That depends on whether your franchisor has a cooperative ad program. Today, the common charge for a national or regional cooperative advertising program is from as low as 1 percent to more than 7 or 10 percent of your monthly gross sales. It would appear that adding an additional several (2–5) percent of your gross sales for local advertising would be appropriate under most circumstances. That total should include the cost of professionally prepared signs for your windows as well as any media advertising.

Consider the nature of your franchise. What are you selling and to whom? If you run a popcorn stand in a shopping mall, your advertising may consist only of coupons or handouts you give to customers as they walk by or when they shop in the store. And that's likely all you need.

But if you run an industrial cleaning franchise, your potential customers may be large factories or real-estate management firms scattered around a metropolitan area. You may need to concentrate on direct sales pitches or mail-order solicitations to the building engineers and maintenance directors.

Know all about the franchisor's advertising program and what it does for you and requires from you. The major franchisors have long-established, well-known, and very effective advertising programs. Wendy's "Where's the Beef?" ad even helped set the tone for a national (and unsuccessful) political campaign, and Coca-Cola and Pepsi's campaigns became worldwide legends and entered our daily vocabulary. Their franchisees can't help but benefit.

Find out what your franchisor's ad program consists of and take advantage of all it offers. In the low-cost-startup franchises, the program may be no more than signs and fixtures for your store, advertising "slicks" for use in local newspapers, brochures, pamphlets and handouts, "grand opening" signs, bunting, and advertising copy and messages for local radio or television stations. You help pay for all of these in your franchise fee. The franchisor may have additional regional or national campaigns of its own. These may be the broad-based "institutional" type, like the Wendy's "Where's the Beef?" ads, or they may be regional, allowing you to participate specifically in the advertising for a small charge.

Five Low-Cost Advertising Methods

Like many other franchisees, you may have a very small ad budget you aren't quite sure what to do with. You fear you may make mistakes and waste this valuable resource. You can overcome all these negatives, however, by learning and using a host of low-cost, yet very effective and easily measured, advertising methods. Here are the basics:

Method #1: Develop a Mailing List

The most effective way to sell your product or service is, of course, to have as a potential customer a person who must have your product or a person who really wants to buy your product. How do you find these practically guaranteed customers? By finding the names of people who have bought the same or a similar product in the past, and selling to them again. You do this by developing a mailing list.

You could go out and buy expensive mailing lists from companies that sell such lists including targets as specific as all one-eyed dentists who buy green tooth polish or those as general as the entire population of New York City. Generally, finding a mailing list offering names of your precisely targeted customers will be difficult. And even if it is available, it will be very expensive—50 cents to $1 per name, or $500–$1,000 for 1,000 names. There are a lot of very expensive fish in that ocean, and for all you know, some of them may be extinct.

For a small franchise, the best way to obtain a mailing list is to build one from scratch. If you own a retail store, the best, simplest, and cheapest way to build a mailing list is to write down the name, complete address, and telephone number of every customer who walks into your store. Of course, if you own a fast-food franchise where hundreds run in and out every hour, this is impractical. But if you run a retail outlet where the customer traffic is slower—a florist or bookstore, for example—you or your salespeople can politely ask for the customer's name and address and write it on the sales ticket. Or ask the customer to write it on a credit-card charge slip.

An equally easy way, and one more motivating to the customer, is to hold a contest, drawing, or raffle if they're legal in your area. Every entrant will give a name, address, and phone number you can later compile into a mailing list. And you've doubled your advertising mileage. The event itself will help build traffic during slack periods, and make your name better known, if you do some public relations and promotion with the advertising for the event.

You can also build a list by using newspaper advertising. Include a coupon that requires name, address, and telephone number to be redeemed for a product or service discount. This too does double duty as a traffic builder.

To turn the names and addresses collected into a mailing list, simply transcribe them onto note cards, make photocopies of the credit slips or coupons, or enter them into a personal computer with a mailing list management program. Alphabetize the names and addresses to keep them in order.

When you have collected several hundred to a thousand or more names, begin to send these proven customers direct mail to encourage them to return to your store.

You can also use the list to do further market research surveys, to advertise a special promotion, to give away coupons or special premium items such as a calendar imprinted with your name, or simply to send holiday greetings, which will remind people about you at a time when they are likely to shop.

Use the slack periods to add to your list using telephone directories, local club membership rosters or chamber of commerce listings, city directories—in short, any source of the names of your potential customers.

Remember, however, that your goal is to make your mailing list as specific as possible. You want only the names of actual customers or people who are very likely to become customers. Why? You want the biggest return possible on your investment in sending out direct-mail solicitations. Direct mail can be relatively expensive (up to several hundred dollars per 1,000 letters), and the rate of return can be very low (only a few percent of the people on the list may redeem coupons or take advantage of special offers).

Targeting is mandatory to avoid the wasteful possibility that you will try to sell aluminum siding to apartment dwellers. Everyone has had that happen to him. Decide it won't be with your money.

Methods #2 & #3: Take to the Streets

Using Handouts Effectively. A second, very inexpensive yet effective, way to attract customers is to give away handouts on street corners, at your shopping center, or along the mall if this practice is approved by the center or mall owner and by local ordinance. For example, in New York City, the major fast-food franchises and exercise salons have long distributed on the street corners coupons and handouts announcing the daily or weekly special. Some of them use actors in bear or chicken costumes—even in jaded Gotham—and it works.

These handouts are usually very inexpensively, yet attractively, printed. Adding coupons to the flyer can boost impulse buying and customer traffic through your store.

Door Stuffers. A similar approach for franchises in suburban areas where foot traffic is low is stuffing doors with brochures, pamphlets, coupons, one-page catalogs, or lists of weekly specials. Use family members to do this during the afternoons or weekends, or pay a distribution service to do it for you. However, if you pay a service, it may put your advertisement in a plastic bag with many other handouts, and your results may not be as good as when you distribute it yourself. This method is time-consuming, but it remains a good way to blanket a neighborhood. *Caution:* Do *not* put the handouts in the mailbox. This is illegal, and the U.S. Postal Service could have you arrested for it.

A variation of the door-stuffer routine is putting handouts on wind-shields of cars parked in shopping centers or mall lots, or parked along the side of the road. This technique, however, is annoying to many people, and often has negative results. The best way to use this technique is if your store is in the mall where you put the handouts, or you sell automotive products or services. For some reason, people do not mind having car-oriented flyers stuck on their cars, while they resent car flyers for almost everything else. Adding a coupon to the flyer, for any business, will sweeten the pot.

Method #4: Work the Phones

Telemarketing is a fancy name for selling by telephone. It is likely your franchisor has developed or can get for you several effective telephone sales pitches related to your products and services. You can train your sales staff to make the calls during the day, get your family to help at night, or hire housewives or students at the minimum wage to make the calls. However, it is not a good idea to do this without professional assistance, so go to your franchisor first. Your local telephone company should also have telemarketing specialists on staff who will train you free or for a small charge.

Do not use this method if you have to pay per-call charges or make long-distance calls. The returns may simply not be worth the expense.

Method #5: Dress a Window

An often overlooked advertising medium is the store window itself. A recently opened video franchise outlet in a Connecticut suburb made this mistake. After a month in business, which depended on drive-in traffic, it had not a single large sign or poster advertising its selections—and some very "sexy" posters are available from the movie producers. It had one grand opening sign and one store name sign; that was it.

A better use of store windows is Burger King's practice of advertising its new menu choices, not only with signs, but with banners and bunting. Discount liquor stores and grocery stores also make very effective use of their store windows, as do most large department stores. Saks Fifth Avenue in New York City, for example, has window displays on three sides and changes each of them once a week. It keeps a revolving display of the latest fashions—men's and women's—attuned to the season and the upscale market from which its customers come.

Of course, Burger King has marketing experts to design its advertising windows; Saks employs window designers. You need not do anything on so grand a scale. But be sure that whatever you do, it is true to the character of your business, is attractive enough to entice people inside, and is changed often enough not to be boring.

The advertising "space" on your store windows is essentially free and the best space you have. Use it to generate walk-in traffic and impulse buying.

Keep Your "WITS" About You: A Simple, Powerful, Coordinated Ad Campaign

To get the maximum impact from your market research and advertising and sales promotion dollars and effort, you must coordinate them. This does not mean you should run "sales" continuously. In fact, running sales constantly—except in discount outlets that base their success on low prices, low service, and hyped advertising—can damage your image. Excessive sales may convince people you need money badly or are in financial difficulties. In fact, running more than two major seasonal sales a year could be a mistake.

However, you can run a successful, ongoing program of "weekly specials." A little-used but inexpensive program, WITS, coordinates window display, interior display, timing of ads, and suggestive selling.

To use WITS, simply choose a mixture of 10 or 12 strong-selling items. Each week, put into action a coordinated campaign pushing one of those products. Always use good sellers; never try to push stale or slow-selling goods with this program. Your goal is to reap the maximum return for your advertising expenditure, and trying to push a dog out the door will not achieve it.

First, design your advertising, even if it consists only of handouts, to emphasize each weekly special. Make sure the ads are printed, broadcast, received in the mail, or handed out at the beginning of the week, preferably Sunday or Monday. Use words such as *special value* or *weekly feature* in your ads, but use the same term consistently. Never call the event a "sale," though, or the products "discount" items. Although you may sell it for a few cents off, you just as well can sell the product at regular price.

Second, make the featured product the centerpiece of your window display. Use the window area that every customer sees, perhaps near the door, for this display. The display itself can be something as simple as a hand-painted poster or as creative as a custom-made moving display. What you use depends on your budget. But use the key words—*special, value, feature*—in the display. Put a copy of your advertising—a tear sheet from the newspaper or your direct-mail brochure, for example—in the display as well.

Third, using attractive signs, again with your tear sheet or brochure added, create an interior display that immediately grabs the customer's attention. This should be in the middle of the path customers follow as they enter your store and/or positioned so their line of sight cannot miss it. Whether it is a small stand near the cash register or a stack of boxes eight feet high, this is called a "point-of-purchase" (POP) display.

The interior display is a perfect place to use any special advertising bunting, banners, or posters your franchisor provides. Or ask the vendor of the product you are featuring if it provides any POP displays to which you can add your franchise logo.

Follow the KISS rule—"*keep it sweet and simple*"—in all four parts of the WITS program, but especially in the POP display. Cluttering the POP with too many messages or a garish display will distract the buyer's attention from the product.

And don't be like Mr. Whipple: Encourage customers to touch the product, use it, try it on, thumb through it. People are more likely to buy something with which they have made a personal connection. So do not stack the WITS product in a precarious heap, ready to collapse at the merest touch. This is a common error grocery stores continue to make to this day. In short, make your POP attractive and neat, but touchable.

Last but not least is the clincher of the WITS program: suggestive selling. These days, using courteous suggestive selling at the cash register is an essential tool for any franchisee. Of course, you do not strong-arm a customer, but politely ask, "Excuse me, sir. Have you noticed this week's special on running shoes? We have our top-of-the-line shoes available in many sizes and colors. Would you like to try on a pair?"

If the customer says no, let it go at that. But if the customer shows mild interest, ask probing questions such as, "Do you jog very often?" Use the opening to describe features and, more important, benefits. "This shoe was proved to last 30 percent longer than a similarly priced competitor; it will save you money in the long run," you might add. (*Hint:* The lasting power of the shoe is a *feature*. The fact that it will save money is a *benefit*.)

And always put a small sign next to the cash register, saying something like, "Have you asked about our special value of the week?" You and your staff could wear small buttons made up with the same question. An astoundingly successful weight loss and diet company (not a franchise but a distributorship) gained national attention with its simple: "Lose Weight Now? Ask Me How." campaign. The entrepreneurs who developed that program made tens of millions of dollars in one year.

A Proven and Popular WITS Program

Learning by experience is the best way; by example, second best. So before you begin your own WITS program, experience a successful example of a WITS program from the customer's side. Visit a random sample of movie theaters and watch how the counter help sells popcorn and sodas, undoubtedly the most popular refreshments at the movies. Many theaters today use a one-two "punch," beginning with interior displays and ending with suggestive selling to overcome the last little bit of resistance.

In many movie theaters, you will:

1. See a POP display advertising a popcorn and soda special as soon as the ticket taker tears your ticket.
2. See a small sign near the cash register, reinforcing the special and promoting the popcorn-soda combination.
3. Be asked by the counter help, politely: "Would you like the medium soda? It is only 10 cents more and a much better value." or "Would you like a super-size popcorn? You can get a large soda for only 50 cents with the super size."

Just in case you have resisted the purchase so far, as soon as you sit down, you will see slides advertising popcorn and sodas. The ad may even tell you that you still have time before the feature to get to the snack bar.

Movie theater owners do this because they make the highest percentage of profit from selling popcorn and sodas; with their WITS plans, they do better still. Follow the example of their success to design and implement your own WITS plan.

Using WITS to Move "Dead" Products

Many people err by using ad dollars to push slow-moving merchandise. Remember that "dead" products won't sell well at any price. Customers want to see new products, so your WITS plan must promote new, strong-selling products.

But you can move slow and dead merchandise as an adjunct to a WITS plan. Simply lower the price and display it near the WITS special. Interest will likely spill over, and you've got nothing to lose from that.

This plan has been worked by bookstores for years, especially the chains. For example, visit any modern bookstore chain, such as Waldenbooks or B. Dalton. As you come in the door, the best-sellers will seem to leap out to grab you. But immediately behind or next to the best-sellers, you will find a table of bargain books or remainders. The books on this table will usually be hardback copies of older best-sellers that have been published in paperback or picture books (*The Great Trains of South America*) selling for a fraction of their original retail prices. Most readers are suckers for these bargain-book tables. The whole plan enables them to increase the purchasing power of their book dollars; they get a best-seller and feel they are getting a good deal more reading with the remainders for just a little bit more.

Notice also that the same bookstore will have a POP of the best-selling paperbacks next to or underneath the cash register counter. And the counter will be filled with hot-selling and profitable items, such as Garfield bookmarks.

In midtown Manhattan, an Irish restaurant uses this same WITS technique on its menu. Entrées come with mashed potato and vegetable. However, printed in a leap-out box at the top of the menu is this statement: For a little bit more, a baked potato and fresh garden salad, $1.50. It's amazing how many people are willing to pay it, or maybe not. Baked potatoes and salad seem to go naturally with steak. And they still get the vegetable.

The Secrets of PR: Building the Image of Your Franchise

The last block in the foundation of your marketing program is public relations and promotion. A simple, well-planned public relations campaign can establish or enhance a positive image for your franchise in your community. McDonald's has garnered tens of millions of dollars of free advertising with its establishment and support of Ronald McDonald Houses for children recuperating from serious illnesses and for their families. This very worthwhile program is basically an offshoot of the hospice concept. A hospice provides a homelike setting in which seriously ill or dying people can live relatively normal lives while receiving the medical attention they require.

This doesn't mean you should mortgage the house and fund a day-care center or anything nearly as fabulous as the things franchisors can do. But you can create an enormous amount of positive impact by helping your community. It will, in turn, help your business, but there is certainly nothing wrong with doing good, especially if everyone benefits.

Of course, most franchises come with an established public image, and the franchisor will go to great lengths to maintain and improve this image. At your training sessions, you will undoubtedly be repeatedly encouraged to live by this image. The franchisor's own national and regional advertising and promotional campaigns will constantly reinforce this positive image for you.

But however much the franchisor does for you, you are still responsible for maintaining and boosting your own image in your own backyard. It is crucial to your long-term success.

Some franchises are household names, but most are not. You and your operation will be the first encounter most people will have with your franchise. The impression they get from you will be the way they will remember, possibly better even than the commercials on national television. A bad impression will not only harm you in the short run, but it will create a ripple effect, damaging the franchise's reputation in the long run.

The One-Word Solution

The solution to building an image is just one word, but it is a word many franchisees do not understand or act upon. That word is *promotion*. To build a positive image and maintain it requires that you pay close and constant attention to promoting yourself, your franchise, and your employees. Fortunately, promotion is simpler than advertising, and it can be lots more fun, too.

In any case, as soon as you open your doors, you will be given a chance to promote yourself, often while helping others. You will be surprised by how many representatives of community organizations show up as soon as you open for business. Of course, you will have to pick and choose which you prefer to support, but the key point is this: Always—in public—promote the good things about your town or neighborhood. Whether you do so in word and deed, or money as well, depends on your budget and which charities you personally feel comfortable helping.

But first and foremost, avoid negative political situations like the plague.

If you do not, you run the very real risk of dividing your customer base into those who agree with your politics and those who do not. Politics is a personal, sensitive area, and people who disagree with you will probably "vote" with their feet and their dollars.

Avoiding political conflict differs from working with the chamber of commerce or a local industry group to boost business fortunes. Even then, you must always "accentuate the positive," as the old song goes. You can and should still be involved politically—contribute to your favorite candidate and vote, but do it quietly. You may notice in the news reports that many large lobbying groups, especially those sponsored by business executives, contribute to all major political parties. They may give more to those candidates who vote in favor of business issues, but they rarely burn their bridges behind them. You can follow a similar path in your local political arena, spreading the wealth, but spreading it deeper in the directions you feel will benefit you most. But always do it without fanfare.

Getting Involved in Your Community

Next, make sure your franchise is a good neighbor. Don't allow things such as noisy garbage pickups to annoy your business neighbors and particularly people living near you, but do keep the garbage out of the street. If you run a fast-food restaurant, make sure the kids who hang out there remain well behaved. Sweep your sidewalk. Keep your plate glass shiny. Don't test your burglar alarm on Sunday morning at 4:00. Clean your vent filters regularly. Redecorate your exterior *before* it goes to seed. In short, follow the Golden Rule even when others don't.

Consider too the damage to your reputation that can occur from unneighborly acts outside your store. Avoid petty conflicts with neighbors and strangers. If you were the one to fly off the handle in a fender bender, calling the other fellow names, imagine the field day the local reporters could have with that—especially after they find out you own the local franchised auto body shop. Your franchisor wouldn't think much of it either.

Another opportunity in the community is sponsorship of a local sports team. Franchises have long led the way in helping Little Leagues, but you may find other ways to help, too. Perhaps there is a Special Olympics group in your area or a less well known activity, such as Double-Dutch Jump Rope, that would be very pleased with a $25 contribution. Be at the forefront of businesses helping with special occasions, such as sending a local team to a state, regional, or national championship.

Coordinate your charity giving with your regular advertising budget on appropriate occasions. Most local radio stations will broadcast such championship games or contests live. So you could run ads that mention how proud you are to support the team. That will definitely help build your image, and it will give the team a boost as well.

Consider also letting local groups use your facilities at a nominal rent, time and space allowing. Most nonprofit, self-help groups use rooms in churches or community centers, but their members will think highly of you if you let them use a spare dining room once a week for an hour for their meetings. Before doing this, however, do check to be sure your insurance policies cover use of the facilities in this manner.

Schools give you another excellent promotion avenue. For example, Junior Civitan, Key Club, and similar high school civic clubs are sponsored by their local adult counterparts. If you belong to Kiwanis, Lions, Rotary, Civitan, or another group, you can improve your image with the children (future customers) as well as their parents (today's customers) by working with them on fund-raisers or at least buying ads in their publications. If you have a parking lot, loan it to school groups for car washes, tag sales, cake sales, and other fund-raisers on Saturday mornings or holidays. Once again, make certain your insurance allows for such a use of the property.

After a while, you may never want to taste a Girl Scout cookie, a Civitan fruitcake, or Key Club candy again as long as you live. You can and should still buy their products, once you've started; share them with your employees, family, or even customers. By sharing them with customers, and letting local groups put up notices on a bulletin board or in windows, you publicize your neighborliness as much as you publicize the group's activity.

Keeping in mind two more old clichés will help you with promotion. First, remember that a picture is worth a thousand words—and maybe a thousand dollars in new business, particularly if the picture in question is of you and appears in the local paper. If you're attending a worthwhile event and the photographer wants to snap you, smile away.

Second, refuse to hide your light under a bushel. You work hard to run a good business, and you should get all due credit for it. For you to get that credit, however, other people have to know about it. Although word-of-mouth advertising helps, it's often up to you to give someone the word to spread. Don't be shy about telling the news media about awards you've won, either in business or personally.

Some inexperienced franchisees may feel that such open PR and promotion is somehow dishonest. This feeling is simply false. Look at it dispassionately if you have these tendencies. First, you will probably get involved in activities you like, whether Little League or the local theater group or arts council. That's not dishonest. You are associating with people you like, performing a service they want or need, and boosting your business at the same time. There are definite benefits to all concerned. Even if you occasionally feel compelled to contribute to a group with which you have little in common, you can still do yourself and your business some good, and you are certainly not doing them any harm.

In short, promotion offers opportunity to everyone. Use it.

Secrets of Attracting Media Coverage

Attracting media coverage is not as hard as it seems. You don't need a high-powered press agent to do it. Local newspapers are, in fact, very suspicious of the hard sell. The top secret of attracting media coverage is to remember that media people have a desperate need for "news"—something new and unusual, some unique event, some different discovery or invention, anything out of the ordinary that will catch the reader's eye. To understand this need for news, consider that the most often read parts of a newspaper are obituaries, horoscopes, weather, comics, and sports. The most popular news items concern celebrities, while local politics, national and international politics, and community news are way down the list.

So, to get significant press coverage requires that you think of a "hook," something new and unusual on which to hang your news story. You can get on the business pages or in local weeklies fairly easily with stories about new products, new processes, new consumer savings or credit plans, new public relations efforts, and the like.

Getting on the front pages and on local television usually requires news of significant breakthroughs in technology. Or if you can arrange a visit by a nationally known celebrity, that might do it. But remember, you can get attention with a celebrity only once in a while; if you bring one through each month, the local paper will say "Not you again" and ignore the story.

Remember too that it is up to you to bring any news to the attention of the local media. They have dozens of people, organizations, and events clamoring for their attention. So you have to persist with press releases, personal calls, and perhaps a personal visit with the editor. If you want good publicity from a local weekly, take the editor to lunch and keep in touch every few months with a card or phone call. If you want good publicity in a daily newspaper, approach the managing editor or business editor in a professional and straightforward manner. Staff members of daily newspapers are often prevented by management from accepting lunch, no matter how innocent, in order to avoid potential conflict of interest charges. Weeklies and magazines generally do not operate under these strictures. Tailor your approach to the receptivity of your audience.

When you meet the editors, if you have any special expertise or knowledge about an important local issue, volunteer to give it to them. Become a sort of unpaid consultant in your field; your contributions will very likely be acknowledged, one way or another, in print. And that's more important to you than a few dollars of straight pay.

What are the possibilities in this? If you sell products or services that affect people's business success, health and well-being, or family life, volunteer to write a semimonthly column or feature for the publication, or do a weekly broadcast on a local radio station, or do a guest appearance on local television. If you sell business services—accounting, for example—offer a family finance column. Cars are your trade? A Mrs. Fixit column might do well. It has been popular since 1980 for local computer-store owners to prepare columns on how to use personal computers. Franchisees in the restaurant business can write nutrition articles; sportswear store owners can offer exercising tips.

Be creative. Become in the public mind an acknowledged expert in your field of endeavor. You will be pleasantly surprised to find there are probably several local publications or broadcast outlets that will be glad to use your services.

Offer Free or Low-Cost Seminars

An offshoot of writing articles can be sponsoring educational seminars on subjects related to your franchise. Computer stores have even developed microcomputer training classes into profit centers since the demand for these services has outstripped the supply of competent instructors. Food franchises can teach nutrition; sportswear, exercise, and similar franchises can teach fitness practices; business service franchises can teach "Finance for the Nonaccountant" or "How to Prepare a Budget for Your Business"; auto repair services can teach people how to do basic emergency repairs—changing flat tires, for example; and so forth through every type of business. You can often charge a small fee to cover the cost of any materials you may want to hand out.

Finally, to make the most of your public relations and promotion efforts, you must coordinate them with the other pillars of your marketing foundation. For example, computer-store franchises use a WITS approach to advertise hot new products, give seminars and training sessions to introduce them to customers and the curious, and conduct PR campaigns to discuss these hot, new products in the local media. Coordinate and conquer!

Pace Yourself

But beware of overcommitment. There will be many demands on your time and money, especially after it becomes known you plan to be actively involved in your community. However, you would do well to budget your time and community promotion dollars as closely as you budget the rest of your finances. You can easily lose track of the main goal: running an increasingly profitable franchise.

Set aside an amount of time and money for public relations and community involvement in your advertising and promotion budget, and add to it gradually as your growth and profits allow. Manage that budget as you do every other line item, and check into the *bona fides* of groups with which you are not familiar. Ask for references, and call the local chamber of commerce, Better Business Bureau, or central charity organization before you give to a new group or charity. Many communities also require canvass-ers for charitable groups to carry identification cards or buy inexpensive permits. Ask to see them before you contribute. And don't be afraid to be firm if a group takes advantage of your neighborliness or abuses your property. Being a good neighbor does not mean being a pushover.

But it is unlikely you will have much trouble from most local groups or charities, so you can relax and enjoy the business and personal benefits of sharing your time and money with others. Being well respected and well known in your community is one of the best results—in addition to becom-ing affluent—owning a franchise can offer.

Summary of the Marketing Structure

Here is a summary of the steps to follow to build a profitable structure on your firm marketing foundation:

1. Identify your real customers with market research.
2. Track your best-selling products.
3. Plan your coordinated WITS program.
4. Coordinate your public relations and promotional program with your WITS plan.
5. Launch your coordinated efforts.
6. Measure results.
7. Follow through and be flexible, changing your program as results dictate, expanding or contracting it as seems best to fit your overall goal—profits.

12

Still the Second Sex: A Realistic Look at Franchising and Women

At the American Booksellers' Convention in Chicago in 1980, many of the women there—authors, publicists, even the few women publishers—wore buttons saying "59 cents." This was to publicize the fact that women, that year, were said to be making 59 cents for every dollar men made. I picked up one of the buttons and, though I'm not prone to wearing words and numbers on my body, inexplicably wore it, albeit with mixed feelings.

Until the advent of the women's movement, I had thought that, like men, women could make it on their own, using wits and skill and courage and knowledge. I always intended to do that. And for years I acted accordingly, and was frustrated to say the least. Why didn't it all work? I had read numerous books in my youth about reporters, private eyes, moguls, scientific geniuses (I particularly recall one named *Steinmetz, Genius of Light*), even knights. I identified with the protagonists completely.

I only recently concluded that the problem was that they were Men and I was Not. An ample analogy. Somethingness and Nothingness. For a while, I despaired. Could a Not reach its goals? How?

Reality told me that my goals would have to be different. Sure, I could set the goals of making lots of money. But I'd better do it in a field where I wouldn't be using half my energy simply staying alive, a field in which men would not knock me out of the box every time I spoke too loudly or was too smart or, God forbid, too right. A field, in short, men didn't care much about. Aha! Then, I could live the way I wanted to, not having to conform my rounded femaleness to the taut stringiness of the male. At least, not often.

I am not unique. In fact, I suspect I discovered all this later than most. In many businesses, especially in franchising, pink is still a "girl's" color. Indeed, it appears that Pink-Around-the-Collar is an indelible feature in franchising. How many women own Midas Muffler shops? How many, for that matter, own McDonald's? I do not know; there are no statistics kept on this subject. The Department of Commerce, which compiles extensive reports on franchising's impact on the economy, does not break down franchising into male and female occupational data statistics. Nor is the information available from the United States Department of Labor. So all there is to go on is gut feeling. But that's all right: Women are supposed to be intuitive.

In sum, as pertains to franchising and women, there is still a pink-collar ghetto. The symbolism of Mary Kay Ash's pink Cadillacs, perks for her best cosmetics distributors, is not lost. Indeed, there are dozens of franchises marketed to women as franchisees (although most of these accept males). Most of these woman-tailored opportunities require relatively low investments.

Earlier, I said that the lower the investment, the lower the final gross income would be. Although that's certainly true in male-dominated and mainstream franchises, many of the almost-for-women-only ones circumvent this rule—a factor greatly in their favor. For example, Jazzercise, Inc. asks only a $500 initial fee. It is payable in at least two portions, with accommodation often made for franchisees who have trouble with that. Income? Not bad. Having spoken to several of its franchisees, my own estimate is that the energetic ones in upscale territories net at least $15,000 a year out of a gross of about two-and-a-half times that. The return on investment is a whopping 3000 percent! (The franchise fee does not include equipment. This consists of a record player, microphone, and VCR, another $1,000 tops. And there is some expense for training. But it's minimal. Jazzercise tries to have monthly training for new recruits in regional locations. Some of the new people can even go home at night during the approximately four days of training. So at worst, we're talking about a return on investment of 1,500 percent. Who wouldn't take it?)

Jazzercise itself indicates that there may be as much as a $10,000 investment required, but that would include leasing a space and other extras most of their franchisees avoid by renting by-the-hour spaces such as school gymnasiums or civic centers.

Wendy DeVries, a Boynton Beach, Florida, Jazzercise franchisee, is one of the latter, and she put the attractions in a nutshell. "I love to dance, and I like to help people. With this, I can do both. It really is a great feeling to see all those logy bodies come into class after the winter holidays and watch as they get back in shape.

"And the timing is convenient for me. I can teach a morning class after my daughter goes to school. I can teach an evening one at 6 P.M. after my husband is home to take care of her, and he can either feed her, or we can all eat together at 7:30. My husband is a fireman, so he often gets two days off in a row. With my middays free, we can do things—go to the beach, work on the house, shop, go to an afternoon movie.

"Of course, the work I do on stage in the seven classes a week I teach is not all of it. You're expected to put in 40 hours a week, and I generally do. There's paperwork, and learning new routines, which come to me by videotape. And Jazzercise in this area does volunteer work, too. We take phone calls for the public TV station during their membership drives. But that also helps get us recognition, which helps bring in new clients.

"I'm very happy with it. It sure beats working in an office, where I was so bored I just wanted to cry most of the time. I never could have had this house if I were still working for someone else.

[The DeVries family has recently moved to a custom home they built themselves; Wendy's income from the franchise helped, as did being able to arrange her hours to help her husband work on it.]

"And then, of course, there are the intangible assets. For instance, I'm working now—getting publicity—sitting with you in my own living room, eating my own cheese and crackers," she added, with a Cheshire-cat smile.

This sounds like an advertisement for Jazzercise. It isn't; but it is undoubtedly certain that of true franchises, this one is the least expensive to get into that I've found, and returns the greatest percentage on investment I've ever come across. Nonfranchise opportunities—distributorships such as Avon and Mary Kay—have been known to do as well too. But then they're not, strictly speaking, franchises. The drawback to Jazzercise is that you need special abilities to run one. Wendy has had some formal dance training (and continues to take classes when she can), and she also works out on her own and stays in good shape. The franchisor doesn't require specialized dance or athletic background but obviously, one needs to be in shape to conduct all those classes and to do it right.

In any case, Jazzercise is one of the fastest-growing franchises—and the market usually is not wrong. In 1984, it opened 344 new territories, for a total of 2,770 units today. It was number two in *Venture* magazine's top ten franchisors. The others were, number one, Domino's Pizza, and from three to ten, in order: Hardee's Food Systems, Rainbow International, Burger King, Adventureland Video, Jani-King, Baskin-Robbins, National Video, and Ugly Duckling Rent-A-Car. (McDonald's, Wendy's, Dunkin' Donuts, Mister Donut, and Taco Bell, which may be assumed to be fast-growing as well, refused to take part in the magazine's poll.)

Except for Jazzercise, what's the common denominator in these businesses? Big bucks. To get in, that is. They are all in the male-dominated fast-food, heavy cleaning, video, or automotive franchises. Take a look at their initial investments, including franchise fee and other costs:

> Domino's: $55,700–$131,500
> Hardee's: $750,000
> Rainbow: $15,000
> Burger King: $283,500
> Adventureland Video: $15,500
> Jani-King: $2,500–$6,000 (a relative bargain!)
> Baskin-Robbins: $50,000–$100,000
> National Video: $67,300–$165,000
> Ugly Duckling Rent-A-Car: $4,000–$14,500, plus premises, fleet of
>   vehicles, and working capital

There are precious few women who could take that kind of capital out of the food budget; those who could probably wouldn't want to. They could invest the money in cleaner stuff—stocks and bonds or even use it to buy in as silent partners—for a decent return. The fact is, most working women have families to think about. The world offers no gender utopias, and most of them have to think about who will make dinner (they will), who will do the ironing, errand running, and so on. They will. Spending the time needed to run any of those enterprises, even if they could afford the entry fee, would likely make them into one-parent families pretty quickly.

In fact, women have lately been better at founding franchises than buying them. A California woman whose chocolate chip cookies were smashing founded her own franchise. Jazzercise's founder is a former professional dancer who began her exercise system partially to keep herself in shape after she married. Another woman founded a franchise because she could find no decent lingerie at affordable prices and figured others were in the same boat. One found that it was hard for mothers of tots to get away to exercise; she capitalized on that and the interest in early childhood education to begin a franchise that offers exercise sessions to both simultaneously. I have written about each of these franchises in the past year. At least two of them seem to have folded, however. Female-owned businesses are subject to at least the same failure rate as male-owned ones, it seems.

Of course, that's no wonder. Women are often undercapitalized. Earlier, I pointed out that a lack of capital could be overcome with good management. That is true, in general, but perhaps less true for women. Despite the breakthroughs, women founding or buying franchises are less likely than men to have extensive management experience. Add to that their greater problems in getting bank loans, and you have a prescription for very hard sledding at best.

There are, to be sure, laws governing the granting of loans. It is my personal feeling that any law that is made will give rise to a hundred ways around it. With these laws, it isn't even hard. Remember that women now make only 53 cents for every dollar of male income—a spectacular drop in just six years—and so there is a built-in bias against their getting the business loans and financing they need.

Jazzercise, successful as it is and as valuable to both its franchisees and clients, is unfortunately an apt symbol of the continuing ghettoization of women in the workforce. For years, women like Wendy DeVries, who wanted satisyfing, lucrative work but had young families, had direct selling to fall back on. Avon and Mary Kay and a few others—which were mainly distributorships rather than franchises and thus demanded no initial investment to speak of—were their lifeblood. Today, because 64 percent of all women between the ages of 18 and 44 are working, this avenue is all but closed off. Women are no longer home: How can selling door-to-door work? Indeed, those who continue to succeed in the cosmetic-selling business do so by selling during work hours on company premises.

Today, Jazzercise and its counterparts are catering to women's needs the same way Avon and the other "war paint" companies once did. But today's woman wants to be beautiful from the inside out, molding the body with exercise rather than the cheekbones with makeup. The exercise classes are a way to overcome the boredom and ennui of the dead-end jobs so many are stuck in. It is a way to get away from Mr. Dad and the kids for a while and cheaply. It is a way to relieve the stress of juggling business and "Mommy" demands as cosmetics were a way to put a face on for a world, even if one seldom saw that world. Female franchising (including distributorships) has segued from the truly fanciful to the grindingly realistic.

The evidence is overwhelming. Franchising is the last stand of the pink-collar ghetto. What does this mean to you, if you are a woman who wants to go into franchising? The same thing life means: Decide what you want, set your goals, and go after them. No excuses, no fair crying foul, despite the fact that unfairness, in reality, exists. If you want a fast-food outlet, go after it. But be realistic. If you must, get your husband to cosign, but make sure those papers are drawn up with you as at least an equal partner and as inheritor, either in death or divorce.

Or set your sights lower at first, raising them as your experience and capital increase. There is no reason you couldn't begin with Jazzercise and, if your needs and finances rise to greater heights, "trade up" in a few years to a full-fledged studio, such as Elaine Powers. (Elaine Powers Figure Salons require a franchise fee of $15,000, with needed capital totaling about $65,000.) Although the dollars you earn from this may be larger, remember that the return on investment may be lower. *Entrepreneur* magazine assigns ratings to franchises on the basis of rates of return on investment. The higher the rating, the better the income to investment ratio will be. For example, *Entrepreneur* gives Elaine Powers a rating of 643; Jazzercise gets 1,120, a conservative figure that comes close to my locally developed estimate of 1,500.)

The last word is this: Profit is the aim of anyone going into business for herself, whether on her own or through franchising. The bottom line is the bottom line. If you can reach it in a pink collar, why not? It's a flattering shade for most women in any case. And in this case, it goes well with "long green."

Below is a listing of franchises that offer either relatively low investments, flexible arrangements as to time spent, negotiable requirements for space, fairly decent return on investment, help with financing, or a combination of some or all of these. Mainly women-oriented, here are the pick of the pinks:

- Nu-Concept Body Wrap, 603 Cleveland Street, Elyria, OH 44035; body wrapping materials and training, $2,500 franchise fee, up to $10,000 total investment, help with financing available.
- Nails 'n' Lashes Studio, 4801 Keele Street, #60 Downsview, Ontario, Canada M3J 3A4; $5,000–$15,000 franchise fee, $10,000–$75,000 initial investment. No help with financing, but the whole thing can be done for less than $15,000.
- Sun Tan/Tanarama, 5475 Crestview, Memphis, TN 38134; tanning salons, no franchise fee, total investment $10,000 and up, no financing. However, it is rated by *Entrepreneur* magazine at 2,640. On the other hand, tanning parlors, along with hair-care franchises, are on the Department of Commerce's "beware" list. The former are fad and seasonal businesses, and there may be problems later with the safety approval and regulation of equipment. The latter? There's a huge glut of hair-care outlets.
- Our Weigh, 3340 Poplar Avenue, #G110, Memphis, TN 38111; weight reduction program, no franchise fee, up to $10,000 investment, no help with financing.
- Great Earth Vitamin Stores, 1801 Parkcourt Place, Bldg. A, Santa Ana, CA 92701; vitamin and mineral supplements, initial investment $15,000, total investment up to $70,000. This is fairly hefty to be a "pick," but the firm does offer help with financing. The ratio rating is 478, not bad.
- Lomma Championship Miniature Golf, 1120 S. Washington, Scranton, PA 18505; no franchise fee, up to $10,000 investment. *Notes:* This is portable, can be operated on cheap rented land, run by teenagers or family members, and help with financing is available.

- Mini-Golf, 202 Bridge St., Jessup, PA 18434; similar to above.
- Mr. Build, 2114 N. Broadway, Santa Ana, CA 92706; commercial, home construction and repair, $4,000–$7,000 franchise fee, $10,000 total capital, and the company offers help with financing. It has a quite respectable 634 rating. But what's it doing among pink-collar picks? Remember, pink collars are also turning blue, with more and more women becoming skilled in the construction trades. Today too, with more and more mechanical help in building, it is often brains and manual dexterity that take precedence over brawn. Besides, you can get a muscular male helper with no skills pretty inexpensively; you be the master and make him the apprentice.
- Almost Heaven Hot Tubs, Rt. 5 FF, Renick, WV 24966; hot tubs, spas, saunas, and whirlpools, no franchise fee, up to $10,000 initial cash needed. Of course, there's no financing help since there's no franchise fee, but this is rated at 938, very nice. And these things are modular for easy installation. A nice adjunct to the building-trades opportunity above.
- Sexton Educational Centers, 34 W. 32nd Street, New York, NY 10001; graduate-test preparation, $5,000 franchise fee, $10,000–$75,000 further investment, help with financing available, very good return on investment possible.
- Arthur Murray Dance Studios, 1077 Ponce de Leon Blvd., Coral Gables, FL 33134; no franchise fee, additional investment ranges from $10,000 to $75,000, no financing help available, but the return on investment can be very good to excellent.
- Chem Clean Furniture Restoration, P.O. Box 423, Union, ME 04862; furniture stripping, no franchise fee, up to $10,000 additional financing needed, with which this franchisor will help. However, only a modest return on investment is predicted for this one.
- Cleanmark, 185 Green's Farms Road, Westport, CT, 06880; carpet and furniture cleaning and janitorial services, $2,300 franchise fee, $9,500 additional investment, and the company will help with financing. It is possible to make a good return on investment. But there is a caution: The firm had only one company-owned and three franchise units in operation in 1985.
- The Maids International, 5015 Underwood Avenue, Omaha, NE 68132; maid service, $7,500–$9,500 franchise fee, $10,000–$100,000 additional investment, but the company does help with financing. However, it shows only a moderate return on investment ratio.
- Sara Care Sitting Services, 1200 Golden Key Circle, #227, El Paso, TX 79925; full range of "sitting services," $10,500 franchise fee, $10,000–$75,000 additional cash needed. The company will help

with financing, but offers a very low return on investment, it seems. Why is it here? It's a franchise anyone who can "sit" or even train others to "sit" can do. No trouble fitting that into a schedule; most women get lots of practice both sitting and telling others to sit. May as well make money from it.

This is by no means a complete list of the pink-collar franchises available. These are merely a few of the particularly low investment ones that offer a fair or better rate of return. For a more complete listing, see Chapter 14.

Part III

The Best Franchises in the United States

13

The Ratings Game: How to Rate a Franchise *Before* You Buy

One question often asked about franchises is how you can quickly and easily tell whether a franchise is worth buying. As this book shows, there is no quick or easy way to make a decision, nor should you. But there are thousands of franchises available, and prospective franchisees do need a relatively straightforward way to begin to evaluate a franchise. This chapter describes a simple (but by no means foolproof) rating system with which you can *begin* your search for a franchise that will suit your taste and budget.

It is based on nine factors, ranging from the number of years in business to whether the franchise company offers financing to franchisees. Frankly, these nine are weighted toward the older, larger, and more successful franchises. But in two key factors—amount of franchise fee and minimum capital required—the system is weighted toward the small investor.

To determine how well a franchise in which you are interested scores, add the points it earns for each factor. There is no maximum score because the highest score depends on how many franchises a company offers, although McDonald's scores almost 1,100 points. The minimum score would be 9 points.

Instead of going on a straight point basis to find the best franchise, it is better to use the point scores and ratings to compare franchises within categories.

In fact, it is better used as a tool to compare franchises within one category and across factors. Obtain the needed information for five to ten franchises in one category of franchise. Compute their scores under this rating system. Then, instead of comparing their final totals, compare them across factors—for example, Company X's fee to capital ratio compared to Company Y's and so forth. This will give you a better idea of what is most important to you, and then you can give those factors the consideration they deserve.

In brief, here are the nine factors and how they are weighted and scored:

1. *Years in business.* One point for every year in business and one point for every year franchises have been offered. For example, McDonald's has been in business and offering franchises since 1955, so it gets 60 points (30 for each category) in 1985.

2. *Number of franchises.* One point for every 10 franchises, with one point given to small or new firms with fewer than 10 franchises. This is weighted toward the large franchises—for example, Servicemaster gets 205 points for its 2,050 franchises (at the end of 1984)—but the rating leans less heavily toward the large franchises than a one point per franchise method.

3. *Minimum franchise fee.* This category is weighted toward the small investor and gives ten points to the franchises with the lowest fee. The table is set like this:

Points	Franchise Fee
10	$0 to $10,000
9	$10,001 to $15,000
8	$15,001 to $20,000
7	$20,001 to $30,000
6	$30,001 to $40,000
5	$40,001 to $50,000
4	$50,001 to $60,000
3	$60,001 to $75,000
2	$75,001 to $100,000
1	$100,001 or more

4. *Minimum capital required.* This does not include the franchise fee, but includes the estimated or required minimum amount of cash and financing needed to begin the franchise operation. It too is weighted toward the small investor, with the less expensive operations getting more points.

Points	Minimum Capital Required
10	$0 to $25,000
9	$25,001 to $35,000
8	$35,001 to $50,000
7	$50,001 to $75,000

6	$75,001 to $100,000
5	$100,001 to $125,000
4	$125,001 to $150,000
3	$150,001 to $200,000
2	$200,001 to $300,000
1	more than $300,001

5. *Franchise fee as a percentage of minimum capital required.* This factor may seem somewhat complicated, but it simply rates how small the franchise fee is. The lower the franchise fee is compared to the capital required, the more money you have to spend to start your franchise. For example, if a franchise company charges a $10,000 franchise fee and requires $100,000 capital, then the ratio is 10 percent, a low amount. Your total investment would be $110,000. If another franchise company charged a fee of $10,000, and required only $10,000 in additional capital, you would have to spend half of your cash on the fee, and you could only put half into the operation. Admittedly, this is somewhat weighted to the expensive operations, such as fast-food restaurants, that require a lot of capital, and it somewhat penalizes firms with low total startup costs.

Points	Percentage
10	0 to 10%
9	11 to 20%
8	21 to 30%
7	31 to 40%
6	41 to 50%
5	51 to 60%
4	61 to 70%
3	71 to 80%
2	81 to 90%
1	91 to 100%

6. *Company-owned franchises as a percentage of the total.* I believe that the fewer company-owned operations there are, the better, and this category is weighted toward those franchise companies with the fewest company-owned operations. If a franchisor's profits are coming from actual franchise operations, it will tend to pay more attention to the franchisee.

Points	Percentage
10	0 to 10%
9	11 to 20%
8	21 to 30%

7	31 to 40%
6	41 to 50%
5	51 to 60%
4	61 to 70%
3	71 to 80%
2	81 to 90%
1	91 to 100%

7. *Growth patterns*. This gives one point for each new franchise opened between 1983 and 1984. Final figures for 1985 were not available. This seems to favor the large franchisors, unless a particular franchise company actually reduced the number of franchises it has. Then this factor is severely weighted against that company, since one point is *deducted* for each franchise that was closed.

8. *Total royalty fees*. This factor is weighted toward those franchise companies that charge the smallest amount of *total* royalties and includes monthly royalties and payments, advertising royalties, and any other payment by the franchisee to the parent franchisor. The total is given as a percentage of the monthly gross profit.

Points	Total Royalties/Month
10	0–1 percent
9	2–3 percent
8	4–5 percent
7	6–7 percent
6	8–9 percent
5	10–11 percent
4	12–13 percent
3	14–15 percent
2	16–17 percent
1	18 or more percent

9. *Financing provided*. This factor gives five points to a franchise company that may provide financial assistance to a franchisee. If it does not provide financing, it does not receive any points.

Examples. Using this rating system, McDonald's receives a total of 1,093 points, with these points for each factor: (1) 60 points for combined years in business; (2) 596 (based on 5,959 active franchises at the end of 1984); (3) 9 points for a relatively low franchise fee; (4) 1 point for a very high capital requirement; (5) 10 points for a very good ratio of franchise fee to capital required; (6) 8 points for a very good ratio of company-owned outlets compared to franchisee-owned; (7) 407 points for adding that many new franchises during 1984; (8) 2 points for a high combined royalty fee; and (9) no points for not providing financing.

McDonald's, of course, has one of the highest ratings of all available franchises. Even most of the best do not receive ratings above 1,000, but a leading franchise should definitely score above 100. Here are examples of the ratings of several more of the best franchises: Servicemaster, Taylor Rental Center, and Jazzercise.

Servicemaster scores 153 points, a very respectable rating, broken down this way: 74 points for being in business 37 years and offering franchises for the same 37 years; 201 points for having 2,005 operating franchises; 10 points for its low $9,750 fee; 10 points for its low $10,000 capital requirement; only 1 point because the ratio of franchise fee to capital (97.5 percent) is so high; 10 points for having *no* company-owned franchises; minus 163 points for losing that many franchises between 1983 and 1984; 5 points for its 7–10 percent royalty; and 5 points for offering financing.

Taylor Rental Center scores 141 points, also a respectable rating: 63 points for being in business 40 years, and offering franchises for 23 years; 55 points for a total of 545 franchises; 7 points for its $20,000 franchise fee; 6 points for its $75,000 and up capital requirement; 8 points for its relatively low (26.7 percent) ratio of franchise fee to capital; 10 points for its low number of company-owned outlets (20 of 545); minus 14 points for losing that many franchises between 1983 and 1984; 6 points for its variable royalty rate; and no points for not offering financing.

Jazzercise, a relatively new and rapidly growing franchise mostly for women, scores 255 points: 16 points for being in business 13 years and franchising for 3 years; 28 points for its 2,770 franchises; 10 points for its very low $500 franchise fee; 10 points for its less than $10,000 capital requirement; 10 points for the very low fee to capital (5 percent) ratio; 10 points for having *no* company-owned franchises; plus 170 points for adding that many new franchises between 1983 and 1984; only 1 point for a very high 30 percent royalty; and no points because it does not offer financing.

Try this system on any franchise in which you have a budding interest. It is *not* a substitute for serious, careful, and lengthy investigation into purchasing a specific franchise. It is a simple guide to help point you in the right direction.

14

The Best Franchises in the United States

This special chapter rates the best franchises in the United States: *by category*. People want to know the best available franchise in their field of interest. Many rating systems list the best overall franchises, leaving many categories out. This makes it difficult for people *not* interested in the most popular or best-established franchises, such as the fast-food chains, to determine the best franchise to match their interests, such as advertising, travel, or educational products. These categories also appeal more to women.

For those people searching for less expensive franchises, a list of the best inexpensive franchise opportunities is given at the end of this chapter.

The Best Franchises in the United States

Note: The number of franchises equals the total as of the end of 1984, the time for which complete figures were available.

Category: Advertising
Name: Money Mailer
Address: 15472 Chemical Lane, Huntington Beach, CA 92649
Product/service: Cooperative direct-mail marketing
Year Began Franchising: 1980
Number of Franchises: 84
  a. Individual owners: ALL
  b. Company-owned: 0
Minimum Franchise Fee: $17,500
Minimum Capital Required: $10,000-$75,000
Total Royalty/Fees: 5%
  a. Monthly percentage: 0
  b. Advertising fee: 5%
Financing Available: NO

Category: Auto and Truck Rental
Name: Budget Rent-A-Car
Address: 200 North Michigan Avenue, Chicago, IL 60601
Product/service: Auto and truck rentals
Year Began Franchising: 1960
Number of Franchises: 1,012
  a. Individual owners: 1,000
  b. Company-owned: 12
Minimum Franchise Fee: $10,000
Minimum Capital Required: $10,000-$75,000
Total Royalty/Fees: 7.5%
  a. Monthly Percentage: 7.5%
  b. Advertising Fee: 0
Financing Available: NO

Category: Auto and Truck Rental
Name: National Car Rental
Address: 7700 France Avenue South, Minneapolis, MN 55435
Product/service: Auto and van rentals
Year Began Franchising: 1947
Number of Franchises: 971
  a. Individual owners: 646
  b. Company-owned: 325
Minimum Franchise Fee: Variable
Minimum Capital Required: Variable
Total Royalty/Fees: 6.8%
  a. Monthly percentage: 5.3%
  b. Advertising fee: 1.5%
Financing Available: NO

Category: Auto and Truck Rental
Name: Avis Rent-A-Car
Address: 900 Old Country Road, Garden City, NY 11530
Product/service: Auto rentals
Year Began Franchising: 1949
Number of Franchises: 3,500
  a. Individual owners: 2,300
  b. Company-owned: 1,200
Minimum Franchise Fee: Variable
Minimum Capital Required: Variable
Total Royalty/Fees: Variable
  a. Monthly percentage: —
  b. Advertising fee: —
Financing Available: NO

Category: Auto and Truck Rental
Name: American International Rent-a-Car
Address: 4241 Sigma Road, Dallas, TX 75234
Product/service: Auto rentals
Year Began Franchising: 1969
Number of Franchises: 1,400
  a. Individual owners: ALL
  b. Company-owned: 0
Minimum Franchise Fee: $5,000
Minimum Capital Required: $10,000-$75,000
Total Royalty/Fees: 2% minimum
  a. Monthly percentage: 2% minimum
  b. Advertising fee: 0
Financing Available: NO

Category: Auto and Truck Rental
Name: Dollar Systems
Address: 6141 West Century Boulevard, Los Angeles, CA 90045
Product/service: Auto and truck rentals
Year Began Franchising: 1966
Number of Franchises: 414
  a. Individual owners: 400
  b. Company-owned: 14
Minimum Franchise Fee: $7,500
Minimum Capital Required: Variable
Total Royalty/Fees: 9%
  a. Monthly percentage: 9%
  b. Advertising fee: 0
Financing Available: NO

Category: Auto and Truck Rental
Name: Rent-A-Wreck
Address: 1089 Wilshire Boulevard, Suite 1260, Los Angeles, CA 90024
Product/service: Used-car rentals
Year Began Franchising: 1977
Number of Franchises: 300
  a. Individual owners: 245
  b. Company-owned: 55
Minimum Franchise Fee: $3,000
Minimum Capital Required: $76,000 or more
Total Royalty/Fees: Per-car basis
  a. Monthly percentage: $15 per car per month
  b. Advertising fee: $5 per car per month
Financing Available: NO

Category: Auto and Truck Rental
Name: Thrifty Rent-a-Car System
Address: P.O. Box 35250, Tulsa, OK 74153
Product/service: Auto rentals
Year Began Franchising: 1964
Number of Franchises: 460
    a. Individual owners: 457
    b. Company-owned: 3
Minimum Franchise Fee: $7,500
Minimum Capital Required: $10,000-$75,000
Total Royalty/Fees: 8%
    a. Monthly percentage: 5%
    b. Advertising fee: 3%
Financing Available: YES

Category: Auto Parts and Services—Auto Parts Stores
Name: Western Auto
Address: 2107 Grand Avenue, Kansas City, MO 64108
Product/service: Automotive parts and home merchandise
Year Began Franchising: 1935
Number of Franchises: 2,455
    a. Individual owners: 2,238
    b. Company-owned: 217
Minimum Franchise Fee: 0
Minimum Capital Required: At least $75,000
Total Royalty/Fees: 0
    a. Monthly percentage: 0
    b. Advertising fee: 0
Financing Available: YES

Category: Auto Parts and Services—Automobile/Truck Sales
Name: TRIEX
Address: 701 North Parkcenter Drive, Suite 200, Santa Ana, CA 92705
Product/service: Used-auto sales and service
Year Began Franchising: 1982
Number of Franchises: 350
    a. Individual owners: 211
    b. Company-owned: 139
Minimum Franchise Fee: $10,000
Minimum Capital Required: Up to $75,000
Total Royalty/Fees: $800 per month
    a. Monthly percentage: $800 per month
    b. Advertising fee: 0
Financing Available: YES

Category: Auto Parts and Services—Body Work, Painting, and Rustproofing
Name: MAACO Auto Painting and Bodyworks
Address: 381 Brooks Road, King of Prussia, PA 19406
Product/service: Car painting and body shops
Year Began Franchising: 1972
Number of Franchises: 360
  a. Individual owners: ALL
  b. Company-owned: 0
Minimum Franchise Fee: $15,000
Minimum Capital Required: $115,000
Total Royalty/Fees: 8% and weekly ad fee
  a. Monthly percentage: 8%
  b. Advertising fee: $500 per week
Financing Available: NO

Category: Auto Parts and Services—Body Work, Painting, and Rustproofing
Name: Ziebart Appearance and Protection Services
Address: 1290 East Maple Road, Troy, MI 48007
Product/service: Rust protection and car appearance shops
Year Began Franchising: 1962
Number of Franchises: 371
  a. Individual owners: 358
  b. Company-owned: 13
Minimum Franchise Fee: $15,000
Minimum Capital Required: $40,000
Total Royalty/Fees: 13%
  a. Monthly percentage: 8%
  b. Advertising fee: 5%
Financing Available: NO

Category: Auto Parts and Services—Brakes and Mufflers
Name: Midas Muffler Shops
Address: 225 North Michigan Avenue, Chicago, IL 60601
Product/service: Mufflers, brakes, and shock absorber installation
Year Began Franchising: 1956
Number of Franchises: 1,831
  a. Individual owners: 1,795
  b. Company-owned: 36
Minimum Franchise Fee: $10,000
Minimum Capital Required: $142,000 minimum
Total Royalty/Fees: 10%
  a. Monthly percentage: 5%
  b. Advertising fee: 5%
Financing Available: NO

Category: Auto Parts and Services—Brakes and Mufflers
Name: Meineke Discount Mufflers
Address: 12013 Wilcrest, Houston, TX 77031
Product/service: Mufflers, exhaust systems, and shock absorbers
Year Began Franchising: 1972
Number of Franchises: 394
   a. Individual owners: 393
   b. Company-owned: 1
Minimum Franchise Fee: $20,000
Minimum Capital Required: $75,000 and up
Total Royalty/Fees: 8%
   a. Monthly percentage: 7%
   b. Advertising fee: 1%
Financing Available: NO

Category: Auto Parts and Services—Car Washes
Name: Hanna Car Wash
Address: 2000 South East Hanna Drive, Portland, OR 97222
Product/service: Automatic car washes and buildings
Year Began Franchising: 1955
Number of Franchises: 7,915
   a. Individual owners: 7,888
   b. Company-owned: 27
Minimum Franchise Fee: $24,000
Minimum Capital Required: Up to $75,000
Total Royalty/Fees: 5%
   a. Monthly percentage: 3%
   b. Advertising fee: 2%
Financing Available: YES

Category: Auto Parts and Services—Lubrication and Oil Changes
Name: Jiffy Lube
Address: 7008 Security Blvd., Baltimore, MD 21207
Product/service: Quick oil changes and lube jobs
Year Began Franchising: 1980
Number of Franchises: 143
   a. Individual owners: 142
   b. Company-owned: 1
Minimum Franchise Fee: $25,000
Minimum Capital Required: $75,000 or more
Total Royalty/Fees: 5%
   a. Monthly percentage: 5%
   b. Advertising fee: 0
Financing Available: NO

Category: Auto Parts and Services—Repairs
Name: Great Bear Automotive Centers
Address: 97-45 Queens Blvd., Rego Park, NY 11374
Product/service: Auto service and repairs
Year Began Franchising: 1947
Number of Franchises: 60
    a. Individual owners: ALL
    b. Company-owned: 0
Minimum Franchise Fee: $15,000
Minimum Capital Required: $75,000 or more
Total Royalty/Fees: 10%
    a. Monthly percentage: 5%
    b. Advertising fee: 5%
Financing Available: NO

Category: Auto Parts and Services—Tires and Tire Retreading
Name: B. F. Goodrich
Address: 500 South Main Street, Akron, OH 44318
Product/service: Tire sales and installation
Year Began Franchising: 1925
Number of Franchises: More than 2,000
    a. Individual owners: ALL
    b. Company-owned: 0
Minimum Franchise Fee: 0
Minimum Capital Required: Variable
Total Royalty/Fees: 0
    a. Monthly percentage: 0
    b. Advertising fee: 0
Financing Available: NO

Category: Auto Parts and Services—Tires and Tire Retreading
Name: Goodyear Tire Centers
Address: 1144 East Market Street, Akron, OH 44316
Product/service: Tire sales and auto service
Year Began Franchising: 1968
Number of Franchises: 536
    a. Individual owners: ALL
    b. Company-owned: 0
Minimum Franchise Fee: 0
Minimum Capital Required: $50,000 or more
Total Royalty/Fees: 1.5%
    a. Monthly percentage: 1.5%
    b. Advertising fee: 0
Financing Available: YES

Category: Auto Parts and Services—Transmission Services
Name: AAMCO Transmissions
Address: One Presidential Blvd., Bala-Cynwyd, PA 19004
Product/service: Transmission repairs and installation
Year Began Franchising: 1963
Number of Franchises: 940
    a. Individual owners: ALL
    b. Company-owned: 0
Minimum Franchise Fee: $22,500
Minimum Capital Required: About $75,000
Total Royalty/Fees: 9% plus
    a. Monthly percentage: 9%
    b. Advertising fee: Variable
Financing Available: YES

Category: Auto Parts and Services—Tune-Up Services
Name: Precision Tune
Address: 755 South 11th Street, Beaumont, TX 77705
Product/service: Auto tune-up centers
Year Began Franchising: 1978
Number of Franchises: 233
    a. Individual owners: 228
    b. Company-owned: 5
Minimum Franchise Fee: $15,000
Minimum Capital Required: $56,500 and up
Total Royalty/Fees: 16.5%
    a. Monthly percentage: 7.5%
    b. Advertising fee: 9%
Financing Available: NO

Category: Auto Parts and Services—Miscellaneous
Name: Harley-Davidson Motors
Address: P.O. Box 653, Milwaukee, WI 53201
Product/service: Motorcycle sales, accessories, and services
Year Began Franchising: 1907
Number of Franchises: 720
    a. Individual owners: ALL
    b. Company-owned: 0
Minimum Franchise Fee: 0
Minimum Capital Required: $10,000-$75,000
Total Royalty/Fees: 0
    a. Monthly percentage: 0
    b. Advertising fee: 0
Financing Available: NO

Category: Beauty and Health—Body Wrapping
Name: The Body Wrap
Address: 5825 West 6th Avenue, Denver, CO 80214
Product/service: Beauty and weight loss treatments
Year Began Franchising: 1981
Number of Franchises: 119
  a. Individual owners: ALL
  b. Company-owned: 0
Minimum Franchise Fee: $39,900
Minimum Capital Required: $60,000
Total Royalty/Fees: $350 per month
  a. Monthly percentage: $350 per month
  b. Advertising fee: 0
Financing Available: YES

Category: Beauty and Health—Cosmetics and Skin Care
Name: "i" Natural Cosmetics
Address: 355 Middlesex Avenue, Wilmington, MA 01887
Product/service: Cosmetics and beauty boutiques
Year Began Franchising: 1972
Number of Franchises: 113
  a. Individual owners: 70
  b. Company-owned: 43
Minimum Franchise Fee: $17,500
Minimum Capital Required: $10,000-$75,000
Total Royalty/Fees: 5%
  a. Monthly percentage: 3%
  b. Advertising fee: 2%
Financing Available: NO

Category: Beauty and Health—Hair Care
Name: Haircrafters
Address: 125 South Service Road, Jericho, NY 11753
Product/service: Hair salons
Year Began Franchising: 1967
Number of Franchises: 304
  a. Individual owners: 274
  b. Company-owned: 30
Minimum Franchise Fee: $18,000
Minimum Capital Required: $71,000-$125,000
Total Royalty/Fees: 8%
  a. Monthly percentage: 6%
  b. Advertising fee: 2%
Financing Available: YES

Category: Beauty and Health—Hair Care
Name: Fantastic Sam's/Original Family Haircutters
Address: P.O. Box 18845, Memphis, TN 38181-0845
Product/service: Family hair-care centers
Year Began Franchising: 1976
Number of Franchises: 365
  a. Individual owners: 349
  b. Company-owned: 16
Minimum Franchise Fee: $20,000
Minimum Capital Required: As much as $75,000
Total Royalty/Fees: $183 per week
  a. Monthly percentage: $125 per week
  b. Advertising fee: $58 per week
Financing Available: NO

Category: Beauty and Health—Opticians and Optical Services
Name: Pearle Vision Center
Address: 2534 Royal Lane, Dallas, TX 75229
Product/service: Full-service optical stores
Year Began Franchising: 1980
Number of Franchises: 804
  a. Individual owners: 384
  b. Company-owned: 420
Minimum Franchise Fee: $10,000
Minimum Capital Required: $31,000-$350,000
Total Royalty/Fees: 14.5%
  a. Monthly percentage: 8.5%
  b. Advertising fee: 6%
Financing Available: YES

Category: Beauty and Health—Suntan Parlors
Name: Eurotan International
Address: 3701 Montrose Blvd., Houston, TX 77006
Product/service: Suntanning equipment and services
Year Began Franchising: 1980
Number of Franchises: 615
  a. Individual owners: 613
  b. Company-owned: 2
Minimum Franchise Fee: 0
Minimum Capital Required: $5,000 minimum
Total Royalty/Fees: 0
  a. Monthly percentage: 0
  b. Advertising fee: 0
Financing Available: YES

Category: Beauty and Health—Weight Control
Name: Nutri/System Weight Loss Centers
Address: Old York and Rydal Roads, Jenkintown, PA 19046
Product/service: Weight loss programs
Year Began Franchising: 1972
Number of Franchises: 709
  a. Individual owners: 549
  b. Company-owned: 160
Minimum Franchise Fee: $49,500
Minimum Capital Required: More than $75,000
Total Royalty/Fees: 8%
  a. Monthly percentage: 7%
  b. Advertising fee: 1%
Financing Available: NO

Category: Beauty and Health—Miscellaneous
Name: Great Earth Vitamin Stores
Address: 1801 Parkcourt Place, Building A, Santa Ana, CA 92701
Product/service: Natural vitamins and minerals
Year Began Franchising: 1978
Number of Franchises: 163
  a. Individual owners: 151
  b. Company-owned: 12
Minimum Franchise Fee: $15,000
Minimum Capital Required: $70,000
Total Royalty/Fees: 6% plus ad fee
  a. Monthly percentage: 6%
  b. Advertising fee: $1,000 per month
Financing Available: YES

Category: Beverages
Name: The Coca-Cola Company
Address: 310 North Avenue, P.O. Drawer 1734, Atlanta, GA 30301
Product/service: Soft drinks
Year Began Franchising: About 1900
Number of Franchises: Hundreds of licensed bottlers worldwide
  a. Individual owners: —
  b. Company-owned: —
Minimum Franchise Fee: Variable
Minimum Capital Required: Variable
Total Royalty/Fees: Variable
  a. Monthly percentage: —
  b. Advertising fee: —
Financing Available: NO

Category: Bookstores
Name: Little Professor Book Centers
Address: 21333 Haggerty Road, Suite 305, Novi, MI 48050
Product/service: Family bookstores
Year Began Franchising: 1969
Number of Franchises: 74
   a. Individual owners: 73
   b. Company-owned: 1
Minimum Franchise Fee: $11,500
Minimum Capital Required: $65,000
Total Royalty/Fees: 2.75% plus ad fee
   a. Monthly percentage: 2.75%
   b. Advertising fee: $15 per month
Financing Available: NO

Category: Business Services—Accounting and Consulting
Name: General Business Services
Address: 51 Monroe Street, GBS Building, Rockville, MD 20850
Product/service: Accounting services, business and management consulting
Year Began Franchising: 1962
Number of Franchises: 790
   a. Individual owners: ALL
   b. Company-owned: 0
Minimum Franchise Fee: $18,500
Minimum Capital Required: $21,500
Total Royalty/Fees: 7%
   a. Monthly percentage: 7%
   b. Advertising fee: 0
Financing Available: NO

Category: Business Services—Accounting and Consulting
Name: Comprehensive Accounting/Business Services
Address: 2111 Comprehensive Drive, Aurora, IL 60507
Product/service: Bookkeeping, accounting, income tax, and management services
Year Began Franchising: 1965
Number of Franchises: 406
   a. Individual owners: ALL
   b. Company-owned: 0
Minimum Franchise Fee: $68,000
Minimum Capital Required: $25,000 and up
Total Royalty/Fees: 12.5%
   a. Monthly percentage: 12.5%
   b. Advertising fee: 0
Financing Available: YES

Category: Business Services—Business Brokers
Name: VR Business Brokers
Address: 197 First Avenue, Needham, MA 02194
Product/service: Business and franchise brokers
Year Began Franchising: 1979
Number of Franchises: 300
  a. Individual owners: ALL
  b. Company-owned: 0
Minimum Franchise Fee: $35,000
Minimum Capital Required: $10,000-$75,000
Total Royalty/Fees: 8%
  a. Monthly percentage: 6%
  b. Advertising fee: 2%
Financing Available: NO

Category: Business Services—Credit and Collection
Name: American Lenders Service Co.
Address: 312 East Second Street, Odesa, TX 79760
Product/service: Credit and collateral adjustment services
Year Began Franchising: 1979
Number of Franchises: 72
  a. Individual owners: ALL
  b. Company-owned: 0
Minimum Franchise Fee: $5,000 and up
Minimum Capital Required: Up to $75,000 more
Total Royalty/Fees: 5% plus ad fee
  a. Monthly percentage: 5%
  b. Advertising fee: $66 per month
Financing Available: YES

Category: Business Services—Temporary Personnel Agencies
Name: Manpower Temporary Services
Address: 5301 North Ironwood Road, Milwaukee, WI 53201
Product/service: Temporary-help services
Year Began Franchising: 1954
Number of Franchises: 1,050
  a. Individual owners: 477
  b. Company-owned: 573
Minimum Franchise Fee: $4,500
Minimum Capital Required: Up to $75,000
Total Royalty/Fees: 3%-6%
  a. Monthly percentage: 3%-6%
  b. Advertising fee: 0
Financing Available: NO

Category: Children's Services
Name: Gymboree
Address: 872 Hinckley Road, Burlingame, CA 94010
Product/service: Parents' and children's play programs
Year Began Franchising: 1979
Number of Franchises: 125
  a. Individual owners: 118
  b. Company-owned: 7
Minimum Franchise Fee: $10,000
Minimum Capital Required: $45,000
Total Royalty/Fees: 9%
  a. Monthly percentage: 6%
  b. Advertising fee: 3%
Financing Available: YES

Category: Clothing, Shoes, and Accessories
Name: T-Shirts Plus
Address: 3630 Interstate 35 South, Waco, TX 76706
Product/service: T-shirts, letters, and put-ons
Year Began Franchising: 1976
Number of Franchises: 251
  a. Individual owners: 242
  b. Company-owned: 9
Minimum Franchise Fee: $17,500
Minimum Capital Required: $75,000 and up
Total Royalty/Fees: 6%
  a. Monthly percentage: 5%
  b. Advertising fee: 1%
Financing Available: NO

Category: Computer Stores and Services
Name: ComputerLand
Address: 30985 Santana Street, Hayward, CA 94544
Product/service: Personal computer hardware, software, and services
Year Began Franchising: 1977
Number of Franchises: 635
  a. Individual owners: ALL
  b. Company-owned: 0
Minimum Franchise Fee: $75,000
Minimum Capital Required: $250,000 or more
Total Royalty/Fees: 9%
  a. Monthly percentage: 8%
  b. Advertising fee: 1%
Financing Available: YES

Category: Computer Stores and Services
Name: Entré Computer Centers
Address: 1951 Kidwell Drive, Vienna, VA 22180
Product/service: Personal computer hardware, software, and services
Year Began Franchising: 1982
Number of Franchises: 211
  a. Individual owners: 210
  b. Company-owned: 1
Minimum Franchise Fee: $40,000
Minimum Capital Required: $300,000 or more
Total Royalty/Fees: 9%
  a. Monthly percentage: 8%
  b. Advertising fee: 1%
Financing Available: NO

Category: Construction—Energy Products and Services
Name: American Energy Managers
Address: 1515 Michigan Avenue, Grand Rapids, MI 49503
Product/service: Insulation and energy management services
Year Began Franchising: 1983
Number of Franchises: 55
  a. Individual owners: ALL
  b. Company-owned: 0
Minimum Franchise Fee: $5,000
Minimum Capital Required: $15,000
Total Royalty/Fees: 0
  a. Monthly percentage: 0
  b. Advertising fee: 0
Financing Available: NO

Category: Construction—Prefabricated Housing
Name: Lincoln Log Homes
Address: 6000 Lumber Lane, Kannapolis, NC 28081
Product/service: Log home kits and services
Year Began Franchising: 1978
Number of Franchises: 417
  a. Individual owners: ALL
  b. Company-owned: 0
Minimum Franchise Fee: 0
Minimum Capital Required: $10,000 and up
Total Royalty/Fees: 0
  a. Monthly percentage: 0
  b. Advertising fee: 0
Financing Available: NO

Category: Construction—Building Materials
Name: Davis Paint
Address: 1311 Iron Street, Kansas City, MO 64116
Product/service: Paint stores
Year Began Franchising: 1947
Number of Franchises: 70
    a. Individual owners: 60
    b. Company-owned: 10
Minimum Franchise Fee: 0
Minimum Capital Required: $10,000 and up
Total Royalty/Fees: 0
    a. Monthly percentage: 0
    b. Advertising fee: 0
Financing Available: NO

Category: Construction—Remodeling
Name: Mr. Build
Address: 2114 North Broadway, Santa Ana, CA 92706
Product/service: Commercial and home construction and repair
Year Began Franchising: 1981
Number of Franchises: 550
    a. Individual owners: ALL
    b. Company-owned: 0
Minimum Franchise Fee: $4,000
Minimum Capital Required: Up to $10,000
Total Royalty/Fees: $650 per month
    a. Monthly percentage: $350 per month
    b. Advertising fee: $300 per month
Financing Available: YES

Category: Construction—Miscellaneous
Name: Almost Heaven Hot Tubs
Address: Route 5 FF, Renick, WV 24966
Product/service: Hot tubs, spas, whirlpools, and saunas
Year Began Franchising: 1974
Number of Franchises: 684
    a. Individual owners: ALL
    b. Company-owned: 0
Minimum Franchise Fee: 0
Minimum Capital Required: About $10,000
Total Royalty/Fees: 0
    a. Monthly percentage: 0
    b. Advertising fee: 0
Financing Available: NO

Category: Dental Clinics
Name: Dwight Dental Care
Address: 280 Railroad Avenue, Greenwich, CT 06830
Product/service: Dental centers
Year Began Franchising: 1982
Number of Franchises: 63
  a. Individual owners: ALL
  b. Company-owned: 0
Minimum Franchise Fee: $20,000
Minimum Capital Required: $75,000
Total Royalty/Fees: 6% plus ad fee
  a. Monthly percentage: 6%
  b. Advertising fee: $15,000 per year
Financing Available: NO

Category: Drugstores and Pharmacies
Name: The Medicine Shoppe
Address: 10121 Paget Drive, St. Louis, MO 63123
Product/service: Pharmacy and health care centers
Year Began Franchising: 1971
Number of Franchises: 505
  a. Individual owners: ALL
  b. Company-owned: 0
Minimum Franchise Fee: $16,000
Minimum Capital Required: $65,000
Total Royalty/Fees: 5%
  a. Monthly percentage: 5%
  b. Advertising fee: 0
Financing Available: YES

Category: Educational Products and Services
Name: Sylvan Learning Centers
Address: 1407 116th Avenue, N.E., Suite 200, Bellevue, WA 98004
Product/service: Reading and mathematics instruction
Year Began Franchising: 1981
Number of Franchises: 65
  a. Individual owners: 64
  b. Company-owned: 1
Minimum Franchise Fee: $27,500
Minimum Capital Required: $75,000
Total Royalty/Fees: 9%
  a. Monthly percentage: 8%
  b. Advertising fee: 1%
Financing Available: NO

Category: Employment Agencies
Name: Snelling & Snelling
Address: 4000 South Tamiami Trail, Sarasota, FL 33581
Product/service: Employment agencies and services
Year Began Franchising: 1955
Number of Franchises: 435
  a. Individual owners: ALL
  b. Company-owned: 0
Minimum Franchise Fee: $29,500
Minimum Capital Required: $35,000 and up
Total Royalty/Fees: 8%
  a. Monthly percentage: 7%
  b. Advertising fee: 1%
Financing Available: YES

Category: Exercise and Fitness Centers—Exercise
Name: Jazzercise
Address: 2808 Roosevelt Street, Carlsbad, CA 92008
Product/service: Dance fitness programs
Year Began Franchising: 1983
Number of Franchises: 2,770
  a. Individual owners: ALL
  b. Company-owned: 0
Minimum Franchise Fee: $500
Minimum Capital Required: Less than $10,000
Total Royalty/Fees: 30%
  a. Monthly percentage: 30%
  b. Advertising fee: 0
Financing Available: NO, but deferred payment of initial fee

Category: Exercise and Fitness Centers—Dance Instruction
Name: Arthur Murray Dance Studios
Address: 1077 Ponce de Leon Blvd., Coral Gables, FL 33134
Product/service: Dance studios and lessons
Year Began Franchising: 1938
Number of Franchises: 255
  a. Individual owners: ALL
  b. Company-owned: 0
Minimum Franchise Fee: 0
Minimum Capital Required: $10,000 and up
Total Royalty/Fees: 5.8%
  a. Monthly percentage: 5.8%
  b. Advertising fee: 0
Financing Available: NO

Category: Florist Shops
Name: Flowerama
Address: 3165 Airline Way, Waterloo, IA 50703
Product/service: Flower shops
Year Began Franchising: 1970
Number of Franchises: 90
  a. Individual owners: 77
  b. Company-owned: 13
Minimum Franchise Fee: $17,500
Minimum Capital Required: $10,000 and up
Total Royalty/Fees: 5.6%
  a. Monthly percentage: 5.6%
  b. Advertising fee: 0
Financing Available: NO

Category: Food—Baked Goods
Name: Pepperidge Farms
Address: 595 Westport Avenue, Norwalk, CT 06856
Product/service: Baked goods and bakery outlets
Year Began Franchising: 1941
Number of Franchises: 1,780
  a. Individual owners: 1,735
  b. Company-owned: 45
Minimum Franchise Fee: 0
Minimum Capital Required: $75,000
Total Royalty/Fees: 0
  a. Monthly percentage: 0
  b. Advertising fee: 0
Financing Available: YES

Category: Food—Candy, Nuts, Fruits, and Confections
Name: Jo-Ann's Nut House/Chez Chocolat
Address: Route 79 & Tennent Road, Box 255, Morganville, NJ 07751
Product/service: Candies and nuts
Year Began Franchising: 1974
Number of Franchises: 225
  a. Individual owners: 195
  b. Company-owned: 30
Minimum Franchise Fee: $1,500 per year
Minimum Capital Required: $75,000 and up
Total Royalty/Fees: 6%
  a. Monthly percentage: 6%
  b. Advertising fee: 0
Financing Available: YES

Category: Food—Candy, Nuts, Fruits, and Confections
Name: Karmelkorn Shoppe
Address: P.O. Box 1059, Rock Island, IL 61204-1058
Product/service: Popcorn and confections
Year Began Franchising: 1930
Number of Franchises: 258
   a. Individual owners: 256
   b. Company-owned: 2
Minimum Franchise Fee: $12,500
Minimum Capital Required: $70,000 and up
Total Royalty/Fees: 6%
   a. Monthly percentage: 6%
   b. Advertising fee: 0
Financing Available: NO

Category: Food—Cheese and Special Foods
Name: Hickory Farms of Ohio
Address: P.O. Box 219, Maumee, OH 43537
Product/service: Cheese, gifts, and specialty foods
Year Began Franchising: 1960
Number of Franchises: 555
   a. Individual owners: 304
   b. Company-owned: 251
Minimum Franchise Fee: $20,000
Minimum Capital Required: $275,000
Total Royalty/Fees: 8%
   a. Monthly percentage: 6%
   b. Advertising fee: 2%
Financing Available: NO

Category: Food—Cookies
Name: Original Great American Chocolate Chip Cookies
Address: 4685 Frederick Drive, SW, Atlanta, GA 30336
Product/service: Chocolate chip cookie stores
Year Began Franchising: 1978
Number of Franchises: 277
   a. Individual owners: 254
   b. Company-owned: 23
Minimum Franchise Fee: $20,000
Minimum Capital Required: $75,000
Total Royalty/Fees: 7%
   a. Monthly percentage: 7%
   b. Advertising fee: 0
Financing Available: NO

Category: Food—Donuts
Name: Dunkin' Donuts
Address: P.O. Box 317, Randolph, MA 02368
Product/service: Donuts and bakery products
Year Began Franchising: 1955
Number of Franchises: 1,290
  a. Individual owners: 1,225
  b. Company-owned: 65
Minimum Franchise Fee: $30,000 and up
Minimum Capital Required: $75,000
Total Royalty/Fees: 8.5-9%
  a. Monthly percentage: 4.5-5%
  b. Advertising fee: 4%
Financing Available: NO

Category: Food—Donuts
Name: Mister Donut
Address: Box 2942, Multifoods Towers, Minneapolis, MN 55402
Product/service: Donut shops
Year Began Franchising: 1956
Number of Franchises: 602
  a. Individual owners: ALL
  b. Company-owned: 0
Minimum Franchise Fee: $15,000 and up
Minimum Capital Required: $50,000
Total Royalty/Fees: 5.4% per week
  a. Monthly percentage: 4.9% per week
  b. Advertising fee: .5% per week
Financing Available: YES

Category: Food—Grocery and Convenience Stores
Name: Convenient Food Mart
Address: 9701 West Higgins Road, Suite 850, Rosemont, IL 60018
Product/service: Superette grocery stores
Year Began Franchising: 1958
Number of Franchises: 1,143
  a. Individual owners: 1,130
  b. Company-owned: 13
Minimum Franchise Fee: $10,000
Minimum Capital Required: $10,000 and up
Total Royalty/Fees: 4.5-5%
  a. Monthly percentage: 4.5-5%
  b. Advertising fee: 0
Financing Available: NO

Category: Food—Grocery and Convenience Stores
Name: 7-Eleven Food Stores
Address: 2828 North Haskell Avenue, Dallas, TX 75221
Product/service: Convenience stores
Year Began Franchising: 1964
Number of Franchises: 7,200
   a. Individual owners: 2,760
   b. Company-owned: 4,440
Minimum Franchise Fee: Variable
Minimum Capital Required: $37,500 or more
Total Royalty/Fees: Variable
   a. Monthly percentage: Variable
   b. Advertising fee: Variable
Financing Available: YES

Category: Food—Grocery and Convenience Stores
Name: Junior Food Mart
Address: P.O. Box 3409, Jackson, MS 39207
Product/service: Convenience stores
Year Began Franchising: 1919
Number of Franchises: 474
   a. Individual owners: 412
   b. Company-owned: 62
Minimum Franchise Fee: $7,500 and up
Minimum Capital Required: $40,000 and up
Total Royalty/Fees: 1%
   a. Monthly percentage: 1%
   b. Advertising fee: 0
Financing Available: YES

Category: Food—Ice Cream
Name: Dairy Queen/Dairy Queen Brazier
Address: P.O. Box 35286, Minneapolis, MN 55435
Product/service: Dairy desserts and hamburgers
Year Began Franchising: 1941
Number of Franchises: 4,787
   a. Individual owners: 4,780
   b. Company-owned: 7
Minimum Franchise Fee: $25,000
Minimum Capital Required: $85,000
Total Royalty/Fees: 7.5%
   a. Monthly percentage: 4%
   b. Advertising fee: 3.5%
Financing Available: NO

Category: Food—Ice Cream
Name: Baskin-Robbins 31 Flavors Ice Cream
Address: 31 Baskin Robbins Place, Glendale, CA 91201
Product/service: Ice cream stores
Year Began Franchising: 1949
Number of Franchises: 3,205
  a. Individual owners: 3,155
  b. Company-owned: 50
Minimum Franchise Fee: 0
Minimum Capital Required: $75,000 and up
Total Royalty/Fees: Variable
  a. Monthly percentage: 0
  b. Advertising fee: Variable
Financing Available: NO

Category: Food—Ice Cream
Name: Carvel Ice Cream Stores
Address: 4151 State Road 84, Fort Lauderdale, FL 33314
Product/service: Soft ice cream
Year Began Franchising: 1945
Number of Franchises: 844
  a. Individual owners: 842
  b. Company-owned: 2
Minimum Franchise Fee: $20,000
Minimum Capital Required: $75,000
Total Royalty/Fees: 6.5%
  a. Monthly percentage: 3.5%
  b. Advertising fee: 3%
Financing Available: YES

Category: Food—Ice Cream
Name: Tastee-Freez
Address: P.O. Box 162, Utica, MI 48087
Product/service: Ice cream and fast-food restaurants
Year Began Franchising: 1950
Number of Franchises: 561
  a. Individual owners: ALL
  b. Company-owned: 0
Minimum Franchise Fee: $10,000
Minimum Capital Required: $40,000-$150,000
Total Royalty/Fees: 5-6%
  a. Monthly percentage: 4%
  b. Advertising fee: 1-2%
Financing Available: NO

Category: Food—Ice Cream
Name: Swensen's Ice Cream Parlour
Address: 2408 East Arizona, Biltmore Center, Phoenix, AZ 85016
Product/service: Ice cream parlors and restaurants
Year Began Franchising: 1963
Number of Franchises: 379
  a. Individual owners: 374
  b. Company-owned: 5
Minimum Franchise Fee: $20,000-$30,000
Minimum Capital Required: $40,000-$150,000
Total Royalty/Fees: 6.5-8.5%
  a. Monthly percentage: 5.5%
  b. Advertising fee: 1-3%
Financing Available: NO

Category: Food—Ice Cream
Name: Bresler's 33 Flavors
Address: 4010 West Belden Avenue, Chicago, IL 60639
Product/service: Ice cream shops
Year Began Franchising: 1968
Number of Franchises: 390
  a. Individual owners: 380
  b. Company-owned: 10
Minimum Franchise Fee: $10,000
Minimum Capital Required: $75,000
Total Royalty/Fees: 8.5%
  a. Monthly percentage: 6%
  b. Advertising fee: 2.5%
Financing Available: YES

Category: Food—Miscellaneous
Name: J.T.'s General Store
Address: 511 Lake Zurich Road, Barrington, IL 60010
Product/service: Home delivery of groceries
Year Began Franchising: 1981
Number of Franchises: 979
  a. Individual owners: ALL
  b. Company-owned: 0
Minimum Franchise Fee: 0
Minimum Capital Required: Up to $10,000
Total Royalty/Fees: 0.25%
  a. Monthly percentage: 0
  b. Advertising fee: 0.25%
Financing Available: YES

Category: Family-Style Restaurants—Dinner
Name: Benihana of Tokyo
Address: 8685 N.W. 53rd Terrace, Miami, FL 33102-0210
Product/service: Japanese steakhouses
Year Began Franchising: 1970
Number of Franchises: 47
   a. Individual owners: 10
   b. Company-owned: 37
Minimum Franchise Fee: $50,000
Minimum Capital Required: $1,130,000
Total Royalty/Fees: 8%
   a. Monthly percentage: 4%
   b. Advertising fee: 4%
Financing Available: NO

Category: Family-Style Restaurants—Italian
Name: Noble Roman's Pizza
Address: P.O. Box 1089, Bloomington, IN 47401
Product/service: Pizza restaurants
Year Began Franchising: 1972
Number of Franchises: 84
   a. Individual owners: 44
   b. Company-owned: 40
Minimum Franchise Fee: $12,500
Minimum Capital Required: $210,000
Total Royalty/Fees: 4%
   a. Monthly percentage: 4%
   b. Advertising fee: 0
Financing Available: NO

Category: Family-Style Restaurants—Pancakes
Name: Village Inn Pancake House
Address: 400 West 48th Avenue, Denver, CO 80216
Product/service: Breakfast and pancake shops
Year Began Franchising: 1961
Number of Franchises: 191
   a. Individual owners: 120
   b. Company-owned: 71
Minimum Franchise Fee: $25,000
Minimum Capital Required: $75,000 or more
Total Royalty/Fees: 5-6%
   a. Monthly percentage: 5%
   b. Advertising fee: 0-1%
Financing Available: NO

Category: Family-Style Restaurants—Steakhouses
Name: Ponderosa Steakhouse
Address: P.O. Box 578, Dayton, OH 45401
Product/service: Steakhouse family restaurants
Year Began Franchising: 1966
Number of Franchises: 661
  a. Individual owners: 223
  b. Company-owned: 438
Minimum Franchise Fee: $15,000
Minimum Capital Required: $75,000 or more
Total Royalty/Fees: 8%
  a. Monthly percentage: 4%
  b. Advertising fee: 4%
Financing Available: YES

Category: Family-Style Restaurants—Steakhouses
Name: Bonanza Family Restaurants
Address: 8350 North Central Expressway, Suite 1000, Dallas, TX 75206
Product/service: Family steak restaurants
Year Began Franchising: 1963
Number of Franchises: 555
  a. Individual owners: 550
  b. Company-owned: 5
Minimum Franchise Fee: $30,000
Minimum Capital Required: $75,000 or more
Total Royalty/Fees: 6.8%
  a. Monthly percentage: 4.8%
  b. Advertising fee: 2%
Financing Available: NO

Category: Family-Style Restaurants—Miscellaneous
Name: Hardee's Restaurants
Address: 1233 North Church Street, Rocky Mount, NC 27801
Product/service: Family restaurants
Year Began Franchising: 1961
Number of Franchises: 2,083 (Northeast only)
  a. Individual owners: 1,258
  b. Company-owned: 825
Minimum Franchise Fee: $15,000
Minimum Capital Required: $650,000
Total Royalty/Fees: 8.5-9%
  a. Monthly percentage: 3.5-4%
  b. Advertising fee: 5%
Financing Available: NO

Category: Family-Style Restaurants—Miscellaneous
Name: Bob's Big Boy Restaurants
Address: One Marriott Drive, Washington, D.C. 20058
Product/service: Full-service family restaurants
Year Began Franchising: 1952
Number of Franchises: 1,106
  a. Individual owners: 883
  b. Company-owned: 223
Minimum Franchise Fee: $25,000
Minimum Capital Required: $75,000 or more
Total Royalty/Fees: 5%
  a. Monthly percentage: 3%
  b. Advertising fee: 2%
Financing Available: NO

Category: Family-Style Restaurants—Miscellaneous
Name: Howard Johnson Restaurants
Address: One Monarch Drive, North Quincy, MA 02269
Product/service: Family restaurants
Year Began Franchising: 1933
Number of Franchises: 615
  a. Individual owners: 204
  b. Company-owned: 411
Minimum Franchise Fee: $30,000
Minimum Capital Required: $75,000 or more
Total Royalty/Fees: 3%
  a. Monthly percentage: 3%
  b. Advertising fee: 0
Financing Available: NO

Category: Family-Style Restaurants—Miscellaneous
Name: Roy Rogers Restaurants
Address: One Marriott Drive, Washington, D.C. 20058
Product/service: Family restaurants
Year Began Franchising: 1967
Number of Franchises: 517
  a. Individual owners: 127
  b. Company-owned: 390
Minimum Franchise Fee: $25,000
Minimum Capital Required: $75,000 or more
Total Royalty/Fees: 8%
  a. Monthly percentage: 4%
  b. Advertising fee: 4%
Financing Available: NO

Category: Family-Style Restaurants—Miscellaneous
Name: Perkins Restaurants
Address: 6401 Poplar Avenue, Memphis, TN 38119
Product/service: Full-service 24-hour restaurants
Year Began Franchising: 1966
Number of Franchises: 308
    a. Individual owners: 214
    b. Company-owned: 94
Minimum Franchise Fee: $25,000
Minimum Capital Required: $150,000
Total Royalty/Fees: 8%
    a. Monthly percentage: 4%
    b. Advertising fee: 4%
Financing Available: NO

Category: Fast-Food Restaurants—Delicatessens
Name: Mr. Dunderbak's
Address: 1740 First Union Plaza, Charlotte, NC 28282
Product/service: Delicatessens and cafés
Year Began Franchising: 1974
Number of Franchises: 37
    a. Individual owners: 34
    b. Company-owned: 3
Minimum Franchise Fee: $24,000
Minimum Capital Required: $150,000
Total Royalty/Fees: 4.9%
    a. Monthly percentage: 4.9%
    b. Advertising fee: 0
Financing Available: YES

Category: Fast-Food Restaurants—Ethnic Foods
Name: Appetito's
Address: 629 West Pierson, Phoenix, AZ 85013
Product/service: Italian fast food
Year Began Franchising: 1976
Number of Franchises: 22
    a. Individual owners: 20
    b. Company-owned: 2
Minimum Franchise Fee: $40,000
Minimum Capital Required: $75,000
Total Royalty/Fees: 8%
    a. Monthly percentage: 4%
    b. Advertising fee: 4%
Financing Available: NO

Category: Fast-Food Restaurants—Fish and Chips
Name: Long John Silver's Seafood Shoppes
Address: 101 Jerrico Drive, Lexington, KY 40579
Product/service: Fast-food seafood
Year Began Franchising: 1970
Number of Franchises: 1,358
   a. Individual owners: 545
   b. Company-owned: 813
Minimum Franchise Fee: $10,000
Minimum Capital Required: $75,000
Total Royalty/Fees: 8.5%
   a. Monthly percentage: 4%
   b. Advertising fee: 4.5%
Financing Available: NO

Category: Fast-Food Restaurants—Fried Chicken
Name: Kentucky Fried Chicken
Address: P.O. Box 32070, Louisville, KY 40232
Product/service: Fried chicken and related foods
Year Began Franchising: 1952
Number of Franchises: 7,750
   a. Individual owners: 6,300
   b. Company-owned: 1,450
Minimum Franchise Fee: $10,000
Minimum Capital Required: $400,000
Total Royalty/Fees: 8.5%
   a. Monthly percentage: 4%
   b. Advertising fee: 4.5%
Financing Available: NO

Category: Fast-Food Restaurants—Fried Chicken
Name: Church's Fried Chicken
Address: P.O. Box BH001, San Antonio, TX 78284
Product/service: Fried chicken restaurants
Year Began Franchising: 1976
Number of Franchises: 1,605
   a. Individual owners: 273
   b. Company-owned: 1,332
Minimum Franchise Fee: $15,000
Minimum Capital Required: $400,000
Total Royalty/Fees: 9%
   a. Monthly percentage: 4%
   b. Advertising fee: 5%
Financing Available: NO

Category: Fast-Food Restaurants—Fried Chicken
Name: Popeye's Famous Fried Chicken & Biscuits
Address: 1333 South Clearview Parkway, Jefferson, LA 70121
Product/service: Cajun fried chicken and related foods
Year Began Franchising: 1976
Number of Franchises: 450
  a. Individual owners: 367
  b. Company-owned: 83
Minimum Franchise Fee: $25,000
Minimum Capital Required: $500,000
Total Royalty/Fees: 8%
  a. Monthly percentage: 5%
  b. Advertising fee: 3%
Financing Available: NO

Category: Fast-Food Restaurants—Hamburgers
Name: McDonald's
Address: McDonald's Plaza, Oak Brook, IL 60521
Product/service: Hamburgers and fast food
Year Began Franchising: 1955
Number of Franchises: 7,935
  a. Individual owners: 5,959
  b. Company-owned: 1,976
Minimum Franchise Fee: $12,500
Minimum Capital Required: $325,000
Total Royalty/Fees: 15.5%
  a. Monthly percentage: 11.5%
  b. Advertising fee: 4%
Financing Available: NO

Category: Fast-Food Restaurants—Hamburgers
Name: Burger King
Address: P.O. Box 520783, Miami, FL 33152
Product/service: Hamburgers and fast food
Year Began Franchising: 1955
Number of Franchises: 3,827
  a. Individual owners: 3,278
  b. Company-owned: 549
Minimum Franchise Fee: $40,000
Minimum Capital Required: $75,000 and up
Total Royalty/Fees: 7.5%
  a. Monthly percentage: 3.5%
  b. Advertising fee: 4%
Financing Available: NO

Category: Fast-Food Restaurants—Hamburgers
Name: Wendy's Old-Fashioned Hamburgers
Address: P.O. Box 256, Dublin, OH 43017
Product/service: Hamburgers and fast food
Year Began Franchising: 1972
Number of Franchises: 2,900
  a. Individual owners: 1,925
  b. Company-owned: 975
Minimum Franchise Fee: $20,000
Minimum Capital Required: $500,000
Total Royalty/Fees: 8%
  a. Monthly percentage: 4%
  b. Advertising fee: 4%
Financing Available: NO

Category: Fast-Food Restaurants—Mexican
Name: Taco Bell
Address: 16808 Armstrong Avenue, Irvine, CA 92714
Product/service: Mexican fast food
Year Began Franchising: 1964
Number of Franchises: 1,837
  a. Individual owners: 869
  b. Company-owned: 968
Minimum Franchise Fee: $45,000
Minimum Capital Required: $75,000 and up
Total Royalty/Fees: 10%
  a. Monthly percentage: 5.5%
  b. Advertising fee: 4.5%
Financing Available: NO

Category: Fast-Food Restaurants—Pizza
Name: Domino's Pizza
Address: 1968 Green Road, Ann Arbor, MI 48105
Product/service: Pizza by home delivery
Year Began Franchising: 1967
Number of Franchises: 1,460
  a. Individual owners: 995
  b. Company-owned: 465
Minimum Franchise Fee: $6,500
Minimum Capital Required: $75,000 and up
Total Royalty/Fees: 8.5% per week
  a. Monthly percentage: 5.5% per week
  b. Advertising fee: 3% per week
Financing Available: NO

Category: Fast-Food Restaurants—Pizza
Name: Pizza Hut
Address: P.O. Box 428, Wichita, KS 67208
Product/service: Pizza and Italian-food restaurants
Year Began Franchising: 1959
Number of Franchises: 4,315
  a. Individual owners: 2,340
  b. Company-owned: 1,975
Minimum Franchise Fee: Variable
Minimum Capital Required: $75,000 and up
Total Royalty/Fees: Variable
  a. Monthly percentage: Variable
  b. Advertising fee: Variable
Financing Available: NO

Category: Fast-Food Restaurants—Pizza
Name: Pizza Inn
Address: 2930 Stemmons Parkway, Dallas, TX 75247
Product/service: Pizza, pasta, and salad bar restaurants
Year Began Franchising: 1963
Number of Franchises: 727
  a. Individual owners: 431
  b. Company-owned: 296
Minimum Franchise Fee: $17,500
Minimum Capital Required: $75,000 and up
Total Royalty/Fees: 7%
  a. Monthly percentage: 4%
  b. Advertising fee: 3%
Financing Available: NO

Category: Fast-Food Restaurants—Pizza
Name: Little Caesar's
Address: 24120 Haggerty Road, Farmington Hills, MI 48024-1059
Product/service: Pizza and similar foods
Year Began Franchising: 1961
Number of Franchises: 563
  a. Individual owners: 403
  b. Company-owned: 160
Minimum Franchise Fee: $12,500
Minimum Capital Required: $75,000 and up
Total Royalty/Fees: Variable
  a. Monthly percentage: Variable
  b. Advertising fee: Variable
Financing Available: NO

Category: Fast-Food Restaurants—Pizza
Name: Round Table Pizza
Address: 601 Montgomery, Suite 500, San Francisco, CA 94111
Product/service: Pizza restaurants
Year Began Franchising: 1962
Number of Franchises: 410 (West and Southwest)
  a. Individual owners: 408
  b. Company-owned: 2
Minimum Franchise Fee: $20,000
Minimum Capital Required: $250,000
Total Royalty/Fees: 7%
  a. Monthly percentage: 4%
  b. Advertising fee: 3%
Financing Available: NO

Category: Fast-Food Restaurants—Sandwiches, Subs, and Salads
Name: Schlotzsky's
Address: 200 West 4th Street, Austin, TX 78701
Product/service: Sandwich shops
Year Began Franchising: 1976
Number of Franchises: 178
  a. Individual owners: 170
  b. Company-owned: 8
Minimum Franchise Fee: $12,500
Total Royalty/Fees: 5%
  a. Monthly percentage: 4%
  b. Advertising fee: 1%
Financing Available: NO

Category: Fast-Food Restaurant—Sandwiches, Subs, and Salads
Name: Subway Sandwiches & Salads
Address: 25 High Street, Milford, CT 06460
Product/service: Submarine sandwiches and salads
Year Began Franchising: 1974
Number of Franchises: 373
  a. Individual owners: 360
  b. Company-owned: 13
Minimum Francise Fee: $7,500
Minimum Capital Required: $10,000 and up
Total Royalty/Fee: 10.5%
  a. Monthly percentage: 8%
  b. Advertising fee: 2.5%
Financing Available: NO

Category: Fast-Food Restaurants—Sandwiches, Subs, and Salads
Name: Blimpie
Address: 1414 Avenue of the Americas, New York, NY 10019
Product/service: Submarine sandwiches
Year Began Franchising: 1965
Number of Franchises: 226
   a. Individual owners: 225
   b. Company-owned: 1
Minimum Franchise Fee: $15,000
Minimum Capital Required: $10,000 and up
Total Royalty/Fees: 9%
   a. Monthly percentage: 6%
   b. Advertising fee: 3%
Financing Available: NO

Category: Fast-Food Restaurants—Miscellaneous
Name: Arby's Roast Beef
Address: 3495 Piedmont Road, NE, Altanta, GA 30305
Product/service: Roast beef sandwiches
Year Began Franchising: 1965
Number of Franchises: 1,337
   a. Individual owners: 1,168
   b. Company-owned: 169
Minimum Franchise Fee: $20,000
Minimum Capital Required: $75,000 or more
Total Royalty/Fees: 4.7%
   a. Monthly percentage: 3.5%
   b. Advertisng fee: 1.2%
Financing Available: NO

Category: Fast-Food Restaurants—Miscellaneous
Name: Sonic Drive-In Restaurant
Address: 6800 North Bryant, Oklahoma City, OK 73121-4444
Product/service: Fast-food restaurants
Year Began Franchising: 1959
Number of Franchises: 969
   a. Individual owners: 876
   b. Company-owned: 93
Minimum Franchise Fee: $7,500-$15,000
Minimum Capital Required: $75,000 or more
Total Royalty/Fees: 4.5%
   a. Monthly percentage: 3%
   b. Advertising fee: 1.5%
Financing Available: NO

Category: Fast-Food Restaurants—Miscellaneous
Name: A&W Root Beer
Address: One Parklane Blvd., Suite 500 East, Dearborn, MI 48126
Product/service: Fast food
Year Began Franchising: 1924
Number of Franchises: 694
  a. Individual owners: 690
  b. Company-owned: 4
Minimum Franchise Fee: $15,000
Minimum Capital Required: $75,000 or more
Total Royalty/Fees: 8%
  a. Monthly percentage: 4%
  b. Advertising fee: 4%
Financing Available: NO

Category: Fast-Food Restaurants—Miscellaneous
Name: Orange Julius
Address: 2850 Ocean Park Blvd., Suite 200, Santa Monica, CA 90405
Product/service: Orange Julius drinks, hot dogs, fast food
Year Began Franchising: 1963
Number of Franchises: 735
  a. Individual owners: 703
  b. Company-owned: 32
Minimum Franchise Fee: $17,500
Minimum Capital Required: $45,000
Total Royalty/Fees: 6%
  a. Monthly percentage: 6%
  b. Advertising fee: 0
Financing Available: NO

Category: Fast-Food Restaurants—Miscellaneous
Name: Captain D's
Address: 1727 Elm Hill Pike, Nashville, TN 37210
Product/service: Fast food
Year Began Franchising: 1969
Number of Franchises: 446
  a. Individual owners: 198
  b. Company-owned: 248
Minimum Franchise Fee: $10,000
Minimum Capital Required: $75,000 or more
Total Royalty/Fees: 5%
  a. Monthly percentage: 3%
  b. Advertising fee: 2%
Financing Available: NO

Category: Gift Shops
Name: The Mole Hole
Address: 217 Howard Street, Petosky, MI 49770
Product/service: Gifts
Year Began Franchising: 1969
Number of Franchises: 122
   a. Individual owners: 120
   b. Company-owned: 2
Minimum Franchise Fee: $20,000
Minimum Capital Required: $75,000 or more
Total Royalty/Fees: $750 per year
   a. Monthly percentage: $750 per year
   b. Advertising fee: 0
Financing Available: NO

Category: Hardware and Home Improvement
Name: Coast-to-Coast Stores
Address: P.O. Box 80, Minneapolis, MN 55440
Product/service: Retail hardware stores
Year Began Franchising: 1928
Number of Franchises: 1,152
   a. Individual owners: 1,150
   b. Company-owned: 2
Minimum Franchise Fee: 0
Minimum Capital Required: $75,000 or more
Total Royalty/Fees: Varies
   a. Monthly percentage: Varies
   b. Advertising fee: Varies
Financing Available: NO

Category: Home Furnishings—Retail
Name: Spring Crest Draperies
Address: 505 West Lambert Road, Brea, CA 92621
Product/service: Custom draperies and window products
Year Began Franchising: 1968
Number of Franchises: 289
   a. Individual owners: ALL
   b. Company-owned: 0
Minimum Franchise Fee: $10,000
Minimum Capital Required: $34,500
Total Royalty/Fees: 3%
   a. Monthly percentage: 3%
   b. Advertising fee: 0
Financing Available: NO

Category: Income Tax Services
Name: H & R Block
Address: 4410 Main Street, Kansas City, MO 64111
Product/service: Income tax preparation
Year Began Franchising: 1958
Number of Franchises: 7,782
  a. Individual owners: 4,243
  b. Company-owned: 3,539
Minimum Franchise Fee: Variable
Minimum Capital Required: $1,000-$2,000
Total Royalty/Fees: Variable
  a. Monthly percentage: Variable
  b. Advertising fee: 0
Financing Available: NO

Category: Insurance
Name: System VII
Address: 14110 East Firestone Blvd., Santa Fe Springs, CA 90670
Product/service: Insurance sales and service
Year Began Franchising: 1981
Number of Franchises: 175
  a. Individual owners: 174
  b. Company-owned: 1
Minimum Franchise Fee: $799
Minimum Capital Required: $5,000-$25,000
Total Royalty/Fees: 10%
  a. Monthly percentage: 6.5%
  b. Advertising fee: 3.5%
Financing Available: YES

Category: Laundry and Dry Cleaning
Name: One Hour Martinizing Dry Cleaning
Address: 2005 Ross Avenue, Cincinnati, OH 45212
Product/service: Dry cleaning service
Year Began Franchising: 1949
Number of Franchises: 1,269
  a. Individual owners: ALL
  b. Company-owned: 0
Minimum Franchise Fee: $16,000
Minimum Capital Required: $10,000 or more
Total Royalty/Fees: $1,500 per year
  a. Monthly percentage: $1,500 per year
  b. Advertising fee: 0
Financing Available: NO

Category: Laundry and Dry Cleaning
Name: King Koin Laundry Center
Address: 5700 West 36th Street, Minneapolis, MN 55416
Product/service: Coin-operated laundries and dry cleaners
Year Began Franchising: 1957
Number of Franchises: 1,212
    a. Individual owners: ALL
    b. Company-owned: 0
Minimum Franchise Fee: 0
Minimum Capital Required: $10,000 or more
Total Royalty/Fees: 0
    a. Monthly percentage: 0
    b. Advertising fee: 0
Financing Available: NO

Category: Laundry and Dry Cleaning
Name: Betty Brite Cleaners
Address: 2243 Bryn Mawr Avenue, Philadelphia, PA 19131
Product/service: Dry cleaning and coin-operated laundries
Year Began Franchising: 1963
Number of Franchises: 818
    a. Individual owners: ALL
    b. Company-owned: 0
Minimum Franchise Fee: 0
Minimum Capital Required: $50,000
Total Royalty/Fees: 0
    a. Monthly percentage: 0
    b. Advertising fee: 0
Financing Available: NO

Category: Lawn and Garden Services
Name: Lawn-A-Mat Chemical and Equipment
Address: 205 Greeley Avenue, Sayville, NY 11782
Product/service: Lawn care chemical and equipment sales
Year Began Franchising: 1960
Number of Franchises: 1,401
    a. Individual owners: ALL
    b. Company-owned: 0
Minimum Franchise Fee: $2,000 or more
Minimum Capital Required: Up to $10,000
Total Royalty/Fees: Variable
    a. Monthly percentage: 0
    b. Advertising fee: 0
Financing Available: NO

Category: Lawn and Garden Services
Name: Lawn Doctor
Address: P.O. Box 512, Matawan, NJ 07747
Product/service: Lawn services automation
Year Began Franchising: 1967
Number of Franchises: 294
   a. Individual owners: ALL
   b. Company-owned: 0
Minimum Franchise Fee: $22,500
Minimum Capital Required: $27,300
Total Royalty/Fees: 15%
   a. Monthly percentage: 10%
   b. Advertising fee: 5%
Financing Available: NO

Category: Liquor and Wine
Name: Foremost Liquors
Address: 5252 North Broadway, Chicago, IL 60640
Product/service: Retail package stores
Year Began Franchising: 1949
Number of Franchises: 68 (South and Midwest)
   a. Individual owners: ALL
   b. Company-owned: 0
Minimum Franchise Fee: $11,400
Minimum Capital Required: $75,000 or more
Total Royalty/Fees: 0
   a. Monthly percentage: 0
   b. Advertising fee: 0
Financing Available: NO

Category: Maintenance, Cleaning, and Sanitation—Carpet, Upholstery, Drapery, and Ceilings
Name: Duraclean International
Address: 2151 Waukegan Road, Deerfield, IL 60015
Product/service: Carpet, furniture, and drapery cleaning service
Year Began Franchising: 1947
Number of Franchises: 1,043
   a. Individual owners: ALL
   b. Company-owned: 0
Minimum Franchise Fee: Variable
Minimum Capital Required: $19,800
Total Royalty/Fees: Variable
   a. Monthly percentage: Variable
   b. Advertising fee: Variable
Financing Available: YES

Category: Maintenance, Cleaning, and Sanitation—Carpet, Upholstery, Drapery, and Ceilings
Name: Rainbow International Carpet Dyeing and Cleaning
Address: 1010 University Parks Drive, Waco, TX 76707
Product/service: Carpet, upholstery, and drapery cleaning and dyeing
Year Began Franchising: 1981
Number of Franchises: 752
   a. Individual owners: 750
   b. Company-owned: 2
Minimum Franchise Fee: $15,000
Minimum Capital Required: $10,000
Total Royalty/Fees: 7%
   a. Monthly percentage: 7%
   b. Advertising fee: 0
Financing Available: NO

Category: Maintenance, Cleaning, and Sanitation—Carpet, Upholstery, Drapery, and Ceilings
Name: ServiceMaster
Address: 2300 Warrenville Road, Downers Grove, IL 60515
Product/service: Carpet, window, drapery, and wall cleaning
Year Began Franchising: 1948
Number of Franchises: 2,005
   a. Individual owners: ALL
   b. Company-owned: 0
Minimum Franchise Fee: $9,750
Minimum Capital Required: Up to $10,000
Total Royalty/Fees: 7-10%
   a. Monthly percentage: 7-10%
   b. Advertising fee: 0
Financing Available: YES

Category: Maintenance, Cleaning, and Sanitation—Exterior Washing
Name: Sparkle Wash
Address: 26851 Richmond Road, Bedford Heights, OH 44146
Product/service: Mobile power cleaning service
Year Began Franchising: 1967
Number of Franchises: 135
   a. Individual owners: 131
   b. Company-owned: 4
Minimum Franchise Fee: $20,000
Minimum Capital Required: $45,000
Total Royalty/Fees: 3%
   a. Monthly percentage: 3%
   b. Advertising fee: 0
Financing Available: YES

Category: Maintenance, Cleaning, and Sanitation—Maid Services
Name: Servpro
Address: 11357 Pyrites Way, Rancho Cordova, CA 95670
Product/service: Office and residential cleaning services
Year Began Franchising: 1967
Number of Franchises: 580
  a. Individual owners: ALL
  b. Company-owned: 0
Minimum Franchise Fee: $33,000
Minimum Capital Required: Up to $75,000
Total Royalty/Fees: 7-10%
  a. Monthly percentage: 7-10%
  b. Advertising fee: 0
Financing Available: YES

Category: Maintenance, Cleaning, and Sanitation—Porcelain Repair
Name: Perma Ceram Enterprises
Address: 65 Smithtown Road, Smithtown, NY 11787
Product/service: Bathroom resurfacing
Year Began Franchising: 1976
Number of Franchises: 168
  a. Individual owners: ALL
  b. Company-owned: 0
Minimum Franchise Fee: $14,500
Minimum Capital Required: Up to $10,000
Total Royalty/Fees: 0
  a. Monthly percentage: 0
  b. Advertising fee: 0
Financing Available: NO

Category: Maintenance, Cleaning, and Sanitation—Home Repairs
Name: Dial One International
Address: 4100 Long Beach Blvd., Long Beach, CA 90807
Product/service: Property maintenance and repair services
Year Began Franchising: 1983
Number of Franchises: 563
  a. Individual owners: 562
  b. Company-owned: 1
Minimum Franchise Fee: $2,300-$5,000
Minimum Capital Required: Up to $10,000
Total Royalty/Fees: Variable
  a. Monthly percentage: Variable
  b. Advertising fee: Variable
Financing Available: NO

Category: Maintenance, Cleaning, and Sanitation—Sewer and Drain Cleaning
Name: Roto-Rooter Sewer & Drain Service
Address: 300 Ashworth Road, West Des Moines, IA 50625
Product/service: Sewer and drain cleaning
Year Began Franchising: 1935
Number of Franchises: 754
  a. Individual owners: 736
  b. Company-owned: 18
Minimum Franchise Fee: Variable
Minimum Capital Required: $7,600-$62,000
Total Royalty/Fees: 0
  a. Monthly percentage: 0
  b. Advertising fee: 0
Financing Available: NO

Category: Medical Services
Name: Miracle Ear
Address: 7731 Country Club Drive, Golden Valley, MN 55427
Product/service: Hearing aids and equipment
Year Began Franchising: 1984
Number of Franchises: 109
  a. Individual owners: 100
  b. Company-owned: 9
Minimum Franchise Fee: Variable
Minimum Capital Required: Up to $75,000
Total Royalty/Fees: $30 per unit
  a. Monthly percentage: 0
  b. Advertising fee: 0
Financing Available: NO

Category: Motels and Hotels
Name: Best Western International
Address: P.O. Box 10203, Phoenix, AZ 85064
Product/service: Hotels
Year Began Franchising: 1946
Number of Franchises: 3,093
  a. Individual owners: ALL
  b. Company-owned: 0
Minimum Franchise Fee: 0
Minimum Capital Required: $450,000
Total Royalty/Fees: 0
  a. Monthly percentage: 0
  b. Advertising fee: 0
Financing Available: NO

Category: Motels and Hotels
Name: Holiday Inn
Address: 3742 Lamar Avenue, Memphis, TN 38195
Product/service: Motels and hotels
Year Began Franchising: 1954
Number of Franchises: 1,698
  a. Individual owners: 1,486
  b. Company-owned: 212
Minimum Franchise Fee: $30,000 or more
Minimum Capital Required: In the hundreds of thousands
Total Royalty/Fees: 6%
  a. Monthly percentage: 4%
  b. Advertising fee: 2%
Financing Available: NO

Category: Motels and Hotels
Name: Quality Inn/Comfort Inn/Quality Royale
Address: 10750 Columbia Pike, Silver Spring, MD 20901
Product/service: Hotels, motels, and resorts
Year Began Franchising: 1950
Number of Franchises: 532
  a. Individual owners: 511
  b. Company-owned: 21
Minimum Franchise Fee: Variable
Minimum Capital Required: Variable
Total Royalty/Fees: 4% minimum
  a. Monthly percentage: 3%
  b. Advertising fee: 1% minimum
Financing Available: NO

Category: Motels and Hotels
Name: Friendship Inns
Address: 739 South 4th West Street, Salt Lake City, UT 84101
Product/service: Motels and hotels
Year Began Franchising: 1961
Number of Franchises: 1,068
  a. Individual owners: ALL
  b. Company-owned: 0
Minimum Franchise Fee: $8,500
Minimum Capital Required: Up to $10,000 for existing motels
Total Royalty/Fees: 0
  a. Monthly percentage: 0
  b. Advertising fee: 0
Financing Available: NO

Category: Pet Shops
Name: Docktor Pet Centers
Address: 355 Middlesex Avenue, Wilmington, MA 01884
Product/service: Pet department stores
Year Began Franchising: 1967
Number of Franchises: 201
  a. Individual owners: 191
  b. Company-owned: 10
Minimum Franchise Fee: $15,000
Minimum Capital Required: $134,800
Total Royalty/Fees: 4.5%
  a. Monthly percentage: 4.5%
  b. Advertising fee: 0
Financing Available: YES

Category: Photography Services and Supplies
Name: Sooter's
Address: 1559 North Mannheim Road, Stone Park, IL 60615
Product/service: Portrait studios and photofinishing
Year Began Franchising: 1968
Number of Franchises: 225
  a. Individual owners: 175
  b. Company-owned: 50
Minimum Franchise Fee: Variable
Minimum Capital Required: $15,000-$20,000
Total Royalty/Fees: 5%
  a. Monthly percentage: 5%
  b. Advertising fee: 0
Financing Available: YES

Category: Printing Shops and Services
Name: Kwik-Kopy
Address: 5225 Hollister, Houston, TX 77040
Product/service: Instant printing centers
Year Began Franchising: 1967
Number of Franchises: 897
  a. Individual owners: ALL
  b. Company-owned: 0
Minimum Franchise Fee: $38,500
Minimum Capital Required: Up to $75,000
Total Royalty/Fees: 6.8%
  a. Monthly percentage: 4.8%
  b. Advertising fee: 2%
Financing Available: YES

Category: Printing Shops and Services
Name: Postal Instant Press
Address: 8021 Beverly Boulevard, Los Angeles, CA 90048
Product/service: Instant printing and copying centers
Year Began Franchising: 1968
Number of Franchises: 923
  a. Individual owners: 917
  b. Company-owned: 6
Minimum Franchise Fee: $40,000
Minimum Capital Required: $54,500
Total Royalty/Fees: 7.8%
  a. Monthly percentage: 6.8%
  b. Advertising fee: 1%
Financing Available: YES

Category: Printing Shops and Services
Name: Sir Speedy Printing Centers
Address: P.O. Box 1790, Newport Beach, CA 92666
Product/service: Instant printing and copying centers
Year Began Franchising: 1968
Number of Franchises: 510
  a. Individual owners: ALL
  b. Company-owned: 0
Minimum Franchise Fee: $12,500
Minimum Capital Required: $75,000 or more
Total Royalty/Fees: 7%
  a. Monthly percentage: 5%
  b. Advertising fee: 2%
Financing Available: YES

Category: Printing Shops and Services
Name: Minuteman Press
Address: 1640 New Highway, Farmingdale, NY 11735
Product/service: Full-service print shops
Year Began Franchising: 1975
Number of Franchises: 445
  a. Individual owners: ALL
  b. Company-owned: 0
Minimum Franchise Fee: $19,500
Minimum Capital Required: Up to $75,000
Total Royalty/Fees: 6%
  a. Monthly percentage: 6%
  b. Advertising fee: 0
Financing Available: YES

Category: Real-Estate Services
Name: Century 21 Real Estate
Address: 18872 MacArthur Boulevard, Irvine, CA 92715
Product/service: Real-estate sales
Year Began Franchising: 1971
Number of Franchises: 6,423
　a. Individual owners: ALL
　b. Company-owned: 0
Minimum Franchise Fee: Variable
Minimum Capital Required: Up to $75,000
Total Royalty/Fees: Variable
　a. Monthly percentage: Variable
　b. Advertising fee: Variable
Financing Available: YES

Category: Recreation and Amusements
Name: Computer Portraits
Address: 11 Melcher Street, Boston, MA 02210
Product/service: Computer portrait systems
Year Began Franchising: 1979
Number of Franchises: 494
　a. Individual owners: 472
　b. Company-owned: 22
Minimum Franchise Fee: $1,500
Minimum Capital Required: More than $10,000
Total Royalty/Fees: 0
　a. Monthly percentage: 0
　b. Advertising fee: 0
Financing Available: YES

Category: Recreation and Amusements
Name: The Athlete's Foot
Address: 24th & A.V.R.R., Pittsburgh, PA 15222
Product/service: Athletic footwear and apparel
Year Began Franchising: 1973
Number of Franchises: 450
　a. Individual owners: 425
　b. Company-owned: 25
Minimum Franchise Fee: $7,500
Minimum Capital Required: $100,000
Total Royalty/Fees: 3%
　a. Monthly percentage: 3%
　b. Advertising fee: 0
Financing Available: NO

Category: Recreation and Amusements
Name: KOA Kampgrounds
Address: P.O. Box 30558, Billings, MT 59114
Product/service: Campground rentals
Year Began Franchising: 1964
Number of Franchises: 709
  a. Individual owners: 695
  b. Company-owned: 14
Minimum Franchise Fee: $20,000
Minimum Capital Required: $75,000 or more
Total Royalty/Fees: 10%
  a. Monthly percentage: 8%
  b. Advertising fee: 2%
Financing Available: NO

Category: Recreation and Amusements
Name: Sport About
Address: 1557 Coon Rapids Blvd., Coon Rapids, MN 55433
Product/service: Sporting goods and apparel
Year Began Franchising: 1978
Number of Franchises: 1,370
  a. Individual owners: 1,369
  b. Company-owned: 1
Minimum Franchise Fee: $7,500
Minimum Capital Required: $58,000
Total Royalty/Fees: 4%
  a. Monthly percentage: 4%
  b. Advertising fee: 0
Financing Available: NO

Category: Rentals—Tools, Equipment, Supplies
Name: Taylor Rental Center
Address: 570 Cottage Street, Springfield, MA 01104
Product/service: Tool and equipment rental stores
Year Began Franchising: 1962
Number of Franchises: 545
  a. Individual owners: 525
  b. Company-owned: 20
Minimum Franchise Fee: $20,000
Minimum Capital Required: $75,000 or more
Total Royalty/Fees: Variable
  a. Monthly percentage: Variable
  b. Advertising fee: 1%
Financing Available: NO

Category: Security Services and Products
Name: Sonitrol
Address: 6161 Lake Ellenor Drive, Orlando, FL 32809
Product/service: Audio security alarm products
Year Began Franchising: 1965
Number of Franchises: 162
   a. Individual owners: ALL
   b. Company-owned: 0
Minimum Franchise Fee: $20,000
Minimum Capital Required: $250,000 or more
Total Royalty/Fees: Variable
   a. Monthly percentage: Variable
   b. Advertising fee: 0
Financing Available: NO

Category: Stereo, Record, Audio, and Video Stores
Name: Curtis Mathes Home Entertainment Centers
Address: P.O. Box 223607, Dallas, TX 75222
Product/service: Televisions, video and audio equipment
Year Began Franchising: 1982
Number of Franchises: 658
   a. Individual owners: 646
   b. Company-owned: 12
Minimum Franchise Fee: $25,000
Minimum Capital Required: $75,000 or more
Total Royalty/Fees: 0
   a. Monthly percentage: 0
   b. Advertising fee: 0
Financing Available: NO

Category: Stores—General Merchandise
Name: Ben Franklin Stores
Address: 1700 South Wolf Road, Des Plaines, IL 60018
Product/service: General retail merchandise
Year Began Franchising: 1927
Number of Franchises: 1,654
   a. Individual owners: 1,653
   b. Company-owned: 1
Minimum Franchise Fee: $125 per month
Minimum Capital Required: $80,000
Total Royalty/Fees: 0
   a. Monthly percentage: 0
   b. Advertising fee: 0
Financing Available: NO

Category: Travel Agencies
Name: International Tours
Address: 5001 East 68th Street, Suite 530, Tulsa, OK 74136
Product/service: Travel services and tour organizers
Year Began Franchising: 1970
Number of Franchises: 222
  a. Individual owners: 219
  b. Company-owned: 3
Minimum Franchise Fee: $25,500
Minimum Capital Required: More than $10,000
Total Royalty/Fees: 0.75-5%
  a. Monthly percentage: 0.75-5%
  b. Advertising fee: 0
Financing Available: NO

Category: Video Rental Stores
Name: Video Connection of America
Address: 22761 Pacific Coast Highway, Malibu, CA 90265
Product/service: Videocassette and equipment rental and sale
Year Began Franchising: 1980
Number of Franchises: 263
  a. Individual owners: 262
  b. Company-owned: 1
Minimum Franchise Fee: $34,900
Minimum Capital Required: $65,000
Total Royalty/Fees: 2.5%
  a. Monthly percentage: 2.5%
  b. Advertising fee: 0
Financing Available: YES

Category: Water Conditioning
Name: Culligan Water Conditioning
Address: One Culligan Way, Northbrook, IL 60062
Product/service: Water treatment and conditioning equipment
Year Began Franchising: 1938
Number of Franchises: 790
  a. Individual owners: 765
  b. Company-owned: 25
Minimum Franchise Fee: 0
Minimum Capital Required: Up to $75,000
Total Royalty/Fees: Variable
  a. Monthly percentage: Variable
  b. Advertising fee: 1-4.1%
Financing Available: NO

Category: Water Conditioning
Name: Rainsoft Water Conditioning
Address: 1225 East Greenleaf Street, Elk Grove Village, IL 60007
Product/service: Water treatment equipment
Year Began Franchising: 1956
Number of Franchises: 267
   a. Individual owners: 265
   b. Company-owned: 2
Minimum Franchise Fee: 0
Minimum Capital Required: Up to $75,000
Total Royalty/Fees: 0
   a. Monthly percentage: 0
   b. Advertising fee: 0
Financing Available: YES

Category: Miscellaneous—Engraving
Name: Craft World
Address: 603 West Plainview Road, Springfield, MO 65807
Product/service: Hot printing, rubber stamps, and engraving
Year Began Franchising: 1976
Number of Franchises: 821
   a. Individual owners: 820
   b. Company-owned: 1
Minimum Franchise Fee: $30,000
Minimum Capital Required: Up to $75,000
Total Royalty/Fees: 0
   a. Monthly percentage: 0
   b. Advertising fee: 0
Financing Available: NO

Category: Miscellaneous—Television Magazines
Name: TV Facts
Address: 1638 New Highway, Farmingdale, NY 11735
Product/service: Local TV magazine and shopping guide
Year Began Franchising: 1971
Number of Franchises: 378
   a. Individual owners: ALL
   b. Company-owned: 0
Minimum Franchise Fee: $14,500
Minimum Capital Required: Up to $75,000
Total Royalty/Fees: $25-$65 per issue
   a. Monthly percentage: $25-$65 per issue
   b. Advertising fee: 0
Financing Available: NO

The Best Low-Investment Franchises

Dozens of reputable, well-established franchises still exist for which the total investment, including franchise fee and startup capital, totals $25,000 or less.

Listed below are the most highly regarded franchises in the country that require a low total investment. These were determined not only by considering their reputations and costs, but also how long they have been in business, the ratio of the total number of franchises compared to the number of company-owned units, their royalty structure, their growth rates, and how actively they are looking for new franchisees.

They come from a variety of franchise businesses, and are given in alphabetical order. Their addresses and details are given in the listings in the previous section.

> Almost Heaven Hot Tubs: Construction—Miscellaneous
> Arthur Murray Dance Studios: Exercise and Fitness Centers
> Dial One International: Maintenance, Cleaning, and Sanitation
> Duraclean International: Maintenance, Cleaning, and Sanitation
> H & R Block: Income Tax Services
> Jazzercise: Exercise and Fitness Centers
> Pepperidge Farm: Food—Baked Goods
> Perma Ceram Enterprises: Maintenance, Cleaning, and Sanitation
> Rainbow International Carpet Dyeing and Cleaning: Maintenance, Cleaning, and Sanitation
> Roto-Rooter Sewer & Drain Service: Maintenance, Cleaning, and Sanitation
> ServiceMaster: Maintenance, Cleaning, and Sanitation

Appendix:
Sources of Assistance
and Information

State Franchise Regulatory Agencies

Fifteen states, from California to New York, require all franchises doing business in the state to register and file disclosure statements. These statements and detailed information about the franchise must be kept on file with the proper state agency and must be given to any prospective franchisee *before* he signs a contract and pays any money to the franchisor. These state agencies can be invaluable sources of help and information as you consider buying a franchise.

If you do not live in one of these states, you can check out the available information on any franchise within your state by contacting the secretary of state, a securities commission or division, a banking division, or the office of attorney general. They should be able to direct you to any information they have about a particular franchisor's activities in that state. The state attorney general's office should also be able to discuss any legal difficulties a franchisor is experiencing in that state; of course, you should check out the complete details before you jump to hasty conclusions, because disgruntled franchisees, who expected too much and did not succeed in the way they thought they should, often try to take advantage of the legal vulnerability of a franchise company.

Of course, you should also write the same agencies in the state where the franchise is incorporated and find out the available details about who is behind the franchise and under what circumstances the company was incorporated and organized.

Given below is a list of the names and addresses of the proper state agencies to which you should go for assistance in each state. Also included is a listing for Canada. This information is current as of the middle of 1985.

California

Department of Corporations
1025 P Street
Sacramento, CA 95814

Hawaii

Corporations and Securities Administrator
Director of Regulatory Agencies & Securities
1010 Richards Street
Honolulu, HA 96813

Illinois

Assistant Attorney General
Chief, Franchise Division
Office of Attorney General
500 South Second Street
Springfield, IL 62706

Indiana

Deputy Commissioner
Franchise Division
Indiana Securities Division
Secretary of State
012 State House
Indianapolis, IN 46204

Maryland

Maryland Division of Securities
Second Floor, The Munsey Building
7 North Calvert Street
Baltimore, MD 21202

Michigan

Office of Franchise and Agent Licensing
Michigan Corporation and Securities Bureau
Department of Commerce
P.O. Box 30222
Lansing, MI 48909

Minnesota

Securities Division
Minnesota Department of Commerce
500 Metro Square Building
St. Paul, MN 55101

New York

Special Deputy Attorney General
Bureau of Investor Protection and Securities
New York State Department of Law
Room 4825-A
Two World Trade Center
New York, NY 10047

North Dakota

Franchise Examiner
Office of Securities Commissioner
Third Floor
Capitol Building
Bismarck, ND 58505

Oregon

Assistant Corporations Commissioner—Franchises
Corporation Division
Commerce Building
Salem, OR 97310
(503) 378-4387

Rhode Island

Chief Security Examiner
Securities Section
Banking Division
100 North Main Street
Providence, RI 02903
(401) 277-2405

South Dakota

Franchise Administrator, Division of Securities
State Capitol
Pierre, SD 57501
(605) 773-4013

Virginia

Examination Coordinator, Franchise Section
Division of Securities and Retail Franchising
11 South 12th Street
Richmond, VA 23219
(804) 786-7751

Washington State

Registrations Attorney, Department of Licensing
Securities Division
Business and Professions Administration
P.O. Box 648
Olympia, WA 98504
(206) 753-6928

Wisconsin

Franchise Investment Division
Wisconsin Securities Commission
P.O. Box 1768
Madison, WI 53701
(608) 266-3414

CANADA

Only the province of Alberta requires franchise disclosure. Contact:

Deputy Director for Franchises
Alberta Securities Commission
10th Floor
10065 Jasper Avenue
Edmonton, Alberta
CANADA T5J 3B1

State Business Opportunity Laws

Many states that do not have franchise disclosure regulations do have laws governing the sale of business opportunities, including dealerships, distributorships, and franchises. The states with these laws and the proper office within the state government to contact for information are listed below:

Connecticut

Securities Division
State Office Building
Hartford, CT 06115
(Governs both Business Opportunity Investment Act and Franchising Fairness Law)

Florida

Two offices are involved:

Division of Consumer Services
110 Mayo Building
Tallahassee, FL 32301
(Franchises and Distributorship Law)

Department of Legal Affairs
Consumer Division
The Capitol
Tallahassee, FL 32301
(Business Opportunity Act)

Georgia

Office of Consumer Affairs
Two Martin Luther King Drive
Suite 356
Atlanta, GA 30334
(Regulates Business Opportunity Law and Sale of Business Opportunities Act)

Maine

Department of Business Regulations
Special Opportunities Section
State House Section 35
Augusta, ME 04330
(Regulates Business Opportunity Act)

Nebraska

Division of Securities
P.O. Box 95006
Lincoln, NE 68509
(Administers both Franchise Practices Act and Business Practices Act)

New Hampshire

Consumer Protection Division
State House Annex
Concord, NH 03301
(Governs Distributorship Disclosure Act)

North Carolina

Department of Justice
Consumer Protection Division
P.O. Box 629
Raleigh, North Carolina 27602
(Enforces Business Opportunities Sales Law)

Ohio

Assistant Attorney General
Consumer Frauds and Crime Section
State Office Tower, 15th Floor
30 East Broad Street
Columbus, OH 43215
(Enforces Business Opportunity Purchasers Protection Act)

South Carolina

Securities Division
816 Keenan Building
Columbia, SC 29201
(Regulates Business Opportunity Sales Act)

Other states with some type of business opportunity act include Arkansas, Delaware, Iowa, Kentucky, Louisiana, Mississippi, Missouri, New Jersey, and Texas.

Franchise and Business Organizations

International Franchise Association
1025 Connecticut Avenue, NW
Suite 707
Washington, DC 20036
(202) 659-0790

Benjamin Thayer, Executive Director
National Alliance of Franchisees
P.O. Box 75416
Washington, DC 20013
(301) 386-3377

The Council of Better Business Bureaus, Inc.
1150 17th Street, NW
Washington, DC 20036

Franchise Education

Franchise Studies Program
School of Business Administration
University of Nebraska
Lincoln, NE 68504

Joseph Mancuso, Executive Director
Center for Entrepreneurial Management
83 Spring Street
New York, NY 10012

Federal Government Agencies

The Federal Trade Commission
Bureau of Enforcement
Sixth Street & Pennsylvania Avenue, NW
Washington, DC 20580

The FTC is an excellent source for information about what should and should not be included in franchise contracts. It also regulates the 1979 Franchise Disclosure Act. Consult its local or regional offices for assistance.

Bibliography

Franchise Books

Bond, Robert E., *The Source Book of Franchise Opportunities*. Homewood, Ill.: Dow Jones-Irwin, 1984.

Dixon, Edward L., Jr., Ed., *The 1983 Franchise Annual*. Lewiston, N.Y.: Info Press, Inc., 1983.

Dixon, Edward L., Jr., Ed., *The 1984 Franchise Annual*. Lewiston, N.Y.: Info Press, Inc., 1984.

Dixon, Edward L., Jr., Ed., *The 1985 Franchise Annual*. Lewiston, N.Y.: Info Press, Inc., 1985.

Finn, Richard P., *Your Fortune in Franchises*. Chicago: Contemporary Books, Inc., 1979.

Franchising: Regulation of Buying and Selling a Franchise. Washington, D.C.: Bureau of National Affairs, CPS Portfolio No. 34, 1984.

Friedlander, Mark, Jr., and Gene Gurney, *Handbook of Successful Franchising*. New York: Van Nostrand Reinhold, 1981.

Glickman, Gladys, *Franchising*. Revised edition. New York: Matthew Bender & Co., 1985.

Hammond, Alexander, *Franchise Rights—A Self-Defense Manual for Dealers, Distributors, Wholesalers and Other Franchisees*. New York: Franchise Publications, 1983.

International Franchise Association, *Directory of Membership, 1982–1983*. Washington, D.C., 1983.

International Franchise Association, *Directory of Membership, 1983–1984*. Washington, D.C., 1984.

International Franchise Association, *Directory of Membership, 1984–1985*. Washington, D.C., 1985.

International Franchise Association, *Franchise Laws, Regulations and Rulings*. Washington, D.C., 1984.

Norback, Peter G., and Craig T. Norback, *The Dow Jones-Irwin Guide to Franchises*. Revised edition. Homewood, Ill.: Dow Jones-Irwin, 1982.

Vaughn, Charles L., *Franchising*. 2nd edition. Lexington, Mass.: D.C. Heath & Co., 1979.

Government Publications

All government publications can be ordered from the Superintendent of Documents, U.S. Government Printing Office, Washington, D.C. 20402.

Federal Trade Commission, *Advice for Persons Who Are Considering an Investment in a Franchise Business*. Consumer Bulletin No. 4, 1970.

Small Business Administration, *Franchise Index/Profile*. (GPO Reference No. N 4500–00125–3.)

Small Business Administration, *Starting and Managing a Small Business of Your Own*, 1985. (GPO Reference No. 045–000–00212–8.)

U.S. Department of Commerce, *The Franchise Opportunities Handbook*. Annual. 1985. (GPO Reference No. 003–008–00194–7.)

U.S. Department of Commerce, *Franchising in the Economy—1981–1983*, 1983.

U.S. Department of Commerce, *Franchising in the Economy—1982–1984*, 1984.

U.S. Department of Commerce, *Franchising in the Economy—1983–1985*, 1985.

General Business Books

Backstrom, Charles H., and Gerald D. Hursh, *Survey Research*. Chicago: Northwestern University Press, 1963.

Caples, John, *How to Make Your Advertising Make Money*. Englewood Cliffs, N.J.: Prentice-Hall, Inc., 1983.

Cohen, William A., *Building a Mail Order Business*. New York: John Wiley & Sons, Inc., 1982.

Cohen, William A., and Marshall E. Reddick, *Successful Marketing for Small Business*. New York: AMACOM, 1981.

Doyle, Dennis M., *Efficient Accounting and Recordkeeping*. New York: David McKay Company, Inc., 1977.

J. K. Lasser Tax Institute, *How to Run a Small Business*. New York: McGraw-Hill, Inc., 1985.

Lewis, Herschell Gordon, *More Than You Ever Wanted to Know About Mail Order Advertising*. Englewood Cliffs, N.J.: Prentice-Hall, Inc., 1983.

Lowry, Albert J., *How to Become Financially Successful by Owning Your Own Business*. New York: Simon & Schuster, 1981.

Pope, Jeffrey, *Practical Marketing Research*. New York: AMACOM, 1983.

Pratt, Stanley E., *How to Raise Venture Capital*. Wellesley Hills, Mass.: Charles Scribner's Sons, 1982.

Pyle, William W., Kermit D. Larson, and Roger H. Hermanson, *A Guide to Elementary Accounting*. Homewood, Ill.: Learning Systems Company, 1981.

Rausch, Edward N., *Financial Keys to Small Business Profitability*. New York: AMACOM, 1982.

Roman, Kenneth, and Jane Maas, *How to Advertise: A Professional Guide for the Advertiser*. New York: St. Martin's Press, 1976.

Winston, Sandra, *The Entrepreneurial Woman*. New York: Bantam Books, 1979.

Franchise and Related Publications

Choice, Entrepreneur, Inc., 2311 Pontius Avenue, Los Angeles, Calif. 90064. New (1986) monthly magazine aimed at women entrepreneurs and franchise buyers and owners.

Continental Franchise Review, P.O. Box 6360, Denver, Colo. 80206. Biweekly newsletter analyzes current franchise market for franchisors and franchisees.

Entrepreneur, Entrepreneur, Inc., 2311 Pontius Avenue, Los Angeles, Calif. 90064. Monthly magazine for entrepreneurs, prospective franchisees, and investors.

Franchise: The Magazine, 1044 Hercules, Houston, Tex. 77058. Monthly magazine aimed at franchisors.

Franchising World, International Franchise Association, 1025 Connecticut Avenue, NW, Suite 707, Washington, D.C. 20036. Monthly newsletter for members with information about trends and membership news.

IFA Franchise Insider, International Franchise Association, 1025 Connecticut Avenue, NW, Suite 707, Washington, D.C. 20036. Monthly newsletter for association members.

Income Opportunities, Davis Publications, 300 Lexington Avenue, New York, N.Y. 10017. Monthly magazine with Franchise Roundtable column by Bryce Webster and frequent articles discussing franchise opportunities.

The Info Franchise Newsletter, Info Press, Inc., 736 Center Street, Box 550, Lewiston, N.Y. 14092. Monthly newsletter with news and discussion of current topics of interest to franchisees.

NAF Newsletter, National Alliance of Franchisees, P.O. Box 75416, Washington, D.C. 20013. Monthly newsletter for members and associates of the NAF.

Index